STRUCTURED PROBLEM SOLVING WITH PASCAL

Lawrence J. Mazlack

Information Systems
University of Cincinnati

Holt, Rinehart and Winston

New York   Chicago   San Francisco   Philadelphia   Montreal
Toronto   London   Sydney   Tokyo   Mexico City
Rio de Janeiro   Madrid

The photograph for the cover is courtesy of Chromatics, Inc.

Copyright © 1983 by CBS College Publishing
All rights reserved.
Address correspondence to: 383 Madison Avenue, New York, NY 10017

Library of Congress Cataloging in Publication Data

Mazlack, Lawrence J.
  Structured problem solving with Pascal.

  Includes index.
  1. PASCAL (Computer program language)   2. Structured
programming.   I. Title.
  QA76.73.P2M36   1983   001.64'24   82-21245
  ISBN-0-03-060153-3

46,669

Printed in the United States of America

Published simultaneously in Canada

3 4 5 6   016   9 8 7 6 5 4 3 2

CBS COLLEGE PUBLISHING
Holt, Rinehart and Winston
The Dryden Press
Saunders College Publishing

TO

Brutus
Zack
Loki
Socko
Susie
Barnabus

who were there for the best
and the worst

CONTENTS

APPENDIXES

PREFACE

A computer language is a tool that can be used for solving many different types of problems. Computer languages are used to communicate with the computer. The language that is used influences the structure of the design of the problem's computer solution. There are a variety of different computer languages. Languages are different because of what they are designed to do, how they go about doing it, and how difficult they are to use.

The structure and form of a computer language have a great deal to do with how a problem is solved on a computer. Some languages encourage programming styles that create programs that are easier to design, implement, and modify. Pascal has been designed to help people learn how to program in the best possible style.

When people first started to use computers, the best method of using them to solve problems was unknown. More and more has been learned about solving problems with the aid of a computer. Recently, a powerful way of using computers to solve problems has been developed. This better way addresses how a problem is to be analyzed before it is written in a computer language and how the problem should be described to the machine. This powerful way of problem analysis is known as *top-down analysis*. The better way of programming that has been developed is known as *structured programming*. This book addresses the technique developed of top-down problem solution design and the structured use of a computer programming language.

Computer languages may be divided into "low" and "high" level langauges. A low level language requires the programmer to be very concerned with precisely how a given computer goes about solving or executing a program. A high level language is intended to resemble human communication forms. A high level language approaches either a "natural" language such as English ("story like") or a mathematical language that has the form of a set of mathematical statements. Consequently, the use of a low level language results in a program which has been developed in terms of the machine being used, whereas a high level language results in a program which has been developed in terms of the problem being solved.

The advantage of using a high level language is that the problem solver can spend more time on how to go about solving a problem and less time on the mechanical details of how the computer executes a given data manipulation. A greater freedom from concern with mechanical details usually allows the problem solver (the programmer) to resolve many more information processing problems in a given time.

There are many high level languages available. This book describes the essential elements of Pascal, a high level language. Pascal was originally introduced by Niklaus Wirth in the early seventies as a first language for students with no programming experience. It is now widely available on both large and small computers. It has the capacity to easily manipulate arithmetic, character, and boolean values. Pascal has significant data description facilities that allow the development of useful data structures. However, more important than its considerable manipulative capability is that the problem solution method can be reflected in the program's structure. Pascal has a variety of powerful "structured" control facilities and useful data structures.

The design of Pascal makes it an ideal tool for writing structured programs. Structured programs generally are simpler in form and are more easily reasoned about. The structured programming technique has been found to have both theoretical and practical advantages. The theoretical advantage in using structured programming is that it produces programs that are closer to being provably correct than any other programming technique.

The practical advantage in structured programming is that the structure of the programs produced is usually simpler and can reflect a top-down/problem solution analysis. Top-down analysis is a progressive problem subdivision analysis technique. This technique produces solutions that are more understandable and allow greater control over errors.

Pascal was designed by one man, Niklaus Wirth. For a period of time, there was no agreed upon standard description of Pascal. Wirth's book (K. Jensen and N. Wirth, *Pascal User Manual and Report,* 2nd ed., Springer-Verlag, New York, 1974) served both as the best description of the goals of Pascal and as a description of what should be in the Pascal language. Several professional groups worked together to develop a standard description of Pascal that all compiler implementations should conform to. The last result of this was ANSI X3J9 "Second Draft Proposal ISO/DP 7185.1." This is available in *Pascal News,* No. 20, December 1980. In 1982, this version became the international standard and is what is referred to as "standard" Pascal in this book.

OF PARTICULAR INTEREST TO THE INSTRUCTOR

This text is oriented towards solving problems that are concerned with handling general collections of data as opposed to problems of a highly mathematical nature. The programming examples have been kept as simple as possible. This focuses attention on what the Pascal program statements are to be doing instead of on the design of the problems that are being solved. The formation of data into groups known as records will be addressed.

The examples and problems in the text require only simple computational skills. Specifically, problems requiring any scientific knowledge or background have been avoided. A few of the problems at the end of the chapters come from scientific or engineering origins; however, the computations required do not include complex equations or background knowledge not provided in the problem statement.

The presentation of the material in the text has been modularized to reduce the need for serial presentation. The shaded box at the start of each section indicates what other sections are suggested as background. This allows the order in which the material is learned to be different than the sequence chosen by the author. Also, some topics can be de-emphasised while others can be eliminated.

The sequence of topics will probably be most satisfactory to a person who is very comfortable with the concepts of top-down analysis and programming. A person who is primarily interested in Pascal as a language, with only a developing interest in the top-down process, may well prefer a different topic order. For example, the first topic in this book that aids in program organization and control is subprograms (Chapter 6, PROCEDURE and FUNCTION Fundamentals). Subprograms are covered before any other control structure (such as iteration or selection). This is somewhat different than the sequence that has been common in the past. Although it is felt that subprograms should be used early, users of this book are not constrained to do so. They can just delay covering the contents of Chapter 6, which introduces subprograms, until just before Chapter 12, which expands the discussion of Chapter 6. Likewise, some people may be more comfortable covering selection (IF, CASE) before iteration (WHILE, REPEAT-UNTIL, FOR). This can be done easily. Also, the topics can be interchanged or delayed since the examples in most of the chapters of the book do not require a complete knowledge of the preceding chapters. In much the same manner, most sections within a chapter do not require that all the previous material in the chapter be covered before a particular section is covered. To aid in course design, the prequisite background required for each section is indicated in the shaded box at the start of each section.

The Pascal standard specifies a set of characters that can be used to construct a Pascal program. The standard also describes a set of alternate characters that can be used for the special purpose symbols. (Appendix C describes the standard and alternate character sets along with character sets available for various computer systems.) As few computer systems are capable of printing the complete Pascal standard character set, virtually all programs written in Pascal that are to run on existing computing systems must use some combination of standard and alternate characters. (Some relatively popular computer systems cannot represent all the necessary characters using a combination of standard and alternate characters.) This book uses the combination of standard and alternate character sets that can be displayed by machines using the EBCDIC representation. Many Pascal implementations for computer systems not using EBCDIC either also use this representation for their character set or will accept all of the alternate characters as valid input. Whatever character set your computer uses, this book can be used with it as long as your Pascal compiler conforms to the Pascal standard.

Lawrence J. Mazlack

Chapter 1

INTRODUCTION

Objectives
Provide a general introduction to computers and to problem solving on computers.

Suggested Background
This chapter does not require any specific background. Although a prior knowledge of computers and the role that they play in the world would be helpful, it is not necessary. This chapter presents a general discussion of the topics included in it. The reader is encouraged to seek additional information in any of the numerous introductory books to computers that are available.

Computers are a part of today's world. Almost every day, they affect us by what they do. They can do some things very well and are inadequate for other tasks. The things that they can do well are often things that are simple for people to do. The computer's strength is that it can do simple things faster, cheaper, and sometimes more reliably than people can.

1.1 THE PARTS OF A COMPUTER

Objectives
Identify the five basic functions of a computer and relate these functions to the major parts of a computer.

Suggested Background
None.

Before a person learns to drive a car, there is a need to have a general idea of the pieces of a car and their functions. For example, the ideas needed include the knowledge that: the engine makes the care move, the brakes stop it, the horn makes a warning noise, the steering wheel is used to change direction, etc. Likewise, before trying to use a computer, a person should have a general idea of what makes up a computer.

There are big computers, small computers, and those that are in between. They all have some things in common. All computers are machines. The type of computers that this book will help a person to use to solve problems is a digital computer. The term *digital* means that the machine manipulates digits or symbols to perform its assigned tasks.

All digital computers can perform five functions: (a) read, (b) write, (c) store data, (d) manipulate data (including arithmetic), and (e) control their own actions and make decisions based on previously supplied instructions. The instructions that tell the computer what to do are called *a program*. How these functions are related is indicated in the diagram shown in Figure 1.1. In the diagram, the direction of the arrows indicates the direction(s) in which data can be passed.

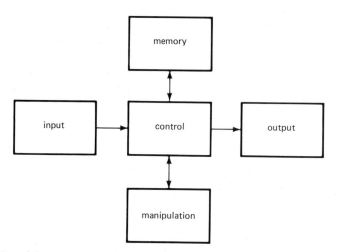

Figure 1.1   Basic parts of a computer.

Precisely how the machine accomplishes its functions is not the concern of this book. This is much the same as a person who knows that flipping a light switch causes the light to come on. How electricity is generated and delivered has little to do with knowing how to turn on a light. The person only need understand the general idea that electricity flows along wires and that a switch can control whether or not the electricity will make the light bulb glow.

The smallest computers perform only one task at a time. Larger computers often do several different things at the same time. For example, one program may be in the process of being read in, another may be manipulating data, and a third may be completed with the results in the output process. When several things are happening at the same time, what is happening needs to be controlled. Control is the job of a powerful program called an *operating system*. An operating system's job is to allocate resources (input devices, output devices, etc.) and to schedule tasks (when to read, what program to run, etc.). The operating system program decides when a Pascal program can do its work.

The operating system program to control the computer handling your Pascal program has already been developed. The course instructor will provide information on how to use it so that Pascal programs can be processed by the computer.

1.2 COMPUTER SYSTEMS

Objective
Provide a general introduction to the hardware and software components of a computer system.

Suggested Background
Section 1.1 should be done before this section. This section is intended to provide a general summary of the topics presented in it. The reader is encouraged to seek supplemental information.

As was discussed in Section 1.1, a computer performs several different functions. Usually a single device does all of these functions. However, modern computers usually are made up of several separate pieces. The pieces are connected together by bundles of wires called cables. There may be many different combinations of pieces that can be used together. When several pieces are connected together, the result is usually called a *computer system*. Sometimes people call the collection of equipment that is used the *hardware* and the programs that are used the *software*.

The hardware that makes up a computer system can include a large variety of input and output devices. Most students will submit their data to a computer using either punched cards or a terminal and the results will be displayed either on a terminal or on a printer. Other input devices include those that read characters optically or magnetically. Computers can also accept data input from devices that read paper tape, magnetic tape, or magnetic disk.

Magnetic tape or disk is used as *auxiliary* storage. Programs and data can be stored temporarily on tape or disk by a computer program during the running of a program or for future use. Data and programs are also often put on tape, and sometimes disk, for transportation from one location to another.

As computer systems grow larger, more and more devices are collected together. Also, external communication capabilities are added to allow people who are not close to the computer to use the computer's facilities. Terminals sometimes communicate with a computer using telephone lines. Making all of the pieces work together is the job of the system software. In large computer systems, a considerable portion of what a computer does is to supervise and control its own activities. (The program called the operating system effects this control.)

1.3 USING A COMPUTER TO SOLVE PROBLEMS

Objective
Discuss how a program is connected to a clear statement of the problem.

Suggested Background
None.

A computer is an extremely powerful device. It can do just about any calculation or series of calculations that are necessary to solve a problem or task. But it can perform tasks only if it is told precisely and exactly what to do. The process of telling a computer what to do can be divided into planning what to do and then specifying the steps necessary to accomplish the plan. The machine must be instructed in its tasks in a way that the computer can use. If the computer was a person, we would say that it has to clearly and unambiguously "understand" what it is to do.

1.3.1 The Role of Algorithms

Objective
Develop the concept of what an algorithm is.

Suggested Background
None.

In order to understand what it is that is to be done, the solution to a problem first must be designed and stated in an algorithm. We all use algorithms. An algorithm is simply a plan of how to solve a problem. A more precise way of defining an algorithm is to say that it is a complete, unambiguous procedure for solving a specified procedure in a finite number of steps. An algorithm should be

(1)   unambiguous
(2)   precisely defined
(3)   finite
(4)   effective
(5)   specified as a series of steps

1.3.2 The Role of Programs

Objective
Connect the use of a program with an algorithm.

Suggested Background
Section 1.3.1.

A program is the way that a problem solver tells a computer the steps that it is to follow to solve a problem. A program is a detailed and explicit set of instructions for accomplishing an algorithmically stated problem. The program has to be stated in a language that the computer can use.

The purpose of a program is to solve a problem. A program that does not work and solve its problem is worthless. Additional goals of a program may include finding the solution in the cheapest and fastest manner possible, but cost and speed are unimportant if the problem has not been solved properly. (It is often the case that the problem is misunderstood by the problem solver and that an algorithm and program are designed to solve the wrong problem. The use of structured walkthroughs, discussed in Chapter 15, helps clarify the understanding of what is to be accomplished.)

1.4 PROGRAMMING LANGUAGES

Objectives
Discuss the purpose of a programming language, how programming languages are described, and the variations in programming languages.

Suggested Background
Sections 1.3, 1.3.1, and 1.3.2

A programming language is used to communicate with a computer. As with any language, there are rules on how a language statement should be formed. The rules for constructing a computer language statement are stricter than those concerning human language statements. For example, people might be instructed to write their ages on a piece of paper in a variety of different valid ways:

"Write your age down."
"Print your age."
"Place your age on the paper."
"Scribble your age there."
"Your age, fill it in."

However, in any given computer language there are only a small number of ways validly to instruct the machine to do the same thing. For example, in Pascal the instructions to write the value of an age are

```
WRITE(AGE)
WRITELN(AGE)
```

1.4.1 Programming Language Syntax and Semantics

Objective
Discuss the purposes of a programming language.

Suggested Background
Section 1.4.

The syntax or grammar of a language consists of rules specifying how to form statements and how the elements in the statements can be related to each other. In a human language, examples of syntax include punctuation, spelling, and the legal ways in which words may be used.

A language's semantics describes the meaning of a statement. In human language, semantics is often difficult to establish in validly formed language statements without a knowledge of the situation. For example, the meaning of the statement

"The girl hit the boy with the bat."

is unclear because we cannot tell if the girl used a bat to hit the boy or the girl hit the boy who was holding a bat. In contrast, in a computer language, a validly formed statement has only one meaning.

1.4.2 High and Low Level Languages

Objectives
Discuss why there are different types of languages.

> **Suggested Background**
> Sections 1.4 and 1.4.1.

Computer languages can be divided into *low* and *high* level languages. A low level language is very close to the machine's construction. Often a low level language can be used only on one model computer. An assembler language is an example of a low level language.

A high level language is usually easier to read. High level language statements are often combinations of English and mathematical statements. Many high level languages can be used on several different models of computers manufactured by different companies. Pascal is an example of a high level language.

It is usually easier and quicker to solve a problem by using a high level language. A program written in a high level language can reflect the form of the problem's solution. It is usually easier to verify the correct execution of a program written in a high level language. Sometimes, when written by a very talented programmer, a program written in a low level language takes less computer time to solve a problem. Sometimes certain manipulations cannot be done in a high level language and must be done in a low level language.

1.4.3 General and Special Purpose Languages

> **Objective**
> Discuss the need for general and special purpose languages.
>
> **Suggested Background**
> Sections 1.4, 1.4.1, and 1.4.2.

People developing high level computer programming languages choose either to (a) design a language to solve a special type of problem or (b) design a language to solve many different types of problems. Languages designed to serve special purposes include:

COBOL	business
FORTRAN	science and engineering
GPSS	simulation
LISP	list processing
SIMSCRIPT	simulation
SNOBOL	character strings and patterns

General purpose languages are used to solve a wide variety of problems. Many problems that a special purpose language can be used to solve can also be solved using a general purpose language. General purpose languages include:

Ada
ALGOL
BASIC
Pascal
PL/I

1.5 HOW A PROGRAM GETS EXECUTED

Objective
Develop an understanding of the steps that take place from when a program is read into the machine to when it is executed.

Suggested Background
Sections 1.1, 1.2, 1.3, 1.3.1, 1.3.2, and 1.4.

When a computer does the tasks specified in a program, the act of doing the tasks is called the *execution* of the program. Several things happen before and after the actual execution of a program.

When someone gives or *submits* a program to a computer, several events happen before the results are known. The result may be one of several things:

(1) messages indicating that the statements making up the program are invalidly written—these are called error or diagnostic messages,
(2) a program that begins to execute, but stops prematurely because of an error in the program's design,
(3) a program that executes and does not prematurely stop, but is unsatisfactory because the program does not do what is desired, or
(4) a program that does what you want it to.

Before a program can be executed, it first must be translated into a language that the computer can use to do its work. This is done by the Pascal *compiler*. The Pascal compiler is a program that translates the Pascal language statements into instructions that the machine is to follow. The compiler also checks to see if the Pascal programmer has followed the rules (*syntax*) specifying how the Pascal language statements were to be written.

After the program is translated, the translated statements are said to be the *object* program. In small computers, the object program is executed right away. In larger computers, the object program may be temporarily stored and then placed or *loaded* into a final place in the machine's memory, from which place the program is then executed. This process is shown graphically in Figure 1.2.

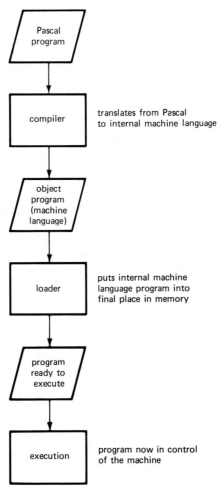

Figure 1.2 Program execution process.

1.6 AN OVERVIEW OF COMPUTER CAREERS
AND PROBLEM SOLVING

Objective
Connect the process of solving problems on the computer with jobs that people perform.

Suggested Background
The previous material in this chapter.

Many people can become involved in the recognition of a problem and its eventual solution on a computer. Figure 1.3 illustrates the roles that people can play when they come together to solve a problem using a computer. For some problems, an individual person can have more than one role. Notice that a written planning document is critical to the process.

A summary of the roles that people can play when a problem is solved on a computer follows.

Application programmer: Takes the solution from the analyst and writes (or codes) the programming language statements necessary to implement the solution plan on the computer. The program is best tested with actual or "live" data supplied by the customer asking for the problem to be solved.

Customer: Needs to have a particular problem solved. A customer may be a person or an organization, from inside or outside the company.

Data entry person: Enters data and/or programs into computer records for eventual input into the computer system. Data entry devices include key punches and terminals. In some places, the person who performs this function is known as a *keypunch operator* or a *tab operator*.

Hardware engineer: Is usually an electrical or mechanical engineer who designs the computer equipment. An engineer usually does not play a direct role in the solution of a particular problem. Most computer equipment is designed and constructed to solve many different problems. However, the equipment is designed to solve specific problem-solving needs that the engineer tries to satisfy.

Maintenance programmer: Once the customer accepts the program, has responsibility for corrections and/or minor enhancements. The maintenance programmer corrects discovered errors and implements changes or improvements.

Salesperson: Acts as an interface between a customer's needs, such as for machines, trained people, and programs, and the supplier who has one or more of these things to offer.

Systems analyst: Prepares a detailed plan of the problem's solution. The plan is then

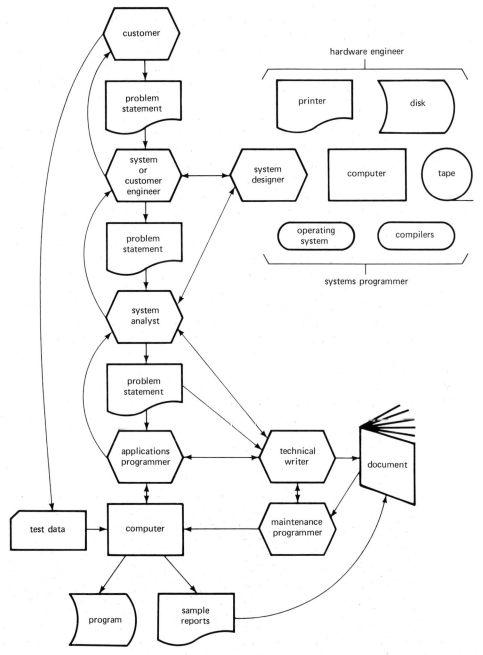

Figure 1.3 Simplified relationship diagram of people solving a computer problem.

given to the application programmer for implementation as a program. The analyst normally refines the solution plan by discussing it with the system engineer and possibly with the customer as well.

System engineer: Discusses the problem with the customer and develops, in consultation with the customer, a statement of the problem. A person performing this function is also sometimes known as a *customer engineer.*

System designer: Is responsible for selecting the computer system's programs (software). This software includes compilers (such as Pascal), operating systems, and prewritten (*packaged*) programs. Most of the system designer's time is spent on keeping the software operating properly.

1.7 ORGANIZING COLLECTIONS OF DATA: DATA ITEMS, RECORDS, FILES

Objectives
Introduce the concept of forming data items into collections of tiems.
Introduce the concept of file organization.

Suggested Background
Sections 1.1 and 1.2.

Computers can be used to store a wide variety of data. In digital computers, the data stored is represented by one or more symbols or characters. One way that the stored data can be represented is by a combination of alphabetic letters, such as a person's name. Computers can also be used to store data that consists entirely of numbers, such as a telephone number. Or the stored data may be a combination of both numbers and letters, such as in a street address.

<name>   CAROL SMITH
<telephone>   505–921–3465
<address>   52 South Elm Road

When computers are used to solve problems, a single problem might involve the use of many different kinds of data. These data are usually collected and stored in an organized manner. Different data items relating to one thing may be grouped together. A collection of all the related data about an area of concern is called a *file.* For example, all the stored data about a company's employees could be known as the employee or personnel file.

If it is possible to divide a file into parts with each part containing several pieces of data describing the same thing, the file subdivisions are called *records.* When records are created, all the data items in a record are related.

When a computer is to store several different data items that describe the same thing, these items are usually placed together in a record. For example, a company might wish to store several different things about an employee: name, birth date, hourly wage, etc. It is convenient to be well organized and keep all the data items about an employee together. All of this data about a single employee can be kept together by placing all of it in a record.

A distinct item of information in a record is known as a *field*. A field can also be known as a *data item*. A field stores a distinct piece of data, such as a person's name. Sometimes a field may be broken up or divided into subfields. For example, the field containing an employee's name could be subdivided into subfields containing the first, middle, and last names.

Usually an organization has a need to keep several records. For example, a company would have several employees and therefore would have a collection of several employee records. A collection of records is known as a file.

This can be summarized by noting that a file contains a collection of records while a record contains a collection of data items. Many organizations have more than one file containing data. Figure 1.4 illustrates the relationship between files, records, and data items by displaying a company's collection of data.

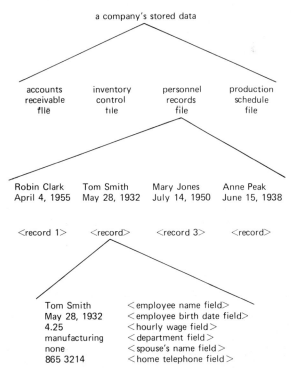

Figure 1.4   Example relationship between a stored information base, files, records, and data items.

Sometimes an organization's collection of files is called its *database*. However, the term database is also often used in conjunction with sophisticated data management systems called *database management systems* or *DBMS*. The data in a DBMS does not always appear to the user as being organized in the form of file-record-item. A full discussion of databases is beyond the scope of this book. You should be aware that different people may have different meanings for the term database.

1.8 QUESTIONS

1.1   Name the five basic parts of a computer.
1.2   What is the difference between computer "hardware" and "software"?
1.3   What is the job of an operating system?
1.4   What is an algorithm supposed to do?
1.5   What is a program supposed to do?
1.6   What is the purpose of a computer programming language?
1.7   What is the job of a compiler?
1.8   In terms of computer languages, define syntax and semantics.
1.9   Why are there special purpose computer programming languages?
1.10 What is meant by program "execution"?
1.11 What is the relationship between a record, a file, and a data item?
1.12 What is the difference between data and information? How does data become information?

Chapter 2

PROBLEM SOLVING BY TOP-DOWN ANALYSIS

Objectives
Introduce the concepts involved with top-down analysis and structured programming. Later in the book, Pascal will be used to solve problems that can be planned by top-down analysis.

Suggested Background
No specific background is required for this chapter.

When people try to plan how they are going to solve a problem, they often begin by defining the general outline of the task. Then the several big pieces that make up the task can be identified. The big pieces can then be seen to be made up of several smaller tasks that need to be done. For example, if our task is to go shopping, we might break the problem into several pieces, such as: (1) go to the store, (2) select the items, (3) pay for them, and (4) bring the purchased items home. Any of these might be broken down further; for example, go to the store might be divided into (a) take the car out of the garage, (b) drive to the store, and (c) park the car in the lot.

In the past few years, people involved in solving problems on the computer have become interested in the technique of problem investigation called top-down analysis. When the solution to a problem has been examined by the use of top-down analysis, programming techniques called structured programming are often used to implement the solution to the problem. The goal is to develop programs that are simple, easy to maintain, and whose results could easily be checked or verified. Pascal was designed to support structured problem analysis and program solution. Pascal encourages the programmer to proceed in a top-down manner.

2.1 TOP-DOWN ANALYSIS

Objectives
Discuss the concept and the usefulness of top-down division of a problem.

Suggested Background
The previous material in this chapter.

A person solving a problem by top-down analysis keeps dividing the problem into smaller and smaller pieces until the resulting pieces can be handled simply and easily. Just as when, in a war, a general might find it easier to "divide and conquer" his opponents, it is usually easier for a problem solver to divide a problem into pieces before "attacking" it.

In top-down analysis, the problem first is broken into a few big pieces (usually three or four). If the tasks to be done in a particular piece can be simply and clearly described in a few statements, then the task does not have to be divided again. If this is not possible, then that task should be broken up into several smaller tasks or parts. The process of breaking up a problem into parts continues until the tasks for each subdivision of the problem can be simply and clearly stated.

Every time that the problem is divided into more pieces, the plan of what needs to be done is further refined. For this reason, top-down analysis is also sometimes known as *stepwise refinement* because each step of the analysis results in greater problem refinement.

2.1.1 Graphic Representation of Top-Down Analysis

Objectives
Present and illustrate a graphic presentation technique that describes top-down analysis.

Suggested Background
The previous material in this chapter.

In some ways, writing a program for a computer to follow is similar to writing cooking instructions for someone to use in a kitchen. A top-down analysis of a simple cooking task might start as shown in Figure 2.1.

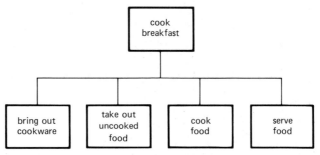

Figure 2.1   First step of a top-down analysis: cooking breakfast.

For some people, this might be enough, but for someone who is doing it for the first time, the task should be stated in finer detail. For example, "bring out cookware" could be further divided as shown in Figure 2.2.

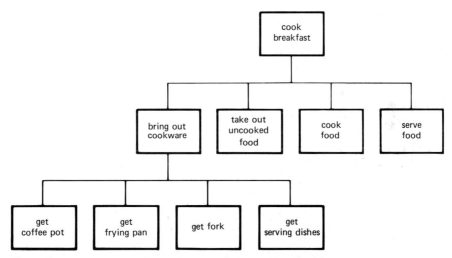

Figure 2.2   Second step of a top-down analysis: cooking breakfast.

At this point, it can be seen that two things are happening to the analysis. One, the number of boxes is growing, making it difficult to refer to specific boxes. And, two, further expansion of the number of boxes may make it difficult to fit them all on the same page.

2.1.1.1 Division Labeling

Objective
Illustrate how the parts of a graphic top-down analysis can be identified. This concept later is used in pseudo-code statement identification.

Suggested Background
The previous material in this chapter.

The first problem is handled by assigning a number for each box, as shown in Figure 2.3. Notice that the "level" of each box is indicated by its labeling number. For example, task 1 is "bring out cookware" and that task is subdivided into tasks 1.1, 1.2, 1.3, 1.4 as shown in Figure 2.3.

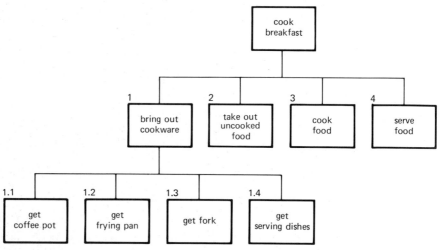

Figure 2.3   Labeled top-down analysis: cooking breakfast.

2.1.1.2 Picture on a Page

Objective
Introduce the concept of picture on a page analysis that enables graphic representations to illustrate the solution plan of a problem where the amount of detail that is to be shown cannot fit on a single page. This concept is intrinsically one of top-down design. It also helps identify modules.

Suggested Background
The previous material in this chapter.

The problem of fitting all the boxes of an analysis onto a page is solved by placing detailed expansion of the boxes on additional pages. A structured graphic analysis should not have lines connecting to additional pages. This expansion technique has been assigned many different names. The one used here is one of the most common: *picture on a page*. Using this technique, a box may be expanded on another page, but no pathways may continue to another page. This is illustrated in Figure 2.4.

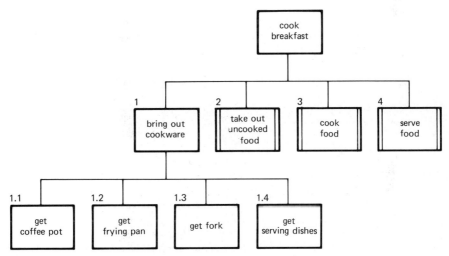

Figure 2.4   Top-down analysis that indicates that tasks 2, 3, and 4 are expanded on another page.

Figure 2.4 indicates that tasks 2, 3, and 4 are expanded on another page. The double vertical lines on the side of each box indicate the task expansion. Figure 2.5 illustrates a possible expansion of task 3. Notice that two tasks (3.2 and 3.3) in this diagram are also indicated as being expanded on another page.

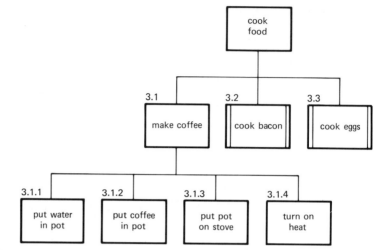

Figure 2.5 Expansion of the "cook food" box.

2.1.2 Outline Form

Objective
Illustrate how a top-down solution of a problem may be stated in an outline form.

Suggested Background
The previous material in this chapter.

Instead of placing the steps of a top-down analysis into a graphical form, the analysis of a problem can be put into an outline form. The top-down outline form of the cooking problem would be

cook breakfast
1   bring out cookware
     1.1   get coffeepot
     1.2   get frying pan
     1.3   get fork
     1.4   get serving dishes
2   take out uncooked food

3   cook food
   3.1   make coffee
      3.1.1   put water in pot
      3.1.2   put coffee in pot
      3.1.3   put pot on stove
      3.1.4   turn on heat
   3.2   cook bacon
   3.3   cook eggs
4   serve food

As can be seen, the outline form produces a clear and detailed explanation of the tasks in the problem solution.

The details of a problem's task definition can be developed by either inserting a new section of detail or by referring to an expansion on another page. For example, item 2 could be expanded as

2   take out uncooked food
   2.1   get coffee
   2.2   get eggs from refrigerator
   2.3   get bacon from refrigerator

An expansion can be either on a separate page or eventually incorporated into a full problem outline. If it is kept on a separate page, the higher level outline should indicate that an expansion exists by referring to the page number of the expansion. For example,

cook breakfast
1   bring out cookware (page A1)
2   take out uncooked food (page A2)
3   cook food (page A3)
4   serve food (page A4)

2.2 PROGRAM PLANNING

Objective
Discuss the general concerns of planning solutions to problems that are to be accomplished with the aid of a computer.

Suggested Background
The previous material in this chapter. Sections 1.3, 1.3.1, and 1.3.2.

The goal of program planning is to provide an exact plan or blueprint for the programmer to follow. A good program plan will ensure that the program does what it is supposed to do and that the job of creating the program will be completed more quickly and accurately.

This text encourages the top-down planning of programs. Different techniques to support top-down planning have been suggested. Some people have argued that a program planning document can also be used successfully to document the program.

Program documentation is used to explain what the program does. This need exists during the program development process as well as after the program has been written. Documentation is an important part of the process of solving problems on the computer. It helps the programmer solve the problem as it makes the problem easier to understand. It can help people other than the first programmer understand the program.

At this point in the text, the primary concern is with how best to plan the solution of a program. If the program's plan can be used again eventually to provide documentation for people other than those involved in the initial program development, that is good, but eventual documentation is not considered the reason for doing program planning. The goal is to effectively and efficiently analyze and plan programs.

Today many people believe that a technique called *pseudo-code* is the best way to explain the solution of a problem to be solved on a computer. The use of pseudo-code in the planning of a program is much the same as the use of the task outline form of a problem's solution discussed in the last section.

A pseudo-code plan of a program breaks up a problem step by step. The statements used in the program plan are in a shortened form of English. These statements are often similar to the language statements of many high level languages. Therefore, when the pseudo-code plan of the program is complete, it is relatively easy to convert the program planning pseudo-code statements into programming language statements.

2.3 USE OF PSEUDO-CODE

Objective
Present the basic planning method of program planning known as pseudo-code. This method is a fundamental part of effective top-down design. This planning method will be used throughout this book.

Suggested Background
The previous material in this chapter.

2.3.1 Pseudo-Code or Outline of a Problem's Solution Design

An outline or pseudo-code form of a problem solution allows the problem solver to easily approach the solution of a problem in a top-down fashion. The creation of pseudo-code is itself a top-down process. Each stage of analysis may be expressed as an outline level. Additionally, the completed analysis may be easily displayed in a combined form that retains the top-down solution methodology used.

When developing the outline form of problem solution design, the highest level divisions of the solution should be expressed first. Then each major subdivision of the problem's solution design should be expressed. The major subdivisions should then be subdivided, and the process continued until the problem solution design is simply and clearly stated.

The steps in this methodology are illustrated by the following AGRICUL-TURAL WAGE example.

Example: Agricultural Wage

Calculate the amount to be paid to several hourly agricultural workers. No taxes or other deductions are to be made. The following data is collected into a record for each worker: NAME, HOURLY RATE, HOURS WORKED. The program is to (1) calculate how much each worker is to be paid, (2) write a check for that amount, (3) produce a summary consisting of a count of the number of workers paid, the total amount paid, and a list of how much was paid to each.

The first step in any problem analysis is to recognize the major portions of the problem. It is best to subdivide each level of the problem's solution into less than four or five divisions. (In considering this example, recall from Chapter 1 that data may be grouped into a record and that records may be grouped into a file.)

1   prepare to calculate this week's payroll
2   as long as there may be a new record to be processed, try to read and process the work record of another person
3   display the summary results
4   store the results and terminate the job

After the major subdivisions of the problem's solution design have been identified, each major division should be divided again. Item 2 can be divided into three major tasks:

2.1   try to read a new work record
2.2   if a new work record was found, calculate the payroll information
2.3   if a new record was not found, write a message indicating that all records have been read

The major item 3 may be divided into

3.1   display count of the people paid
3.2   display total of the wages paid
3.3   display detaled list of all wages paid

The major item 4 may also be divided:

4.1   store the work records
4.2   terminate processing

Subdivisions may themselves be subdivided. For example, the subdivision of 2.2 may be divided into:

2.2.1   read and print name, hourly rate, hours worked
2.2.2   calculate wage by multiplying rate by hours
2.2.3   write check
2.2.4   write name, hourly rate, hours, wage to summary file
2.2.5   add to count of people paid, add wages to total wages paid

The refining process continues until the problem solution plan is sufficiently divided. A problem has been divide up enough when the program can be easily and simply written from the program plan.

The reasons for two of the items in 2.2 of the example plan may not be clear. In 2.2.1 the incoming data is printed directly after it is read in. This is called *echo printing* and helps in the verification of the program's results. This technique is discussed in greater detail in a later chapter. In 2.2.4 the summary results are written to a file that is printed later (under 3.3). The printing of the summary file is delayed as the printer is already being used to print the checks (under 2.2.3).

2.3.2 Column by Column Development of Pseudo-Code

Objective
Illustrate an effective way to develop a top-down pseudo-code solution plan.

Suggested Background
The previous material in this chapter.

When the problem solver is creating the problem solution, a good way to do it is in a column by column format, one column for each subdivision level. All the refinements in a column should be completed before moving on to the next column. The following table displays how the solution to the previous example might be developed.

1 prepare to calculate this week's payroll	1.1 get work records	
	1.2 initialize summary totals	1.2.1 set count of people to zero
		1.2.2 set total wages paid to zero
2 as long as there may be a new record to be processed, try to read the work record of another person	2.1 try to read a new work record	
	2.2 if a new work record was found, calculate the payroll information	2.2.1 read and print: name, hourly rate, hours worked
		2.2.2 calculate wage by multiplying rate by hours
		2.2.3 write check
		2.2.4 write name, hourly rate, hours, wage to summary file
		2.2.5 add to count of people paid, add wages paid to total wages paid
	2.3 if a new record was not found, write a message that all records have been read	
3 display the summary results	3.1 display count of the people paid	
	3.2 display total of the wages paid	
	3.3 display detailed list of all wages paid	
4 store the results and terminate the job.	4.1 store the work records	
	4.2 terminate processing	

2.3.3 Indented Pseudo-Code Format

Objective
Illustrate how a pseudo-code solution plan can be effectively displayed so that the structure of the problem is revealed.

Suggested Background
The previous material in this chapter.

After developing the problem's solution, the design can be displayed in the
indented pseudo-code format that was shown before.

Example: Agricultural Wage: Pseudo-Code

This is the solution design to the AGRICULTURAL WAGE example in the
form of indented pseudo-code. This result can be generated by first developing the results in the column by column format that was shown in the
preceding section.

agricultural wage
1   prepare to calculate this week's payroll
    1.1   get work records
    1.2   initialize summary totals
        1.2.1   set count of people to zero
        1.2.2   set total wages paid to zero
2   as long as there may be a new record to be processed, try to read the work
    record of another person
    2.1   try to read another work record
    2.2   if a new work record was found, calculate the payroll information
        2.2.1   read and print: name, hourly rate, hours worked
        2.2.2   calculate wage by multiplying rate by hours
        2.2.3   write check
        2.2.4   write name, hourly rate, hours, wage to summary file
    2.3   if a new record was not found, write a message that all records have
        been read
3   display the summary results
    3.1   display count of the people paid
    3.2   display total of the wages paid
    3.3   display detailed list of all wages paid
4   store the results and terminate the job.
    4.1   store the work records
    4.2   terminate processing

2.4 AN OVERVIEW OF STRUCTURED PROGRAMMING

Objectives

Provide a general overview of what has come to be known as structured programming. Pascal is a language that was specifically designed to develop structured programming solutions to problems. A more extensive review of structured programming can be found in Jensen (1981). This section provides a general introduction to the theoretical considerations of structured programming that may not be suitable for all readers.

Suggested Background

None. An understanding of the previous material would enhance this chapter. At the same time, some of the topics covered in this chapter are motivating factors for previous material.

Structured programming also helps in the *maintenance* of a program. (Program maintenance means the modification of an already written and running program, often by someone other than the original program author.) Someone who modifies an already existing structured program can concentrate first on the control structure and then on the tasks being done.

Increasing experience with the concepts of structured programming have allowed them to be systematized. Demonstrations of the effectiveness of structured programming have helped it to gain acceptance. Additionally, theoretical work starting with Dijkstra (1965) helped formalize the procedures and in turn led to the development of languages such as Pascal. Pascal was specifically designed to be a structured programming language.

Structured programming helps reduce the complexity of a problem. This helps (a) to increase the amount of work an individual programmer can accomplish, (b) to reduce program testing problems, and (c) to improve program clarity.

The solving of problems through top-down program development is based on step by step refinement. At each level, what is to be done is defined and decomposed and expressed in terms of lower level detail. The process is continued until the level is reached at which it is possible to directly write statements in the computer language being used. This process is often called *stepwise refinement* (Wirth, 1971). It is a fundamental part of structured programming. The highest level of the problem represents the general description of the problem; each subsequent lower level provides greater and greater detail.

A benefit of top-down design is the resulting separation of the statements deciding what happens next from the specific manipulations that are to be done in the program. The top level or controlling modules specify what is to be done and the conditions under which it is to be done. Lower level modules are controlled by the higher level modules and accomplish what needs to be done. This natural separation assists the designer because the problem has been divided into two smaller problems: control and function. An example of this was seen in the preceding payroll program where the control structure selected the payroll calculation steps for execution if a new work record was found.

The parts that make up a higher level program module will eventually become separate groups of program statements whose execution is determined by a control statement. The overall control structure can be designed and programmed before any of the lower levels are written.

Structured programming also helps in the *maintenance* of a program. (Program maintenance means the modification of an already written and running program, often by someone other than the original program author.) Someone who modifies an already existing structured program can concentrate first on the control structure and then on the tasks being done.

In a structured program, the program is limited to language statements that accomplish three functions: sequence, selection, and iteration. That is, when solving a problem, the sequence in which things are done can be changed, some things may be selected to be done while others may not be done, and iteration may result in some things being repeated until a specified condition is satisfied. The idea that programs can be limited to these three types of statements was first presented by Bohm and Jacopini (1966). Top-down designs are often expressed in terms of these funtions as what is happening can be clearly specified.

A strength of the top-down approach is that the stages of the programming process may be carried out independently. For example, once a given module has been defined, it can be programmed and tested, whether or not any of the other program modules are developed. This is accomplished by substituting *stubs* for program modules that still have to be developed.

A stub may be substituted for a block of program statements that have not yet been developed. The stub has the same name as the uncompleted programming for which it substitutes, but it doesn't perform the actual function it represents. What it does is to provide sufficiently similar behavior to "fool" the module that references it. This allows the overall control structure of the program to be developed and tested while individual modules are under separate development. Likewise, it allows the development and testing of a module to proceed separately before it is plugged into the rest of the program.

The major advantage of this phased approach is that at every point there is a partial system that works. It shows the computer analyst and programmer a pretty good picture of what the final system will do and serves as the test bed for the next module to be completed. A second advantage is that problems in the design are more likely to be discovered during the initial analysis and design of the problem solution.

One of the factors that led to the development and acceptance of the structured, top-down approach is that the requirements of a system usually change before the project is finished. Someone gets a new idea, a different mix of equipment is selected, the federal income tax people demand a different form for reporting withholding tax, etc. Design change is inevitable. It doesn't have to ruin the project. A project can be planned to adapt to changes. The top-down approach allows planning for changes by postponing the design of the most volatile system components until they become stable.

The top-down approach is also helpful in isolating critical parts of the problem, whether they are part of the function of the system, such as an algorithm that must be especially efficient, or are part of the environment.

REFERENCES

C. Bohm and G. Jacopini, Flow diagrams, Turing machines and languages with only two formation rules, *Commun. ACM,* vol. 9, no. 5, May 1966, pp. 366–371.

E. W. Dijkstra, Programming considered as a human activity, *Proc. IFIP Congress,* 1965, pp. 213–217.

R. W. Jensen, Structured programming, *IEEE Computer,* vol. 14, no. 3, March 1981, pp. 31–48.

N. Wirth, Program development by stepwise refinement, *Commun. ACM,* vol. 14, no. 4, April 1971, pp. 221–227.

2.5 AN OVERVIEW OF PROGRAM DOCUMENTATION

Objective
Provide a brief introduction to the value of program documentation.

Suggested Background
This section can stand alone. However, Section 1.6, which discusses the need for people solving a problem with a computer to communicate, would be useful.

Over the years, programmers have used various program planning techniques. Often people try to use the plan that was used to develop the program to provide documentation after the program has been developed. Program documentation is used to describe what a program must do, what the program user must do to run the program, and how each part of the program goes about doing what it does. These documentation needs can be respectively identified as: functional specifications, usage instructions, and program analysis/implementation techniques.

Program documentation is especially useful when someone other than the original programmer is to use and/or modify the program. This text considers program planning and documentation as distinct activities.

When problems are to be solved using a top-down approach, a technique of problem analysis that displays the steps that the solution method is to follow is needed. There are several different techniques for displaying the solution concept of a problem. This text uses the method called *pseudo-code*. Pseudo-code is a structured form of English. Pseudo-code is an effective way to plan a top-down solution of a problem. An older method is the use of a semigraphical representation called a *flowchart*. There are several different styles of flowcharting. This book has chosen to use pseudo-code instead of flowcharts as pseudo-code is a significantly more effective tool for planning top-down, structured programs.

2.6 QUESTIONS

2.1 What is the goal of structured programming?
2.2 List the benefits of structured programming.
2.3 What is meant by "top-down" analysis?
2.4 How does the "picture on a page" planning technique relate to the top-down development of pseudo-code?

2.7 PROBLEMS

2.1. Using the picture on a page technique, describe the tasks needed to go grocery shopping.

2.2. Perform a top-down analysis of the tasks needed to wash a car. Display your analysis in the column-by-column pseudo-code form shown in Section 2.3.2.

2.3. Perform a top-down analysis of the tasks required to get input to leave the house in the morning. You should include getting out of bed, bodily cleanliness, eating a breakfast of cornflakes, and getting dressed. Display your analysis in the form of indented pseudo-code.

2.4. The evil Dr. Kcalzam has put you in a room that is rapidly filling with water. The room will stay filled with water for 24 hours. On the table before you are 12 pills. Eleven of them are poisonous. One of them will allow you to successfully and healthily breathe water for 25.2317654 hours. You have been provided with a simple balance scale that will work exactly three times. Each pill is numbered. The pill that will contribute to your continued good health is either heavier or lighter than the poison pills. All the poison pills have the same weight. Describe your algorithm using pseudo-code to identify the "nice pill." No other means of resolving your dilemma will be acceptable.

Note: A simple balance scale consists of two pans. Into each pan objects may be placed. When the scale is released, it indicates
   (a) the two pans contain contents of equal weight, or
   (b) which, if any, pan has heavier contents.

2.5. Thomas Zarok in the second grade was given a problem to add all the numbers from 1 to 100 together. He completed the task in a little over one minute of work. He obviously did not do the necessary 99 additions but instead used an algorithm to answer the problem. (The answer is 5050.) Your job is to design an algorithm to do the same.

Chapter 3

BASIC ELEMENTS OF A PROGRAM

Objectives
Describe the basic building blocks of a Pascal computer program. This is one of the three core chapters on Pascal that are necessary for all the remaining Pascal material. The other chapters are 4 and 5.

Suggested Background
As this is the first chapter on Pascal programming itself, no prior background is necessary. Material in Chapters 1 and 2 would enhance your understanding of this and subsequent chapters. This chapter should be done before any other chapter on the Pascal language.

When discussing how they live, people describe both what they have and the pattern of their activities. Most of the things that we own are not in use at any one time. When an organized person has things that are not in use, they are usually stored in a specific place. Tools may be stored in a toolbox, clothes in a dresser, and a car in the garage. A person using a computer needs to be even more organized.

Someone concerned with a computer program needs to know both how to define what data is available and the basic classification and pattern of activities within a program. This chapter discusses how things are identified and how they are organized.

3.1 DATA

Objective
Introduce the concept of data storage and differing types of data.

Suggested Background
The previous material in this chapter.

Within a computer, data is stored in specific places. The programmer tells the computer where to store the data. Some programming languages require the programmer to tell the computer precisely where the data is to be stored within the machine. This is often a tedious process during which it is easy to make many mistakes.

When using a high level language such as Pascal, the storage spaces within the computer are given names selected by the programmer. The programmer selects the names. The programming language, instead of the programmer, selects the spaces that are to be used. To store or retrieve data, the programmer only needs to know the name of the space where the data is stored. Knowledge of the exact location of the space is not needed.

A computer can store many different kinds of data. In order that the data can be used properly, the computer must be told what the nature of the data is. When using Pascal, this is done by providing a data type for each variable.

Pascal has two different classes of data types: (a) scalar and (b) structured. Structured data types are used to organize individual data elements into groups of data called *data structures*. Structured data is discussed in a later chapter.

3.1.1 Scalar Data Types

Objectives
Introduce the concept of a scalar data type and introduce the different data types.

Suggested Background
The previous material in this chapter.

A scalar data type defines or lists all the possible values of the type. A data type is said to be scalar when between two values of the same data type there can be only one of the following relationships: greater than, less than, or equal. This means that scalar data types can be *ordered*. Ordered data can be put into a list based on whether or not one data item is considered to be less than, equal to, or greater than another data item. For example, the list 1,2,3,3,3,4,7 is ordered from smallest to largest.

There are two classes of scalar data types: (a) standard or (b) user defined. Standard scalar data types provided by Pascal are: INTEGER, REAL, CHARACTER, and BOOLEAN. User defined data types are developed by the programmer for use in solving a specific problem and will be discussed in a later chapter.

3.1.1.1 INTEGER

Objective
Define the scalar data type INTEGER.

Suggested Background
The previous material in this chapter.

INTEGER data is numeric data consisting entirely of whole numbers. Consequently, INTEGER values are not expressed using a decimal point. The largest INTEGER that can be used in a program is usually determined by the computer that is being used. Pascal has available the largest positive INTEGER that can be handled with the computer being used. This information is available through a predefined constant called MAXINT. (In the Waterloo Pascal compiler, the value of MAXINT is defined as 2,147,483,647.)

Examples of valid INTEGERs in Pascal are

$$56340$$
$$+121893$$
$$14$$
$$-75$$
$$0$$
$$-63451$$

Notice that INTEGERs do not carry a decimal point. Also note that commas are not used within a numeric constant in Pascal. This is illustrated in the list above by the first integer being shown as "56340" and not as "56,340". If an INTEGER has a comma in it, Pascal will identify the comma as an error. INTEGERs without a leading sign ("+" or "−") are considered positive.

3.1.1.2 REAL

Objective
Describe REAL scalar data values.

Suggested Background
The previous material in this chapter (Section 3.1.1.1 is not necessary).

REAL numbers are numbers that require the use of a decimal point. In Pascal all REAL numbers must be written with at least one digit on each side of the decimal point. Some valid Pascal REAL numbers are

$$3424.75$$
$$0.16$$
$$-154.32$$
$$1.4$$
$$0.0$$
$$-16.8942$$

As was the case for INTEGERs, REAL numbers in Pascal do not include commas. This is illustrated in the list above by the first real number being shown as "3424.75" and not as "3,424.75".

REAL numbers may also be represented in Pascal by a form similar to scientific representation. This type of representation is most useful for numbers that are very large or very small. However, scientific notation can be used for any size REAL number. In scientific notation, the number is written as a value multiplied by a specified power of 10. The representation

$$6.2E+5$$

tells Pascal that the value of the constant is 6.2 multiplied by 10 to the fifth power, or

$$6.2 \times 100000 = 620000$$

The representation

$$4.31E-3$$

tells Pascal that the value of the constant is 4.31 multiplied by 10 to the −3 power, or

$$4.31 \times 0.001 = 0.00431$$

Constants expressed in Pascal as REAL numbers are not required to have a sign either in front of the number or in the exponent. They are not required to have a decimal point because they have an exponent. Additionally, fractional powers are not valid. Some valid REAL constants expressed in this form are

```
     -26.2E+12
  31.14159E-1
      3.2E23
        5E+12
    37.4E-21
```

The size of the REAL number that can be represented in Pascal depends on the computer being used. The size limit is a combination of range and precision. Range describes the largest and the smallest allowable values. Precision describes the maximum number of digits that can be used to represent a REAL number. Generally, the maximum number of digits that can be used to represent a REAL number is smaller than the maximum number of digits that may be used to compose an INTEGER. (When using the Waterloo Pascal compiler, the largest REAL value is approximately $7.2E+75$ and the smallest positive REAL value is approximately $5.4E-79$.)

3.1.1.3 CHARACTER

Objective
Discuss the CHAR (character) scalar data type.

Suggested Background
The previous material in this chapter (Sections 3.1.1.1 and 3.1.1.2 are not required).

A character data value in Pascal can be any one of the characters defined as being valid for the computer being used. Different computer builders provide different character sets. All manufacturers include at least the 26 capital letters of the alphabet A,B,C, . . .,Z and the ten digits 0,1,2, . . .,9 as well as the blank character. Appendix C presents several different character sets that are often used with Pascal. (When using the Waterloo Pascal compiler, character data is defined to include all 256 EBCDIC character codes. This includes all upper and lower case letters, and special characters.)

The character data type is defined as CHAR in Pascal. If there is a need to store data consisting of more than one character, such as a person's name, a more complex data structure must be used. This is discussed in a later chapter. Character data elements are enclosed in single apostrophe marks. The apostrophe mark itself is represented by two apostrophes. The following are all valid character representations.

```
'2'
'A'
'3'
'+'
'<'
''''     (the apostrophe character)
```

Data stored as a CHAR type is scalar. This means that CHAR values can be placed in a sequence. This sequence is sometimes known as the *sort sequence*. The sort sequence is determined by the inequality relationship between different CHAR values. The sort sequence depends on the computer that is used. In general the following is true

$$' \ ' < 'A' < 'B' < \ldots < 'Z' < '0' < '1' < \ldots < '9'$$

Most people are familiar with the everyday use of a sort sequence. For example, the names in a telephone book are sequenced by the above sort sequence.

3.1.1.4 BOOLEAN

Objective
Discuss and present the BOOLEAN scalar data type. This data type is not used often in the rest of the book as a data variable value. BOOLEAN values will often happen as the result of tests and will in turn be used to control what happens in the program.

Suggested Background
The previous material in this chapter (Sections 3.1.1.1, 3.1.1.2, and 3.1.1.3 are not required).

BOOLEAN scalar data elements have a value of either "TRUE" or "FALSE." The value "FALSE" is considered to have a scalar value less than that of "TRUE" ("FALSE" < "TRUE").

One way that a "TRUE" or "FALSE" value can result is from a scalar relational comparison—for example, a test to see if the value of one variable is greater than the value of another variable. Relational comparisons can be made between any two standard scalar data values of the same type; that is, INTEGER, REAL, CHAR, or BOOLEAN data types. (Relational comparisons are discussed in Section 5.3.) A BOOLEAN variable may be used to store the "TRUE" or "FALSE" value that results from a relational comparison. BOOLEAN data elements may be used to control the order in which program statements are executed. How to do this is discussed in Chapter 6 on flow of control in a program.

3.2 NAMES

Objective
Discuss how Pascal labels and describes what it uses.

Suggested Background
The introductory material at the beginning of this chapter.

People find it necessary to name many different things. Names refer to: (a) people, places, and other physical objects; (b) ideas about how to handle physical objects, such as those in nuclear engineering; (c) nonphysical attributes, such as spirituality; as well as (d) ideas concerned with the development of nonphysical objects, such as theology. Each of these things is named, even though the things named are considerably different. In solving problems on a computer, it is also necessary to name a variety of different things.

3.2.1 Identifiers

Objectives
Discuss why there are identifiers and identify the different classes of identifiers.

Suggested Background
Section 3.2.

Pascal provides three different classes of names: (a) user identifiers, (b) reserved words, and (c) standard identifiers. Each of these serves a different purpose.

For example, when a Pascal programmer manipulates data in the computer, the computer uses the name of the space where the data is stored as a way of identifying the data. When the value of the data that is stored can be changed during the course of a program, the contents of the space are said to be variable. The user defined identifier that names the space is called a *variable name*.

3.2.2 User Identifiers

User identifiers are names defined by the programmer to name a wide variety of different objects such as (a) variables, (b) constants, (c) data types, (d) procedures

and functions, or (e) programs. A user identifier must begin with an alphabetic
character and be composed only of alphabetic and numeric chracters. Alphabetic
characters are defined as "A","B", . . .,"Z" and numeric characters are defined as
"0","1", . . .,"9".

As long as it fits on a line, an identifier may be as many characters long as
desired. However, some Pascal compilers only use the first eight characters of an
identifier to distinguish one identifier from another. (Both standard Pascal and the
Waterloo Pascal compiler use all the characters in the identifier.)

3.3 VARIABLES

Objectives
Discuss the concept of variables and their role.

Suggested Background
The previous material in this chapter.

Variables are usually the most commonly used identifiers in a program. They
are used to refer to a location within the machine where data is kept.

3.3.1 The Role of Variables

One way of visualizing the role that variables play is to think of a set of
mailboxes. Each mailbox may have a name on it. The postman knows where to put
the mail because of the names on the mailboxes. In much the same way, the computer
knows where to store information because the spaces within the machine can be
identified by variable names.

Mailboxes are available in many different sizes. Different mailboxes may be
chosen because of different needs. One person gets a lot of mail and needs a big box;
another may only need a small box. In much the same way, computers can provide
different types of storage space, depending on what is to be stored.

3.3.2 The Need to Declare Variables

Objectives
Identify the reason why Pascal uses variables and discuss the implica-
tions of Pascal being a strongly typed language.

Suggested Background
The previous material in this chapter.

When programming in Pascal, we tell or declare the variable names that are going to be used. Roughly speaking, this is the same as assigning names to mailboxes. All variables that are used in a Pascal program must be declared.

When declaring Pascal variables, it is also necessary to define or declare the data type. Roughly speaking, this can be thought of as choosing the size of the mailbox that will be associated with a given name.

Pascal is a strongly typed language. The term *strongly typed* has a special theoretical meaning when it is used to classify a programming language. The importance of this classification in this book is that strongly typed languages restrict the values that may be assigned to a variable. Strongly typed languages help enhance legibility and program organization. Also, error checking during program compilation and execution is aided by strong typing.

In Pascal the strong typing has the result that:

(a) Each variable can and must be associated with a single data type.
(b) The variable may only have values of its associated variable type. For example, an integer variable may not take on a character value.
(c) Most operators and functions are defined only for specific data types. For example, there is one division operator for integer variables and another for real variables.
(d) Mixing data types in a computation is restricted. For example, a numeric variable cannot be added to a character variable.

3.3.3 Declaring Variables

Objective
Describe how a Pascal programmer is to define variables.

Suggested Background
Section 3.3.2.

In Pascal variables are declared using the VAR declaration. The form of the VAR declaration is

```
VAR
    <name>,...,<name> : <data type>;
    <name>,...,<name> : <data type>;

        .
        .
        .

    <name>,...,<name> : <data type>;
```

(A particular type of notation is used above and will be used elsewhere in this text. Whenever a character string is enclosed between angle brackets, for example <name> or <data type>, it indicates that any object of that class may be used. For example, any of INTEGER, REAL, BOOLEAN, or CHAR could be used as a data type.)

Blank characters generally are not required in Pascal; all necessary separations are indicated by punctuation and restricted names (discussed in Section 3.4). However, no blanks may be included within an identifier. Blanks may be inserted to make a program more readable. For example, the VAR section of

```
VAR
    COUNT, AGE, ROOMNUMBER: INTEGER;
    AVERAGE, SALARY: REAL;
    DEPENDENTS: INTEGER;
```

defines COUNT, AGE, ROOMNUMBER, and DEPENDENTS to be INTEGER variables while AVERAGE and SALARY are defined to be REAL numbers.

The VAR declaration allows the grouping of as many variables of the same type as desired within the same statement. There is no requirement to group names of the same type together. As many statements and lines can be used as desired. For example, the previous VAR declaration can be restated as

```
VAR
    COUNT: INTEGER;
    AGE: INTEGER;
    ROOMNUMBER: INTEGER;
    AVERAGE: REAL;
    SALARY: REAL;
    DEPENDENTS: INTEGER;
```

In general, this text will declare variables on separate lines, primarily to increase program readability.

3.3.4 Meaningful Variable Names

Objective
Encourage the use of constructing variable names that inform the reader as to what the variable is being used for.

Suggested Background
Sections 3.3.2 and 3.3.3.

Programs are much more readable when the programmer uses *meaningful* variable names. A meaningful variable name indicates how a variable is being used. Meaningful variable names make the task of writing and changing a program much easier. For example, compare

```
TOTALSALES/CUSTOMERCOUNT
```

with the equally valid

```
J/K
```

If the data types and values are the same, both statements will result in the same numeric result. However, to someone reading the program, the first statement is certainly much more understandable.

3.4 RESTRICTED NAMES

Objectives
Describe why there are restricted names and identify which names are restricted.

Suggested Background
All parts of Section 3.3.

In daily life, there are many names that have restricted use. Some restrictions are absolute. For example, only one automobile manufacturer can use the name "Morgan." Some names are generally used in one way, but can be used in another way. For example, "George" is usually a male name, but it is occasionally used to name a female, such as "George Sand." Other names can be freely applied; for example, "Skinny."

3.4.1 Reserved Words

Objective
Identify the names in Pascal that can be used for only one purpose in a program.

Suggested Background
All parts of Sections 3.3 and 3.4.

There are some names that the Pascal programmer cannot use for variable or constant names. These are names that Pascal has reserved for a special purpose and cannot be used in a program for any other purpose. They are known as *reserved words* and are

AND	END	NIL	SET
ARRAY	FILE	NOT	THEN
BEGIN	FOR	OF	TO
CASE	FUNCTION	OR	TYPE
CONST	GOTO	PACKED	UNTIL
DIV	IF	PROCEDURE	VAR
DO	IN	PROGRAM	WHILE
DOWNTO	LABEL	RECORD	WITH
ELSE	MOD	REPEAT	

Some Pascal compilers may have additional reserved words such as FORWARD and EXTERN.

3.4.2 Standard Identifiers

Objective
Identify the names in Pascal that have a predefined meaning and use that can have the predefined use redefined.

Suggested Background
All parts of Section 3.3. and Sections 3.4 and 3.4.1.

Standard identifiers are names that have a predefined meaning. Their meaning may be redefined in a Pascal program. When they are redefined, they cannot be used for the original purpose for the rest of the program. For example, the predefined meaning of SQRT in Pascal is square root. However, the programmer can define the meaning of SQRT to be an INTEGER variable name. If this happens, SQRT no longer can be used to find a square root.

One advantage in allowing standard identifiers to be redefined is that the programmer does not have to keep track of what the standard identifiers are. However, redefining a standard identifier could cause some problems by eliminating the programmer's ability to do things that could be done before.

The names of the standard identifiers are

ABS	GET	PAGE	SQR
ARCTAN	INTEGER	PRED	SQRT
BOOLEAN	INPUT	PUT	SUCC
CHAR	LN	READ	TEST
CHR	MAXINT	READLN	TEXT
COS	NEW	REAL	TRUE
DISPOSE	ODD	RESET	TRUNC
EOF	ORD	REWRITE	UNPACK
EOLN	OUTPUT	ROUND	WRITE
EXP	PACK	SIN	WRITELN
FALSE			

3.5 CONSTANTS

Objectives
Present the concept of data values that remain constant throughout the execution of a program and how these constant variables can be defined in a Pascal program.

Suggested Background
All parts of Section 3.3.

Sometimes, in a program, there is a value that is not supposed to change. This type of value is known as a *constant* value. For example, the programmer may wish to use the constant *pi* (3.14159 . . .). One way for the programmer to do this is simply to include the numeric value 3.14159 within the program statements. However, except for well known numeric values such as that for pi, a person reading the program may not be able to understand the role that a given constant is to play.

Pascal provides the programmer with a means of identifying named constants without the concern that the value of the named identifier will change. The form or syntax of the CONST section is

```
CONST

    <name> = <constant>; ... ; <name> = <constant>;
```

For example,

```
CONST
    PI = 3.1415927;
    MOMSAGE = 46;
    NO = FALSE;
    DOLLARSIGN = '$';
```

In these examples, the equal test operator "=" has been used to indicate what value a constant is to be given. For example, the value of the constant PI is established to be 3.1415927. The general use of the equal test operator is discussed in the Chapter 5.

3.6 STRUCTURE OF A PASCAL PROGRAM

Objective
Present an overview of how all the pieces of a Pascal program are to fit together.

Suggested Background
The previous material in this chapter.

A Pascal program is composed of three parts: (a) program heading, (b) declarations, and (c) an executable section.

3.6.1 Program Heading

Objective
Describe how the first statement of a Pascal program is to be written.

Suggested Background
None.

The program heading is the first statement in a program. It begins with the reserved word "PROGRAM." This statement assigns a name to the program and identifies the files that the program will use to acquire data and to supply results.

A program uses a file to communicate the results of what it has done. The most common Pascal file for results is called "OUTPUT." Normally, OUTPUT will be assigned either to the printer or to a terminal. If a program reads in data, this data must also be read in through a file. "INPUT" is the standard Pascal file for data coming into the program. "INPUT" is usually assigned to a card reader or to a terminal. The use of files will be discussed again in a later chapter.

The form of the PROGRAM statement is

```
PROGRAM <name> (<file>,...,<file>);
```

For example,

```
PROGRAM TAXES(INPUT,OUTPUT);
```

names the program "TAXES" and specifies two files for program communication, "INPUT" and "OUTPUT."

3.6.2 Declaration Section

Objectives
Describe where declarations are to be made in a program and introduce the fact that there are more than data declarations.

Suggested Background
The previous material in this chapter.

In the declaration section, the Pascal programmer names all the identifiers that will be used in the program. Everything that is to be named in a Pascal program must be named in the declaration section. The declaration section can include the previously discussed VAR and CONST as well as several other classes of declarations. How a declaration is described varies from declaration class to declaration class. The form of the declaration section is

```
LABEL     <declaration>;
CONST     <declaration>;
TYPE      <declaration>;
VAR       <declaration>;
PROCEDURE <declaration>;
FUNCTION  <declaration>;
```

The inclusion of any declaration is optional. The order of the declarations must be as shown, except that there may be several PROCEDURE and/or FUNCTION declarations and their order may be interchanged.

So far only the CONST and VAR declarations have been discussed. These declarations are directly related to the data types that have been covered. The other declarations are discussed in later chapters.

3.6.3 Executable Section

Objectives
Introduce the concept that there is a separate section of a Pascal program where computations and decisions are made. Also, present the form of the section.

Suggested Background
Sections 3.6, 3.6.1, and 3.6.2.

The executable section of a Pascal program performs the work that the program has been designed to do. All computations, reading of data, and writing of results happen in the executable section.

The executable section is bounded or delimited by the reserved words BEGIN and END. That is, BEGIN must be the first word on the executable section and its matching END terminates the executable section. The terminating END of the executable section must be followed by a period "."—which indicates the end of the program. The executable part of a Pascal program uses terms previously defined either by Pascal or by a declaration.

The form of an executable section is

```
BEGIN
   <statement>;
   <statement>;
   .
   .
   .
   <statement>;
   <statement>
END.
```

3.6.3.1 Statement Separator

Objective
Introduce the concept that statements are separated from each other by
a special punctuation mark.

Suggested Background
Section 3.6.3.

The semicolon ";" in Pascal is used as a statement separator, not as a statement
terminator. It is used to indicate where the separation is between a preceding and a
following statement. The programmer must be careful in using the semicolon, or
serious programming errors can occur. As we proceed in the text, the proper use of
the semicolon will be regularly pointed out.

3.6.3.2 The Use of BEGIN and END

Objectives
Introduce the concept of delimiters as opposed to statements. Also,
discuss the specific roles of the delimiters BEGIN and END.

Suggested Background
Sections 3.6 and 3.6.1.

Notice that the last "<statement>" in the example from Section 3.6.3 was not
followed by a semicolon. This is because the statement does not have to be separated
from END. The reserved word "END" is not considered to be a separate statement. It
acts as a boundary marker or delimiter in the program. The period that follows END
acts both to mark the end of the program and to terminate the last program statement.

Likewise, the reserved word "BEGIN" is not a statement. It is used as a
delimiter to mark or indicate the beginning of a group of statements. Notice that in the
form shown in Section 3.6.3, BEGIN has no punctuation after it. There is no
punctuation because the first executable statement is only completed on the next line
of the example.

The reserved words BEGIN and END can also be used within the executable
section of a Pascal program. There they can be used to group statements together.
This use is explained in Chapter 6.

3.6.4 Comments

Objective
Describe how documentary comments can be included in a Pascal program.

Suggested Background
A general understanding of the previous material in this chapter is desirable; however, this section does not build on any specific other section. A general understanding of the need for documentation (Section 2.5) will enhance an understanding as to why comments are inserted into a program.

Comments are used to help someone reading the program to understand it. They are useful both to the original programmer and to the other people who may read the program.

The entire process of explaining what a program does and how it does it is called *documentation*. One of the advantages of Pascal is that the structure of the language and the ease of constructing meaningful variable names make Pascal partially self-documenting.

To help with documentation, Pascal allows comments to be inserted into programs between pairs of brackets: "{" "}" such as

```
{ THIS IS AN EXAMPLE OF A COMMENT }
```

Not all versions of Pascal have the capability to use brackets. When this happens it is usually because the host computer or the device being used to input the program cannot represent them. Pascal provides that, as an alternative, "(*" and "*)" may be used to enclose a comment. For example,

```
(* THIS IS AN EXAMPLE OF A COMMENT *)
```

This last form of comment construction is used throughout the text.

3.6.5 Complete Program Shell

Objective
Present a description of how all the pieces of a Pascal program are fitted together.

The complete shell of a Pascal program is

```
PROGRAM <program name>(<file>,<file>,...,<file>);
LABEL <declaration>;
CONST <declaration>;
TYPE  <declaration>;
VAR   <declaration>;
PROCEDURE and FUNCTION <declarations>;
BEGIN
   <statement>;
   <statement>;
   .
   .
   .
   <statement>
END.
<input data>
```

The statements following a program heading until the delimiting "." are considered to be a *block*. This is shown in Figure 3.1.

PROGRAM ────▶ heading ├───▶ block ├───▶◉

Figure 3.1 Simplified syntax diagram for a program.

The graphic description shown in Figure 3.1 is known as a *syntax diagram*. All of the constructions in a Pascal program can be described by syntax diagrams. The syntax diagrams that describe Pascal are found in Appendix A.

The following example program TICKETS illustrates a complete Pascal program. It calculates the maximum profit that could be made from selling tickets to an event. This program uses statements that have not been discussed yet. WRITELN is used to print a program's results and is discussed in Chapter 5 on input and output. The general use of ":=" in the assignment statement is discussed in the next chapter.

Notice that the program TICKETS is written using one line per statement and that the statements are organized in a clear fashion. Pascal does not require this organization. Pascal does not limit how many statements there can be on a line. Also, Pascal does not require the use of specific starting columns. However, a clearly organized layout helps in (a) developing the program, (b) correcting any errors (debugging), and (c) understanding what the program is trying to do. The rules that this text uses to organize programs are listed in Appendix F. For now, notice that all the major divisions of the program start on the same column and that each indentation occurs three more columns in.

```
PROGRAM TICKETS(OUTPUT);
   (* THIS PROGRAM CALCULATES THE MAXIMUM PROFIT THAT CAN BE MADE
      FROM SELLING TICKETS TO AN EVENT                            *)
CONST
   (* FIXED FACTORS *)
   MAXPEOPLE:=240;  (* SIZE OF THE AUDITORIUM  *)
   COST:=300;  (* TALENT COST *)
VAR
   MAXPROFIT: INTEGER;
   TICKETPRICE: INTEGER;
BEGIN  (* TO CALCULATE PROFIT *)
   TICKETPRICE := 3;  (* TRY A POSSIBLE TICKET PRICE IN DOLLARS *)
   MAXPROFIT := MAXPEOPLE * TICKETPRICE - COST;
   WRITELN('THE MAXIMUM PROFIT AT ',TICKETPRICE,  (* DISPLAY RESULTS *)
            'DOLLARS A TICKET IS',MAXPROFIT);
END.  (* EXAMPLE *)
```

Notice that the last statement was placed on two different lines. A single Pascal statement may be placed on more than one line.

3.7 QUESTIONS

3.1   What are the two different classes of Pascal data?

3.2   What are the different Pascal scalar data types?

3.3   Why is it necessary to have identifiers?

3.4   Discuss the difference in how the following identifiers are used: variables, restricted names, reserved words.

3.5   What is the difference between a REAL and an INTEGER value?

3.6   What is the difference in how reserved words and standard identifiers can be used?

3.7   Where can the value of a CONSTANT be changed?

3.8   Specify which of the following data representations are
      (a)   INTEGER or REAL
      (b)   correct or incorrect representations in Pascal

```
        5
      -63.4
        0.5
       43.5
       +72
    2,242.18
        0.0000767
       17.
       -5E-3
      5642.6E2
      4,628
```

Chapter 4

BASIC INPUT AND OUTPUT

Objectives
Describe how Pascal reads in data and presents the results of a program's actions. Also, discuss the relationship between data and information. This is one of the three core chapters on Pascal (along with Chapters 3 and 5). Chapters 3, 4, and 5 are all necessary to Pascal material after Chapter 5.

Suggested Background
Chapter 3. Additionally, the general material presented in Sections 1.1 and 1.2 would be helpful.

Accepting and delivering data are fundamental activities of any computer. Data is placed in a computer through the use of a computer's *input* capabilities. Incoming data sometimes is processed immediately with the results then reported by using the computer's *output* capabilities. For this reason, simple computer use was and is often called *data processing*. Not all input data need be processed immediately; sometimes it may be stored for eventual use.

Computers are capable of reading many different types of incoming items. Sometimes just one incoming item is read by a single statement; sometimes several incoming items are read by a single statement.

What is read may be used by itself or as part of a group of items. When desired, items can be grouped together in *structures* or in records.

Items are generally considered to be *data* items until they are given meaning. Meaning is given either through computer processing or by how the items are organized. Once items have an associated meaning, they are sometimes said to be *information*. For example, if the incoming items read are

```
48 81 TOM MIAMI
```

these items can only be initially identified as data items because they have no associated meaning. However, if the data items can be associated with meanings, the data items can be said to be providing information. For example, the previous data can be used so that it is known that

(1) on day 48,
(2) of year 81,
(3) hurricane TOM,
(4) went from the sea to the land near MIAMI.

It can be said that the input items can be used as information.

In short, input items are only considered to be information if they can be associated with a meaning. It should be noted that some people are not concerned with the distinction between data and information. Because of this, computer processing is often simply called data processing. The term data processing is becoming less popular as many computers do more than simple manipulations of data.

Data may be read into a computer from many different devices. Likewise, many different devices may be used to receive output from the computer. Incoming items may come from one type of device and output may well be placed onto another. The input/output devices are usually known as *peripheral devices* or *peripherals*.

Basic Pascal input is usually done by using either a card reader or a computer terminal. Basic output is usually done by using a terminal or a high speed printer. How Pascal uses other devices is discussed in Chapter 14 on files.

4.1 INPUT

Objective
Describe how a Pascal program can be instructed to read in data.

Suggested Background
The previous material in this chapter. All of this section may be done after Section 4.1 on OUTPUT.

Pascal uses the READ and READLN statements to tell the computer to try to find and accept incoming items. If a Pascal program uses the READ or READLN statements, the PROGRAM heading statement at the beginning of the Pascal program must include the INPUT specification. For example,

```
PROGRAM WAGES(INPUT, .. );
```

4.1.1 READ

Objectives
Describe how Pascal reads data using the READ statement and discuss to where the data can be read.

The READ command has the form

```
READ(<variable name>,<variable name>,...,<variable name>)
```

The list of variable names in the read statement is called the *input variable list*.

Every variable name in the input variable list must have been previously defined in a VAR statement. Names that were previously defined in a CONST section cannot be included in an input variable list as the input statement would try to change the value of the constant that had been defined in the CONST section. (Recall that it is illegal to try to change the value of a constant.)

The Pascal statement

```
READ(AGE,HOURSWORKED)
```

tells the computer to find and read values for AGE and HOURSWORKED.

When a Pascal program is reading input items using the READ statement, it reads input data lines until a value is found for all the items in the input variable list. The input items requested by a single input statement may be found on one or more input lines.

4.1.1.1 Numeric Data

Numeric input items should be separated from each other by at least one blank. For example, given the following Pascal program fragment,

```
VAR
   NUMBER: INTEGER;
   AGE: INTEGER;
   HOURLYPAY: REAL;
   SEX: CHARACTER;
   HOURSWORKED: REAL;
   WAGES: REAL;
BEGIN
   .
   .
   .
   READ(NUMBER,AGE,HOURLYPAY,HOURSWORKED);
   .
   .
   .
```

if the first lines of data are

```
86345 23    14.63 41.4
86684 27 8.3       16.2
```

the result would be that NUMBER would be assigned the value of "86345", AGE the value of "23", HOURLYPAY the value of "14.63" and HOURSWORKED the value of "41.4". If, instead, the first few input data lines were

```
86345   23
14.63
41.4 86684 27
8.3
16.2
```

the same values would be obtained as were obtained by the first READ statement. However, it is clear that the first presentation of data is better organized as it represents the natural grouping of the incoming items.

4.1.1.2 Character Data

Objectives
Discuss and illustrate how character data is read.

Suggested Background
The previous material in this chapter (Section 4.1.1.1 is not required).

Recall that the value of a character variable in Pascal is one character long. Because of this, when character data is read in, it is brought in one character at a time.

If character data is to be brought in, neither a blank nor any other character is used to separate one item of character data from another item of character data. Also, there is no separation on the input line between character data and any other type of data. This is because any character could be validly read in as the value of a character variable. When reading character data, a Pascal program will use the first input character found as the input character.

For example, the program fragment

```
VAR
    NUMBER: INTEGER;
    AGE: INTEGER;
    HOURLYPAY: INTEGER;
    GENDER: CHAR
    HOURSWORKED: REAL;
    WAGES: REAL;
BEGIN
    .
    .
    . .
    READ(NUMBER,AGE,GENDER,HOURLYPAY,HOURSWORKED);
    .
    .
    .
```

would read the data input line

$$86345\ 23F14.63\ 41.4$$

with the result that NUMBER would be assigned the value "86345", AGE the value "23", GENDER the value "F", HOURLYPAY the value "14.63", and HOURS-WORKED the value "41.4".

4.1.1.3 Stream Input

Objectives
Discuss the concept of stream input and how Pascal reads stream input using a pointer to keep track of what is to be read next.

Suggested Background
The previous material in this chapter (Section 4.1.1.2 is not required).

The READ statement reads data from what is known as *stream input*. What this means is that input data items are treated as a continuous sequence or stream of items without much concern as to which input line the input item happens to be on. This is done by using a pointer that moves along the input items. The pointer keeps track of which data items have been brought in by a READ statement. If an input statement is satisfied in the middle of an input line of data items, the next item on the line could be read by another READ. For example, in the program fragment

```
VAR
    APPLES: INTEGER;
    ORANGES: INTEGER;
    PEACHES: INTEGER;
BEGIN
    READ(APPLES,ORANGES,PEACHES);
    READ(APPLES,ORANGES,PEACHES);
```

if the input data items were

```
                    5
                    12 23 24
                    14
                    15 67
                    82 104 76
                    18 91
```

the first READ would bring in the value of "5" as the value of APPLES. The input pointer is then moved along to the next line to find "12" for the value of ORANGES. After reading in "12", the pointer is at the blank character immediately after the "12". Next, "23" is read in for the value of PEACHES. The input pointer is then on the blank character immediately after the "23". When the second READ statement is executed, reading begins again at the blank character that the pointer is currently at; that is, the blank immediately after the "23". Consequently, the data item "24" will be brought in as the new value for APPLES. Similarly, the new value of ORANGES will be "14" and the new value of PEACHES will be "15". Once an item has been brought in, the READ statement will not bring it in a second time. The input pointer cannot be moved backwards. How the input pointer was moved in this example is illustrated in Figure 4.1.

Because Pascal READs stream data, a READ asking for more than one data value can be thought of as being broken up or decomposed into a separate READ for each value to be read. For example,

```
READ(APPLES,ORANGES,PEACHES)
```

is handled as

```
READ(APPLES);
READ(ORANGES);
READ(PEACHES);
```

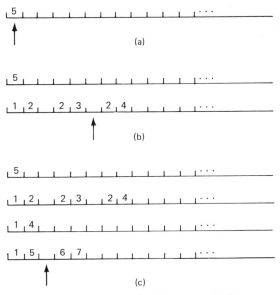

Figure 4.1 (a) Input pointer before any data has been read. (b) Input pointer after the first three data values have been read. (c) Input pointer after two sets of three data values have been read.

4.1.2 READLN

Objective
Differentiate between how READ and READLN read data.

Suggested Background
The previous material in this chapter (Section 4.1.1.2 is not required).

READLN is a special form of the READ statement. READLN is to ensure that the first character read by a following READ or READLN statement will be the first character of the input line after the input line that was used to satisfy the READLN statement. After a READLN is executed, the input pointer is moved to the first character of the next input line. What effect this has on the data values read into the machine can be seen by the following example. If the input data were

```
46 23
17
64 92 27
16 25 48 90
```

the statements

```
READLN(NUMBER,AGE);
READLN(NUMBER,AGE);
READLN(NUMBER,AGE);
```

would result in the first READLN assigning the value of "46" to NUMBER and "23" to AGE. The second READLN would result in the value of "17" as the new value of NUMBER and "64" as the new value of AGE. The third READLN would result in the value of "16" as the new value of NUMBER and "25" as the new value of AGE. Notice that several values on the input lines were skipped when the pointer was moved. How the input pointer was moved in this example is illustrated in Figure 4.2.

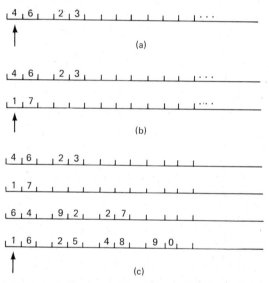

Figure 4.2   (a) Input pointer before any data has been read. (b) Input pointer after the first pair of numbers has been read by a READLN statement. (c) Input pointer after the second pair of numbers has been read by a READLN statement.

The READLN statement may be used without any items in its input variable list. The READLN by itself forces the input pointer to the start of a new input line. This is done to have greater flexibility in controlling the reading process. The previous example could be rewritten as

```
READ(NUMBER,AGE);
READLN;
READ(NUMBER,AGE);
READLN;
READ(NUMBER,AGE);
READLN;
```

Given the same incoming data, the results would be the same as before.

Because Pascal READs stream data, a READLN asking for more than one data value can be thought of as being broken up into a separate READ for each input value followed by a READLN. For example,

```
READLN(NUMBER,AGE);
```

is handled as

```
READ(NUMBER); READ(AGE); READLN;
```

4.1.3 End of File

Objective
Discuss what happens when a Pascal statement tries to read a data item that is not there.

Suggested Background
The previous material in this chapter.

When a Pascal program tries to read an input item and cannot find it, the *end of file condition* occurs. An end of file condition happens in Pascal when an attempt is made to read a new input data line and there is not an input data line to be read. Because the end of file condition happens when the program tries to find a new input line that is not there, a READLN without an input variable list statement can cause this condition when it seeks a new input line.

Pascal has a predefined BOOLEAN FUNCTION that indicates the end of file condition: "EOF". The value is initially established as "FALSE" by the Pascal compiler. When the end of file condition occurs, EOF has the value of "TRUE".

When the end of file condition happens, the program will stop with an execution error unless the program is told what to do. The EOF value can be used to control what happens. This is discussed in the next chapter.

If a single READ or READLN statement is trying to input more than one value, the EOF condition can happen in the middle of the input process. When this happens, an execution error will occur because an attempt was made to read after the value of EOF became TRUE. For example, if the statement

```
READ(APPLES,ORANGES,PEACHES,GRAPES)
```

had only the data

available, the value of 5 would be input for APPLES and then the value of 12 would be input for ORANGES. Then the value of EOF would become TRUE when an attempt was made to find a data value for PEACHES and none was available. Next, even though the value of EOF was TRUE, an attempt would still be made to find a value for PEARS. This last action would cause an error to happen when the program was executing.

There may be more than one file used to supply input data to a Pascal program. Each file that is used for input has an EOF value associated with it. How to read from files other than the standard file INPUT and how to use the EOF variables associated with them are discussed in a later chapter.

4.1.4 End of Line

Objective
Discuss how a Pascal program can come to know when it is at the end of an input line.

Suggested Background
The previous material in this chapter.

Input data items for a Pascal program are found on one or more input data lines. When input is from cards, each one of these lines is 80 characters long. When input is from lines generated from a computer terminal, the length of each line is variable. Each input line is terminated when the "return" or "enter" key on the terminal is hit. The end of each one of the input lines is marked. Exactly how each line is marked depends on the computer system used. Generally, a blank character is placed at the end of each input line just before the "end of line" mark.

Usually it is possible to input data from a file without worrying about which input line an individual data item is from. This is because Pascal data is generally treated as stream. However, when consecutive CHAR data items are being input, it may be useful to know whether or not the end of the line has been reached. The usefulness of doing this is discussed in Section 11.2 (character strings).

When a Pascal program is inputting data, and is at the end of an input data line, the predefined Pascal BOOLEAN FUNCTION identified as EOLN has a TRUE value. Everywhere else, EOLN has a FALSE value.

4.2 OUTPUT

Objectives
Discuss how a Pascal program communicates the results of a program and describe how an output statement should be formed.

Suggested Background
The material at the start of this chapter. The parts of Section 4.1 are not required. Specifically, all parts of this section may be done before any of the parts of Section 4.1 are done.

Basic output in Pascal is accomplished by using the WRITE and WRITELN statements. If a Pascal program uses the WRITE or WRITELN statements, the PROGRAM statement at the beginning of the Pascal program must include the OUTPUT specification. For example,

```
PROGRAM EXAMPLE(OUTPUT)
```

4.2.1 WRITE

Objectives
Discuss and specify how the results of a Pascal program may be communicated by the use of the WRITE statement. Provide illustrations of the use of WRITE.

Suggested Background
The introductory material at the beginning of this chapter and Section 4.2.

The WRITE statement is used to display the program's results or output. The form of the WRITE statement is

```
WRITE(<output item>,<output item>,...,<output item>)
```

What is written is the values of the various output items. Output items may be literal strings, variable names, calculations, or constants.

A literal string is a character string enclosed between single quote marks that is to be written out. For example,

```
WRITE('THIS IS AN EXAMPLE OF A LITERAL STRING')
```

would produce the result

```
THIS IS AN EXAMPLE OF A LITERAL STRING
```

A constant in an output list can be either the value defined in a CONST section or a value expressly placed in the output list. For example, the program fragment

```
CONST
   NUMBER = 5;
BEGIN
   WRITE('NUMBER',NUMBER,5)
```

would result in the following output

```
NUMBER          5          5
```

4.2.1.1 Stream Output

Objective
Discuss how results are written as a stream on an output line by a Pascal program.

Suggested Background
Sections 4.2 and 4.2.1.

Unless told otherwise by a WRITELN statement (discussed in Section 4.2.2), a Pascal program will write as many output values as it has space for on an output line. When a line is filled, the next line will be used. New lines will be used until all the specified output has been written.

The WRITE statement produces what is known as *stream* output. The effect that this has is that a new WRITE statement will write on the same output line as the preceding WRITE statement if there is any more space on the line. (This may be changed using WRITELN.) For example, if the previous program is rewritten as

```
PROGRAM EXAMPLE(OUTPUT);
CONST
   NUMBER = 5;
BEGIN
   WRITE('NUMBER');
   WRITE(NUMBER);
   WRITE(5);
END.
```

the result would still be

```
NUMBER            5            5
```

4.2.1.2 Spaces on the Output Line

Objectives
Specify how many spaces are allocated for each data value that is written on an output line by Pascal and describe how the number of spaces may be controlled.

Suggested Background
Sections 4.2, 4.2.1.1.

When writing output, Pascal reserves a standard amount of space on the output line for each output value. The amount of space used depends on the data type and the convention of each local installation. The compiler that has been used for the examples in this text has the following conventions.

data type	number of columns
INTEGER	12
REAL	16
BOOLEAN	5
CHAR	1
'text string'	length of text string

The amount of space used can be controlled by using an edit specification with an item in the output list. The form of the edit specification is

```
<output item>:<width>
```

For example, if it was desired that each numeric value in the previous example would be three columns wide, the output statement could be rewritten as

```
WRITE('NUMBER',NUMBER:3,5:3)
```

The result would be

```
NUMBER  5  5
```

When specifying the field width for a REAL value, it is necessary to specify both the total width of the field and the number of digits to be allowed to the right of the decimal point. The total width of the field is to include the decimal point. If a negative result is possible, the total width of the field should also include space for the negative sign. The form of the edit specification for REAL values is

```
<output item>:<total field width>:<digits to the right>
```

For example, given the program fragment

```
CONST
   SALARY = 23976.24;
   AGE = 42;
BEGIN
   WRITE('SALARY IS ',SALARY:9:2,' --- AGE IS ',AGE:3);
```

the result would be

```
SALARY IS  23976.24 --- AGE IS  42
```

4.2.2 WRITELN

Objectives
Differentiate and illustrate the Pascal write statements WRITE and WRITELN.

Suggested Background
Sections 4.2, 4.2.1, and 4.2.1.1.

WRITELN is a special form of WRITE. It is used to ensure that the first output item from the next WRITE statement begins in column 1 of the next output line. The difference in results between WRITE and WRITELN can be seen in the following program fragments. The program fragment

```
WRITE('A');
WRITE('B');
WRITE('C');
```

would result in the output of

ABC

when the output line was written. In comparison, the program fragment

```
WRITELN('A');
WRITELN('B');
WRITELN('C');
```

would result in the output of

A
B
C

The WRITELN statement does not have to include a list of output items. It can be used by itself in order to force the start of a new line. For example, the program fragment

```
WRITE('A');
WRITE('B');
WRITELN;
WRITE('C');
```

would result in the output of

AB
C

4.3 QUESTIONS

4.1   On an input record, what is the difference between how numeric and character data items are separated from each other?

4.2   What is the difference between the READ and READLN statements?

4.3   What is the difference between the WRITE and WRITELN statements?

4.4   What is meant by "stream" input?

4.5   Given the following program,

```
PROGRAM QUESTION(INPUT,OUTPUT);
VAR
    A: INTEGER;
    B: INTEGER;
    C: INTEGER;
    D: INTEGER;
BEGIN
    READ(A,B,C,D);
    WRITE(A:2,B:2,C:2,D:2);
    READ(A,D);
    WRITE(A:2,B:2);
    READ(B,C);
    READ(A,D);
    WRITE(A:2,B:2,C:2,D:2)
END.  (* QUESTION *)
```

if the incoming data are the following, what will be displayed as the results?

```
1 2 3
4 5
6
7 8
9 0 9
8 7 6 5
4 3 2 1 0
```

4.6   Given the following program,

```
PROGRAM QUESTION(INPUT,OUTPUT);
VAR
    A: INTEGER;
    B: INTEGER;
    C: INTEGER;
    D: INTEGER;
BEGIN
    READLN(A,B,C,D);
    WRITE(A:2,B:2,C:2,D:2);
    READLN(A,D);
    WRITE(A:2,B:2);
    READLN(B,C);
    READLN(A,D);
    WRITE(A:2,B:2,C:2,D:2)
END.  (* QUESTION *)
```

if the incoming data are the following, what will be displayed as the results?

```
1 2 3
4 5
6
7 8
9 0 9
8 7 6 5
4 3 2 1 0
```

4.7 Given the following program,

```
PROGRAM QUESTION(INPUT,OUTPUT);
VAR
    FIRST: INTEGER;
    SECOND: INTEGER;
    THIRD: INTEGER;
BEGIN
    READ(FIRST,SECOND);
    WRITE(FIRST,SECOND);
    READ(THIRD,FIRST,SECOND);
    WRITELN(THIRD,FIRST,SECOND);
    READLN(SECOND,THIRD);
    WRITELN(FIRST,SECOND,THIRD);
    READ(FIRST,SECOND);
    READLN(FIRST,SECOND,THIRD);
    WRITELN(FIRST,SECOND,THIRD);
    READ(FIRST);
    WRITE(FIRST)
END.  (* QUESTION *)
```

if the data are

```
 1  2  3  4  5
 6  7  8  9 10
11 12 13 14 15
16 17 18 19 20
21 22 23 24 25
26 27 28 29 30
31 32 33 34 35
```

what results will be displayed?

4.8   Given the following program,

```
PROGRAM QUESTION(INPUT,OUTPUT);
VAR SALARY: REAL;
    AGE: INTEGER;
    SEX: CHAR;
BEGIN
    READ(SALARY,AGE,SEX);
    WRITELN(SALARY);
    WRITELN(AGE);
    WRITELN(SEX);
    READ(SALARY,AGE,SEX);
    WRITELN(SALARY,AGE,SEX)
END. (* QUESTION *)
```

if the input data are

$$24756.28 \ \ 25M \ \ 25628.75$$
$$27F \ \ 236.14$$

what results will be displayed?

4.9   Given the following program,

```
PROGRAM QUESTION(INPUT,OUTPUT);
VAR
    FIRST: INTEGER;
    SECOND: INTEGER;
    THIRD: INTEGER;
BEGIN
    READ(FIRST,SECOND);
    WRITE(FIRST,SECOND);
    READ(THIRD,FIRST,SECOND);
    WRITELN(THIRD,FIRST,SECOND);
    READLN(SECOND,THIRD);
    WRITELN(FIRST,SECOND,THIRD);
    READ(FIRST,SECOND);
    READLN(FIRST,SECOND,THIRD);
    WRITELN(FIRST,SECOND,THIRD);
    READ(FIRST);
    WRITE(FIRST)
END. (* QUESTION *)
```

if the data are

```
 1  2  3  4  5  4  3  2  1
 6  7  8  9 10  9  8  7  6
11 12 13 14 15 14 13 12 11
16 17 18 19 20 19 18 17 16
21 22 23 24 25 24 23 22 21
26 27 28 29 30 29 28 27 26
31 32 33 34 35 34 33 32 31
```

what results will be displayed?

4.4 PROBLEMS

4.1. Write a Pascal program that will
  (a) Display an appropriate title.
  (b) Display your name.
  (c) Input and display the integers representing your birthday. The integers should be
input and displayed in the following order.

  day
  month
  year

Make sure that your program identifies the parts of your birthday when it is displayed.
  Note: All programs that you write should use meaningful variable names. Meaningful
variable names are names that tell you what the variable is being used for. For example, in this
problem good variable names might be DAY, MONTH, and YEAR. Good programs also
include comments that explain what is happening in the program.

4.2. Every morning the president of the Purple Passion Shirt and Pants Company wants a
report of the quantity produced the previous day. You are to produce a report displaying the
quantity of shirts and pants produced the previous day. Test your program with the following
data.

Shirts	Pants
1168	1200
2436	2381
1095	1095

In each case, the first number represents shirts, and the second pants. Run your program three
times, each time with the data for a different day.

4.3. Katherine Kelly is planning her Christmas shopping list. She has decided how much
money she wants to spend on the following people.

Aunt Dot:	$5.00
Uncle Jack:	$7.50
Mrs. Matthews:	$12.00
Mom:	$14.50
Dad:	$14.50
Billy:	$16.25

You are to display in a report Katherine's Christmas shopping budget. You do not have to do
any calculations, just develop a computer-generated report.

4.4. Look up which teams your football team played last year and what were the scores. You are to display what the scores were and who won. Finally, you are to display what the team's record was (wins and losses). You do not have to do any calculations, just display the record.

4.5. A personnel manager has collected data on the chief executive officer of the IS Company. Write a program that will
 (a) Input the following data on the chief executive officer.

> age
> years of employment with the firm
> house address
> present salary

 (b) Display the data as it is input using meaningful variable names and comments. Use the following data

> 53
> 12
> 2651
> 22
> 36050

4.6. Input the values for the ages of your immediate family members and then display them along with meaningful titles.

4.7. Write a program that will
 (a) Display your name.
 (b) Display the size of your family in the form:

```
LIVING PARENTS = x
BROTHERS = xx
SISTERS = xx
NEPHEWS = xx
NIECES = xx
PETS = xx
```

4.8. Display the courses that you are taking this academic term in the following form.

```
COURSE NUMBER    COURSE TITLE    DAYS    TIME    CREDIT HOURS
-------------    ------------    ----    ----    ------------
```

4.9. Using WRITE and WRITELN statements, create an attractive image or "artistic" design on your output device.

Chapter 5

FUNDAMENTALS OF ACTING ON VALUES

Objectives
Describe and specify how Pascal changes and compares data values. Along with Chapters 3 and 4, this is one of the three core chapters on Pascal that are necessary for all Pascal material after this chapter.

Suggested Background
Chapter 3. Chapter 4 may be done before or after this chapter. The questions at the end of this chapter do not require a knowledge of Chapter 4. However, as it is necessary to communicate the results of a program, the problems at the end of this chapter do require a knowledge of Chapter 4.

In our daily activities, we often act on things by changing or comparing them. For example, we may combine three large snowballs to make a snowman. Or, we may compare two pieces of pie to see which is larger. In the first case (the snowman), the operation of union or addition is performed. In the second (pieces of pie), a relation comparison or test is performed. Pascal has specific operators to act on the objects within its environment.

Operators are used to indicate when special functions are to be performed and to describe what is to be done. One is used to indicate when a variable is to be assigned a new value. Others are used to manipulate data, such as when two numbers are added together. They can be used to negate a value. Some are also used to test the logical relationship between values, such as when discovering whether one value is larger than another. Some of Pascal's operators can be used for several different variable types. Others, such as INTEGER division, are restricted to a particular variable type.

Stored data values are changed by using statements. How a value or a collection of values is to be acted upon is described in an *expression*. When an expression is used, it is part of a statement.

5.1 ASSIGNMENT

Objectives
Describe what an assignment statement accomplishes and illustrate how it is specified.

Suggested Background
The previous material in this chapter.

The value of a variable is altered by the use of an assignment statement. If a variable has a value, the assignment statement will replace it with a new value. The form of the assignment statement is

```
<variable name> := <expression>
```

An expression, when evaluated, produces a value. This value becomes the new value for the variable in the left hand side of the assignment statement.

In Pascal, the compound symbol ":=" is used to indicate that a variable is to be assigned or provided with a value. For example, the statement

```
AGE := 48
```

tells the computer to store the numeric integer value of 48 in the space in the computer identified by the variable name AGE. The old value of AGE is replaced with the new value of 48. The old value disappears.

When data is copied from one variable to another by the use of an assignment statement, the data is duplicated, not transferred from one to another. For example, the sequence of statements

```
AGE := 18;
MINIMUM := AGE;
```

will result in both AGE and MINIMUM having the value of 18.

5.1.1 Assignment of Constant Values

Objective
Describe a Pascal restriction on changing the value of a constant.

Suggested Background
The previous material in this chapter and Chapter 3.

A Pascal constant may only be given a value in the CONST declaration portion of the program. Once a constant has been given a value, it cannot be changed. If the program attempts to change the value of a constant in the executable section of the program, it will be considered an error.

5.1.2 Assignment of Variable Values

Objectives
Describe what it means for a value to be assigned to a variable and specify how it can happen.

Suggested Background
The previous material in this chapter and Chapter 3. (Section 5.1.1 is not required.)

Variables in a Pascal program may have their values changed during the execution of a program. Variables can be given a value as the result of executing a statement. For example, in the program fragment

```
VAR
    AGE: INTEGER;
BEGIN
    AGE := 21;
    AGE := 48;
```

AGE is defined to be a numeric integer variable. The first statement

```
AGE := 21
```

instructs the machine to assign the integer "21" to AGE as the new value of AGE. Then the statement

```
AGE := 48
```

instructs the machine to assign the integer "48" to AGE as the new value of AGE. The first value of AGE is lost.

5.2 ARITHMETIC OPERATORS

Objectives
Describe the operators that are used in Pascal to perform arithmetic and indicate with what type of data they can be used.

Suggested Background
Introductory material at the beginning of this chapter.

The arithmetic operators perform calculation functions such as addition and multiplication. Arithmetic operators are applied to numeric data types. All the variables and constants in the same calculation must have the same data type. Some arithmetic operators can be used with either REAL or INTEGER data types; others are restricted to one data type. As Pascal ignores blanks while interpreting the meaning of a statement, it is up to the programmer to decide whether blanks are to be used to surround an operator. The arithmetic operators are

operator	description	used with data type(s)
+	addition	INTEGER, REAL
−	subtraction	INTEGER, REAL
*	multiplication	INTEGER, REAL
DIV	division	INTEGER
/	division	REAL
MOD	modulus	INTEGER

The modulus operation produces what is sometimes known as a *remainder*.

The symbols +,−, and * are also used as set operators. Sets and set operators are discussed in a later chapter.

5.2.1 Integer Operators

Objective
Describe and illustrate the operators used to perform INTEGER arithmetic.

Suggested Background
Introductory material at the beginning of this chapter and Section 5.2.

Integer operators are used to manipulate INTEGER scalar type variables and constants. Addition, subtraction, and multiplication are indicated in familiar forms. For example,

```
AGE + WEIGHT
GROSS - COSTS
ORDERED * 5
```

INTEGER division is expressed in a form that is less common. For example,

```
TOTAL DIV COUNT
```

tells the Pascal compiler to divide TOTAL by COUNT. As this is INTEGER division, the results are truncated. A truncated result is one in which the decimal point and anything to the right of the decimal point are disgarded. The result produced is also known as the quotient of a division. The following illustrates some results of applying DIV.

calculation	result
6 DIV 2	3
6 DIV 3	2
6 DIV 4	1
6 DIV 5	1
6 DIV 6	1
6 DIV 7	0

The sign of the resulting value is positive if both values have the same sign, and negative if they are different. It is an error to divide by zero.

The INTEGER MOD function calculates and provides the remainder of a division. The following illustrates some results of applying MOD.

calculation	result
6 MOD 2	0
6 MOD 3	0
6 MOD 4	2
6 MOD 5	1
6 MOD 6	0
6 MOD 7	6

The sign of the result value is always positive. It is an error if the right hand value in a MOD expression is zero or negative.

5.2.2 REAL Operators

Objectives
Describe the operators that are used to perform arithmetic on REAL values and illustrate their use.

Suggested Background
Introductory material at the beginning of this chapter, Section 5.2, and Chapter 3.

The forms of operators that are used for REAL arithmetic manipulations are familiar. For example,

```
12.3 + AREA
VOLUME - 3.6
PI*CIRCUMFERENCE
MILES / GALLON
```

are valid representations of REAL addition, subtraction, multiplication, and division. To the limits of the compiler and the computer being used, digits to the left and right of a REAL value will be kept. For example,

```
VAR
    WEIGHT: REAL;
    VOLUME: REAL;
BEGIN
    WEIGHT := 156.0 + 0.018;
    VOLUME := 14.2 * 8.06;
```

will result in the value of WEIGHT becoming 156.018 and the value of VOLUME becoming 114.452.

5.2.3 Mixing REAL and INTEGER Values

When a statement has both REAL and INTEGER values in an expression, the expression is said to be a *mixed mode* expression. A REAL operator may operate on INTEGER values. For example, in the expression

```
22 * 67.8
```

the multiply operator is considered to be a REAL operator and the expression a REAL expression as one of the VALUES, "67.8", is REAL. Because of this, the value of "22" will be converted to REAL before the multiply operator is applied as both the values in an expression must be of the same type. (The result of 22*67.8 is 1491.6.) The same thing happens for the + and – operators. The division operator may also be used with a pair of INTEGER values; however, the results will be REAL. For example, the result of evaluating 1.8/24 is 0.05 and the result of 18/24 is 0.75.

The strictly INTEGER operators of MOD and DIV cannot be used with REAL values.

When an INTEGER value is assigned to a REAL variable, the INTEGER value is converted to a REAL value by Pascal before the assignment statement is executed. When it is desired to assign a REAL value to an INTEGER variable, the value must first be converted to an INTEGER value by an explicit programming statement. This can be accomplished by using either TRUNC or ROUND. TRUNC truncates any digits to the right of the decimal point and ROUND rounds the value to the closest INTEGER value (either up or down). The following illustrates the results of applying TRUNC and ROUND.

```
                            ---------if----------
                            A := 3.6      A := 3.4
                            --------      --------
        ROUND(A) results in     4             3
        TRUNC(A) results in     3             3
```

5.3 RELATIONAL OPERATORS

Objectives
Describe the relational operators and illustrate the results that can come from applying them.

Suggested Background
Introductory material at the beginning of this chapter, Section 5.2, and
Chapter 3.

Relational operators are used to discover the scalar relationship between
values. The operators and the tests performed follow.

operator	test performed
>	greater than
>=	greater than or equal
<	less than
<=	less than or equal
=	equal
<>	not equal

These operators may also used on several data types that are discussed later in this
book: strings, sets, and pointers. These uses are discussed later as is the use of the
relational set operator "IN".

The resulting value of a relational test is "TRUE" or "FALSE". The following
are examples of relational comparison tests and results.

relational test	result
'A' < 'B'	TRUE
'Z' < 'B'	FALSE
235 <> 235	FALSE
25 >= 36	FALSE
2 = 2	TRUE
5 <= 7	TRUE

5.4 BOOLEAN OPERATORS

Objectives
Describe the operators that can be used with BOOLEAN data values
and illustrate the result of applying them.

Boolean operators act upon BOOLEAN scalar data type values; that is, data values that are either TRUE or FALSE. Operations performed upon BOOLEAN values are said to be *logical* operators. There are three BOOLEAN operators in Pascal:

AND   (logical conjunction)
 OR   (logical disjunction)
NOT   (logical negation)

The following illustrates the results of applying the boolean operators.

operator application	results in
FALSE AND FALSE	FALSE
FALSE AND TRUE	FALSE
TRUE AND FALSE	FALSE
TRUE AND TRUE	TRUE
FALSE OR FALSE	FALSE
FALSE OR TRUE	TRUE
TRUE OR FALSE	TRUE
TRUE OR TRUE	TRUE
NOT FALSE	TRUE
NOT TRUE	FALSE

5.5 UNARY OPERATORS

Most Pascal operators are binary. That is, they operate on two things. For example, in

```
COUNT * PRICE
```

"*" is a binary operator as it is applied to both COUNT and PRICE. Binary operators are also known as *infix* or *dyadic* operators.

Unary operators are applied to only one thing. There are three different scalar unary operators in Pascal. They are "+", "−", and "NOT". Unary operators operate only on single scalar data type values. The following illustrates the results of some applications of unary operators.

calculation	value of A	result
+A	5	5
+A	−5	−5
−A	5	−5
−A	−5	5
3+(−A)	5	−2
3+(−A)	−5	8
NOT A	FALSE	TRUE
NOT A	TRUE	FALSE

Unary operators are also known as *prefix* or *monadic* operators.

5.6 EXPRESSIONS

Objectives
Describe and illustrate the construction where operators are used.

Suggested Background
Chapter 3 and the previous material in this chapter.

A Pascal expression has a value at the time of its use. If it is undefined when used, it is an error.

An expression may be constructed of constants, variables, and function names (functions are discussed in a later chapter). When an expression has been fully evaluated, a single value results. Operators may be used in an expression. For example, the constructions

```
12.5 + 0.62
DISTANCE
-6
AGE >= 15
MILES/GALLON
COUNT + 1
```

are all valid Pascal expressions. Observe that a valid expression may be formed without an operator or a variable.

An expression can have several operators in it; for example,

```
TEST1 + TEST2 + TEST3 + TEST4
```

Even though an expression may have more than one operator in it, only one of the operators is performed at a time. The computer can be told which operator to apply next by using parentheses. For example, in

```
BUSHELS * (COST - DISCOUNT)
```

the parentheses cause the subtraction

```
COST - DISCOUNT
```

to be performed first. The result of the subtraction is then multiplied by BUSHELS. When parentheses are present, the operators are applied from the "innermost" *nested* parenthesized expression "outward." For example, in

```
BUSHELS * (COST - (0.20 * COST) )
```

the double parentheses *nesting* would cause the first calculation to be

```
0.20 * COST
```

as this the innermost nested expression. The result of this calculation would then be subtracted from the value of COST, and the result of that calculation would be subsequently multiplied by the value of BUSHELS.

When there is more than one operator in an expression, the computer chooses which operation to perform next based on what is called precedence.

The precedence for Pascal follows.

order of application	
1	parenthesized expressions
2	NOT
3	*,/,DIV,MOD,AND
4	– (unary),+(unary),+,–,OR
5	<,<=,=,<>,>,>=

All the operators at the same level have the same precedence. When there are two or more operators of the same precedence in an expression, the operators are applied left to right. For example, in the expression

```
HEIGHT - WIDTH + LENGTH
```

the first calculation is

```
HEIGHT - WIDTH
```

The result of this calculation is then added to the value of LENGTH.

5.7 QUESTIONS

Suggested Background
The questions can be answered with a knowledge of this and Chapter 3. Although the information presented in this chapter has not required the background material found in Chapter 4, the problems in this chapter do. This is because Pascal programs that do not communicate their results are not very meaningful. Some of the problems require only a knowledge of WRITE, some require a knowledge of both READ and WRITE.

5.1   What is the purpose of an operator?
5.2   How does the assignment of values of constants and variables differ?
5.3   Can the values of both constants and variables be changed in an assignment statement? If not, why not?
5.4   Indicate which of these expressions is valid. If there is an error, indicate what the error is. If the expression is valid, indicate the result.

```
3 + 4
-3 + 4
3 - * 4
3 * - 4
3.2 * 4
4 * 3.2
3.2 DIV 4
3.2 / 4
3 * (4/3)
3 DIV (4 DIV 3)
3 + 4 (5 + 7)
3 + 4 * (12 - 2) + 3)
```

5.5   What is the resulting value of the following?

```
ROUND(3.2)        TRUNC(3.2)
ROUND(4.7)        TRUNC(4.7)
ROUND(-5.2)       TRUNC(-5.2)
ROUND(-3.8)       TRUNC(-3.8)
ROUND(3.2 + 0.4)  TRUNC(3.2 + 0.4)
```

5.6   In the following expressions, number the first operator that is performed, the second, etc.

```
A + B - C + D * E / F * G + H - K + L

(A + (B - C) + (((D * E) / F) + H) - (K + L) )
```

5.7   How does the result of a scalar operation differ from the result of a relational operation?
5.8   What is the difference between the actions of unary and binary operators?

5.8 PROBLEMS

5.1.   Write a Pascal program that will
   (a)   Input and display the nine digits in your Social Security number. Each digit should be input and displayed separately. The digits may be displayed together on one line or a separate line may be used to display each digit.
   (b)   Calculate and display the total of these digits.

5.2.   Alice is planning to buy a microcomputer to do her homework. The micro that she wants to buy costs $869.43. Each week, from her paper route, Alice can save $23.62. Write a program to calculate and report how long it will take for Alice to save enough money. Also report the total cost and the amount she can save weekly.

5.3.   The Crunchy Cereal Corporation hires a computer consultant and pays the consultant $45 an hour to assist its programming teams. A daily time record is kept and is turned in at the end of the week. Write a program that will input five numbers representing the amount of hours worked, Monday through Friday. Then calculate and report the consultant's weekly pay. Test your program with the following data.

7.5   4.2   12.6   8.0   6.3

5.4. Frank Kuchner owns an apartment complex that consists of 10 buildings. Two buildings have four 3-bedroom apartments each. The other buildings have eight 1-bedroom apartments and three 2-bedroom apartments each. If a 1-bedroom apartment rents for $250 per month, a 2-bedroom apartment for $300 per month, and a 3-bedroom apartment for $350 per month, write a program to calculate and display the monthly rental income from each building and the total from all of them.

5.5. It is said that programmers in industry spend 3% of their time writing requirements, 3% writing specifications, 5% designing, 7% writing programming language statements, 8% module testing, 7% integration testing, and 67% on maintenance. Write a program that will report the number of person-hours spent each week on each of the tasks if the Black Lash Corporation has 15 full-time (40 hours per week) programmers working for it.

5.6. A box has the following dimensions.

$$Length = 7$$
$$Width = 23$$
$$Depth = 16$$

Write a Pascal program to do the following. Your output should be identified by meaningful titles.
   (a) Using READLN, input the value for length.
   (b) Display the value for length.
   (c) Using READLN, input the value for width.
   (d) Display the value for width on the same line as length.
   (e) Calculate area by multiplying length by width.
   (f) Display the area on a new line.
   (g) Using READLN, input the value for depth.
   (h) Display the value for depth on a new line.
   (i) Calculate the volume by multiplying depth by the area.
   (j) Display the value for the volume on a new line.

5.7. Write a Pascal program that will calculate income taxes and display a short tax return. Your program should input the following data.

   The last two digits of last year (YY)
   The number of standard deductions you claim
   Your total pretax income for the year

Follow these rules in calculating your taxes.
   (a) Standard deductions are worth $750 each.
   (b) The federal tax is a flat 19.5% of net federal taxable income. Net federal taxable income is

   (Pretax income for year) – (Number of standard deductions)*750

   (c) The state tax is a flat 5.3% of net state taxable income. Net state taxable income is

   (Federal taxable income) – (Federal taxes)

Your report should be in the following form.

```
TAX FORM FOR 19yy

your full name
street address
city, state  postal code

NUMBER OF DEDUCTIONS CLAIMED = xx
TOTAL EARNINGS FOR THE YEAR  = xxxxx.xx
LESS STANDARD DEDUCTIONS OF  =  xxxx.xx
NET FEDERAL TAXABLE INCOME   = xxxxx.xx


FEDERAL TAX OWED             =          xxxxx.xx
NET STATE TAXABLE INCOME     = xxxxx.xx
STATE TAX PAYABLE            =          xxxxx.xx
TOTAL TAXES OWED             =         xxxxxx.xx
```

5.8. Write and run a Pascal program that will do the following.
   (a) Input values for variables named COST, SALES PRICE, QUANTITY.
   (b) Display the values for COST, SALESPRICE, QUANTITY.
   (c) Calculate the value of PROFIT by the equation

$$\text{PROFIT} := \text{QUANTITY} * (\text{SALESPRICE} - \text{COST})$$

   (d) Display the value for PROFIT.
   (e) Test your program with the data

                  5.73   8.42   26

5.9. Write a Pascal program that will
   (a) Display your name.
   (b) Input and display integer numbers representing the hours (to the nearest hour) you spend in class each day of the week (Monday through Friday); the number of hours for each day should be input and displayed separately.
   (c) Calculate and display the total number of hours you spend in class each week.
   Make sure each piece of information is clearly and properly identified as it is displayed. In addition make sure your program is general enough to work for any person who supplies data to your program.

5.10. Write a Pascal program that will
   (a) Input and display integer numbers representing the number of miles (to the nearest whole mile) that you traveled by car, bike, or bus each day this past week, from Monday through Sunday. Input a number for each day in that order even if you traveled zero miles that day.
   (b) Calculate and display the total number of miles you traveled all week.
   Make sure each piece of information is clearly and properly identified as it is displayed. In addition make sure your program is general enough to work for any person who supplies sufficient data to the program.

5.11.   The Bottlesville Warehouse Company conducts a monthly update of its total inventory of shoe boxes. Construct a program using three variables. One is used for last month's inventory value of 301 boxes. Another is for this month's additions of 53 boxes. Add this month's additions to last month's inventory to find this month's total inventory (represented by the third variable). Display the results with suitable titles.

Your results should have the following form.

```
LAST MONTH'S INVENTORY:   301
NEW ADDITIONS:             53
NEW UPDATED INVENTORY:    354
```

Your program should do the addition.

5.12.   The Fast-Clean Vacuum Company wishes to update its salespersons' records. Write a program that will input one record containing three data values.

Previous sales totals
This month's sales
Salesperson number

Add the previous sales to this month's sales to find the current total sales. Your results should have the form

```
SALESPERSON NUMBER: xx
PREVIOUS SALES TOTAL: xxxx
THIS MONTH'S TOTAL:    xxx
CURRENT TOTAL SALES:  xxxx
```

Test your program with the following data.

```
  25   (salesperson number)
 350   (this month's sales)
1056   (previous sales total)
```

5.13.   Richard spent some time backpacking in the mountains of Colorado. He started hiking Friday morning and finished hiking the following Friday afternoon. Each day he spent a different amount of time hiking. When he did hike, he walked a average of 3 miles per hour.

You are to write a program that will

Input the hours he walked each day.
Calculate and display the total amount of miles that he walked.
Calculate and display how many hours he spent walking.

Test your program with the following data.

```
12   9   15   0   9   21   6   18
```

5.14. The Big Apple Beer Company is preparing an advertising budget for its new beer: Big A. The company intends to advertise on TV and radio, in newspapers, and magazines, and on billboards. Each input record will have the amounts listed in the following sequence.

TV
radio
newspapers
magazines
billboards

Prepare a program that will input the dollar amount in the budget for each of the advertising areas and that will report these amounts along with the percentage spent in each advertising category. Your results should be in the following form.

	TV	RADIO	NEWSPAPERS	MAGAZINES	BILLBOARDS
AMOUNT	xxxx	xxxx	xxxx	xxxx	xxxx
PERCENT	xx	xx	xx	xx	xx

Test your program with the following data.

$$2200 \quad 1400 \quad 1750 \quad 689 \quad 763$$

5.15. During the winter, the Taibleson family feeds three birds: a blue jay, a sparrow, and a finch. They are fed for 101 days. The blue jay eats five seeds a day, the sparrow eats three seeds a day, and the finch eats two seeds a day. Write a Pascal program to
   (a) Calculate and display the total number of seeds each bird eats during the winter.
   (b) Calculate and display the total number of seeds the Taiblesons will have to buy.

5.16. A *magic square* is one of the oldest mathematical number curiosities. In a magic square, the sums of all of the numbers in each row, column, and major diagonal are the same. For example,

12	20	−5	7
4	6	4	20
9	14	10	1
9	−6	25	6

is an example of a magic square with the sum of 34. There are several different ways of constructing magic squares. This example was constructed by using Bergholt's general method. In Bertholt's method, the numbers are generated by assigning any positive or negative numeric values to replace the alphabetic values of A, B, C, D, W, X, Y, Z shown in the square below.

A − W	C + W + Y	B + X − Y	D − X
D + W − Z	B	C	A − W + Z
C − X + Z	A	D	P + X − Z
B + X	D − W − Y	A − X + Y	C + W

You are to develop a program that will generate a magic square. Input the values for A, B, C, D, W, X, Y, Z. Test your program using the following values.

A = 3   B = 6   C = 5   D = 2   W = 4   X = 16   Y = 6   Z = 10

The resulting magic square is considered to be symmetric.

Chapter 6

PROCEDURE AND FUNCTION FUNDAMENTALS

Objectives
Describe PROCEDUREs and FUNCTIONs and the role that they can play in problems solving by modularizing solutions.

Suggested Background
Some people believe that PROCEDUREs and FUNCTIONs are an extremely powerful tool in the structured programming solution process and for that reason should be learned as early as possible. Other people believe that this material should be delayed until the learner is more proficient. This chapter accommodates both views as it can be covered with only the knowledge of the three core Pascal chapters (3, 4, 5). If desired, this chapter can also be delayed until just before the second chapter on PROCEDUREs and FUNCTIONs. It is possible to introduce the concept of PROCEDUREs immediately after the chapter on input/output (Chapter 4) and before the chapter on basic data manipulations (Chapter 5). To support this, many of the problems at the end of this chapter do not require data manipulations. However, for organizational reasons, this text incorporates the use of subprograms for both non-data manipulation uses and simple data manipulation uses.

PROCEDUREs and FUNCTIONs are powerful programming tools. They help the programmer use top-down design to develop programs. Programs developed using the top-down approach are usually developed faster and are easier to understand. PROCEDUREs and FUNCTIONs also allow the same programming statements to be used in several places in the same program, or in many different programs.

This chapter discusses the relatively simple use of PROCEDUREs and FUNCTIONs where the value of any variable or constant is known everywhere in the program. A later chapter discusses how PROCEDUREs and FUNCTIONs are used when a given variable or constant value is not known everywhere in the program.

6.1 USES FOR PROCEDURES AND FUNCTIONS

Objective
Present a general picture of the usefulness of PROCEDUREs and FUNCTIONs.

Suggested Background
The previous material in this chapter.

6.1.1 Grouping Things Together

Objective
Create an awareness that some of the activities that are done in the course of solving a problem can be naturally grouped together.

Suggested Background
The previous material in this chapter.

Most problem solutions require that a variety of different things be accomplished. In many problems, it is best to divide the activities needed to solve the problem into smaller groups of tasks. Breaking the problem into pieces or smaller groups of tasks clarifies what needs to be done. Initially the problem solver needs only to specify what each piece is to do, not all the details needed to do the task. For example, a student's daily activities or tasks might be

s.1   get up
s.2   attend school
s.3   return home
s.4   do homework
s.5   sleep

Clearly, within this list of activities, there is much unspecified detail.
What the activity list provides is the first level of a top-down description. When analyzed each activity can be broken up into other activities. For example,

s.4   do homework

could be subdivided into

s.4.1   write English paper
s.4.2   solve math problems
s.4.3   read history chapters

This type of refinement is what was discussed in Chapter 2 under "top-down design." Good programmers often solve their problems this way. PROCEDUREs and FUNC-TIONs can help a programmer organize the statements in a program by grouping them together so that each group accomplishes a distinct part of the problem's solution.

Grouping statements together is part of the *modularization* process. Modules are groups of statements in which (a) the first statement of the module is always executed before any other statements in the module, (b) the last statement in the module is always executed if any statements in the module are executed, and (c) the only exit from the module is through the last statement of the module. A good program is usually made up of several modules. PROCEDUREs and FUNCTIONs can be used to define the limits of a module.

6.1.2 Standard or Commonly Done Things

Objective
Develop an awareness that some tasks that have to be done to solve one problem may also have to be done to solve another problem.

Suggested Background
The previous material in this chapter.

Often many of the things that are done to accomplish one task can be used to accomplish other tasks as well. For example, if a person is buying a hamburger at any one of several fast food places (Burger Castle, Burger Delight, etc.), many of the things that are done to select and pay for a standard hamburger are the same. For example, a person uses the same technique to pay for a hamburger at Burger Castle as at Burger Delight. Likewise, many things that are done with computers can use the same routines or techniques from one program to another.

In Pascal a routine that is to be used in several different programs only needs to be written once if it is placed in PROCEDURE or a FUNCTION. Chapter 12 on PROCEDUREs and FUNCTIONs discusses how it is possible for a Pascal programmer to develop PROCEDUREs or FUNCTIONs that can be moved from one program to another.

6.1.3 Things Done More Than Once

Objective
Develop an awareness that the same activities may be done more than once while solving a single problem.

Suggested Background
The previous material in this chapter.

Some things that are done to solve a problem are done more than once when solving the problem. For example, if a person is visiting several different fast food restaurants to purchase and compare the food served, the process might be described as

f   visit fast food restaurants and evaluate their hamburgers
    f.1   visit a Burger Castle restaurant
        f.1.1   select a hamburger
        f.1.2   order a hamburger
        f.1.3   pay for the hamburger
        f.1.4   evaluate the hamburger
    f.2   visit a Burger Delight restaurant
        f.2.1   select a hamburger
        f.2.2   order a hamburger
        f.2.3   pay for the hamburger
        f.2.4   evaluate the hamburger
    f.3   visit a Burger Star restaurant
        f.3.1   select a hamburger
        f.3.2   order a hamburger
        f.3.3   pay for the hamburger
        f.3.4   evaluate the hamburger
    f.4   report the results of the evaluations

Computer programs often need to perform identical tasks several places in the program. For example, in one place the average age of a group of apple pickers might be calculated. In another the average number of apples picked might then be calculated. In another the average age of the dogs guarding the apples might also be calculated. In Pascal, the same calculation could be performed using only one set of statements by the use of a PROCEDURE or a FUNCTION.

6.1.4 Subprograms

Objective
Present PROCEDUREs and FUNCTIONs as being subprograms.

Suggested Background
The previous material in this chapter.

A PROCEDURE or a FUNCTION can be thought of as a separate program that is nested within another program. For that reason, PROCEDUREs and FUNCTIONs are called *subprograms*. As will be seen, the parts needed to construct a PROCEDURE or FUNCTION are much the same as those needed to construct a program. The major differences are in the headings and in the different ways that variables can be declared.

Another way of thinking about subprograms is that they provide a way to "invent" new high level instructions using combinations of other instructions. For the most part, this chapter places the emphasis on the use of subprograms for organizational reasons (segmentation, stubs) and places less emphasis on the "invention" of new high level statements (replacing multiple occurrences of groups of statements). The next chapter on subprograms (Chapter 12) has a greater emphasis on data manipulation.

6.2 PROCEDURES

Objectives
Describe the purpose of PROCEDUREs and how they are constructed.

Suggested Background
The previous material in this chapter. This section may be done before or after the section on FUNCTIONs (6.3). The entire chapter may be delayed until just before the next chapter on PROCEDUREs and FUNCTIONs.

PROCEDUREs can be used by programmers to help create readable programs. PROCEDUREs can be used to segment the program by forming and defining groups of statements. A group of statements that are defined by a PROCEDURE can then be invoked for execution by a single program statement. This helps make it easier to understand the organization of the tasks needed to solve the problem for which the program has been written. It also can make the development of the problem solution significantly easier.

If a program has the same group of statements repeated several times, a PROCEDURE can enable the programmer to write the statements only one time, and then invoke them for execution as many times as desired by single program statements.

A PROCEDURE is an independent program unit. It can have its own declarations for LABELs, CONSTants, TYPEs, and VARiables, as well as for other PROCEDUREs and FUNCTIONs.

In a Pascal program, PROCEDUREs are defined after the CONSTant and VARiable declarations, but before the main part of the program. (Chapter 2 describes the order in which all the possible parts of a Pascal program are to be defined.) The form of a Pascal program containing a PROCEDURE is

```
PROGRAM <program name>(<external file names>);
VAR
    <variable definitions>
PROCEDURE <procedure name>;
BEGIN
    <program statements to be executed in the procedure>
END;  (* <procedure name> *)
BEGIN  (* MAIN PART OF PROGRAM *)
    <program statements to be executed in the main program>
END.  (* <program name> *)
```

The line beginning with PROCEDURE and ending with the semicolon is called the *PROCEDURE heading*. The complete PROCEDURE declaration terminates with the END delimiter that is paired with the BEGIN of the PROCEDURE. All PROCEDUREs must have a BEGIN-END pair.

If a program has several PROCEDUREs, they can be all placed in the same area of the program, one after the other. If the program also has FUNCTION definitions (FUNCTIONs are discussed in another section of this chapter), they can be mixed up with the PROCEDURE definitions. Either PROCEDURE or FUNCTION definitions may come first. PROCEDUREs and FUNCTIONs may also be defined within PROCEDUREs and FUNCTIONs. This chapter does not explicitly discuss the definition of PROCEDUREs and FUNCTIONs within other PROCEDUREs and FUNCTIONs; The topic is discussed in Chapter 12. However, when this happens, these definitions are placed in the same way in PROCEDUREs and FUNCTIONs as they are placed in the overall program.

A PROCEDURE can be thought of as a separate program whose statements are not executed until they are invoked. They are invoked by the appearance of the PROCEDURE's name.

If desired, variables and constants can be defined within the PROCEDURE as well as for the main part of the program. Variables that are defined "outside" of a

PROCEDURE can be used within the PROCEDURE. Variables defined inside the PROCEDURE cannot be used outside the PROCEDURE in which they are defined. Variables and constants that are defined within a PROCEDURE are considered to be *locally* defined and are discussed in a later chapter. This chapter only presents examples that do not use locally defined variables and constants.

6.2.1 Using Procedures for Segmentation

Objective
Illustrate how PROCEDUREs can be used to achieve segmentation.

Suggested Background
The previous material in this chapter.

When organizing an activity, we might first start out by stating a general, undetailed organization of the activity. For example, if we are interested in cooking and eating breakfast, we might state the tasks involved as:

x   cooking and eating breakfast
   x.1   get food
   x.2   cook food
   x.3   eat food

After doing this, we could describe the steps involved in the separate tasks in greater and greater detail. This is part of "top-down problem design" and is discussed in Chapter 2.

The same thing can be done in a program. For example,

z   calculate area
   z.1   print titles
   z.2   calculate area
   z.3   print area

One way of doing this would be to write a simple program. For example,

```
PROGRAM AREA(INPUT,OUTPUT);
   (* THIS READS IN VALUES FOR HEIGTH AND WIDTH
      AND THEN CALCULATES THE AREA              *)
VAR
   HEIGHT: INTEGER;
   WIDTH: INTEGER;
   AREA: INTEGER;
BEGIN
   WRITELN('CALCULATE AREA');
   WRITELN('--------------');
   READ(HEIGHT,WIDTH);
   WRITELN('HEIGHT = ',HEIGHT:3,' WIDTH = ',WIDTH:3);
   AREA := HEIGHT * WIDTH;
   WRITELN('AREA = ',AREA:6)
END.  (* AREA *)
```

Although this program isn't very complex, it does serve as an example to show how modular organization can be used. The program can be rewritten to group the title writing statements and the statements concerned with the volume calculations into two groups. For example,

```
PROGRAM AREA(INPUT,OUTPUT);
   (* THIS READS IN VALUES FOR HEIGHT AND WIDTH
      AND THEN CALCULATES THE AREA              *)
VAR
   HEIGHT: INTEGER;
   WIDTH: INTEGER;
   AREA: INTEGER;
(* ============================================================ *)
PROCEDURE TITLES;
BEGIN  (* TITLE PRINTING PROCEDURE *)
   WRITELN('CALCULATE AREA');
   WRITELN('--------------')
END;  (* PROCEDURE TITLES *)
(* ============================================================ *)
PROCEDURE FINDAREA;
BEGIN  (* READING DIMENSIONS AND CALCULATING AREA *)
   READ(HEIGHT,WIDTH);
   WRITE('HEIGHT = ',HEIGHT:3,'WIDTH = ',WIDTH:3);
   AREA := HEIGHT * WIDTH
END;  (* PROCEDURE FINDAREA *)
(* ============================================================ *)
BEGIN  (* MAIN PART OF PROGRAM *)
   TITLES;
   FINDAREA;
   WRITELN('AREA = ',AREA:5)
END.  (* AREA *)
```

The comment statements with " . . . = = = . . ." are not required by Pascal. They have been used to make it easier for a reader to separate the PROCEDUREs from the rest of the program.

Notice that the main portion of the program contains only three statements. These statements clearly tell us what the program is doing. This makes the program easily readable. Thus, the tasks that the second program is to perform are more easily understood than those of the first program.

6.2.2 Replacing Multiple Occurrences of the Same Statements

Objective
Illustrate how PROCEDUREs can be used to replace multiple occurrences of the same group of statements.

Suggested Background
Introductory material at the beginning of the chapter and Section 6.1.3.

Often the same task has to be accomplished several times to solve a problem. For example, when washing dishes, we go through the same actions for each dinner plate. In a program, a PROCEDURE can be used to define what the computer is to do. Then the same statements can be used several times in the program.

For example, if what we want to do is to

t.1   process the first number
    t.1.1   read the number
    t.1.2   write the number
    t.1.3   add the number to a total of all numbers
    t.1.4   write the total so far
t.2   process the second number
    t.2.1   read the number
    t.2.2   write the number
    t.2.3   add the number to a total of all numbers
    t.2.4   write the total of all numbers so far
t.3   process the third number
    t.3.1   read the number
    t.3.2   write the number
    t.3.3   add the number to a total of all numbers
    t.3.4   write the total of all numbers so far
t.4   process the fourth number
    t.4.1   read the number
    t.4.2   write the number
    t.4.3   add the number to a total of all numbers
    t.4.4   write the total of all numbers so far
t.5   finish processing
t.6   write the total of all the numbers

a simple program to do these tasks would be

```
PROGRAM TOTAL(INPUT,OUTPUT);
   (* READ IN NUMBERS AND TOTAL THEM *)
VAR
   NUMBER: INTEGER;
   TOTAL: INTEGER;
BEGIN  (* PROCESSING NUMBERS *)
   TOTAL := O;  (* INITIALIZE TOTAL OF ALL NUMBERS READ *)
   READ(NUMBER);  (* READ FIRST NUMBER *)
   WRITE('NUMBER IS: ',NUMBER:4);  (* ECHO NUMBER *)
   TOTAL := TOTAL + NUMBER;  (* TOTAL OF ALL READ SO FAR *)
   WRITELN(' -- TOTAL = ',TOTAL:6);
   READ(NUMBER);  (* READ SECOND NUMBER *)
   WRITE('NUMBER IS: ',NUMBER:4);  (* ECHO NUMBER *)
   TOTAL := TOTAL + NUMBER;  (* TOTAL OF ALL READ SO FAR *)
   WRITELN(' -- TOTAL = ',TOTAL:6);
   READ(NUMBER);  (* READ THIRD NUMBER *)
   WRITE('NUMBER IS: ',NUMBER);  (* ECHO NUMBER *)
   TOTAL := TOTAL + NUMBER;  (* TOTAL OF ALL READ SO FAR *)
   WRITELN(' -- TOTAL = ',TOTAL:6);
   READ(NUMBER);  (* READ FOURTH NUMBER *)
   WRITE('NUMBER IS: ',NUMBER);  (* ECHO NUMBER *)
   TOTAL := TOTAL + NUMBER;  (* TOTAL OF ALL READ SO FAR *)
   WRITELN(' -- TOTAL = ',TOTAL:6)
END.  (* TOTALING NUMBERS *)
```

This is a simple program and there may be other ways to solve it (such as by using the repetitive control structures discussed in a later chapter). However, it does help to see how a PROCEDURE could be used in the following program both to modularize it and to help make the writing process shorter.

```
PROGRAM TOTAL(INPUT,OUTPUT);
   (* READ IN NUMBERS AND TOTAL THEM *)
VAR
   NUMBER: INTEGER;
   TOTAL: INTEGER;
(* ================================================================ *)
PROCEDURE NUMBERTOTAL;
BEGIN  (* NUMBER PROCESSING ROUTINE *)
   READ(NUMBER);  (* READ NUMBER *)
   WRITE('NUMBER IS: ',NUMBER:4);  (* ECHO NUMBER *)
   TOTAL := TOTAL + NUMBER;  (* TOTAL OF ALL READ SO FAR *)
   WRITELN(' -- TOTAL = ',TOTAL:6)
END;  (* PROCEDURE NUMBERTOTAL *)
(* ================================================================ *)
BEGIN  (* MAIN PART OF PROGRAM *)
   TOTAL := O;  (* INITIALIZE TOTAL OF ALL NUMBERS READ *)
   NUMBERTOTAL;  (* READ AND TOTAL FIRST NUMBER *)
   NUMBERTOTAL;  (* READ AND TOTAL SECOND NUMBER *)
   NUMBERTOTAL;  (* READ AND TOTAL THIRD NUMBER *)
   NUMBERTOTAL   (* READ AND TOTAL FOURTH NUMBER *)
END.  (* TOTAL *)
```

6.2.3 Using Procedures as Stubs

> **Objectives**
> Introduce the fundamental program development concept of stubs and show how PROCEDUREs can be used as stubs.
>
> **Suggested Background**
> Introductory material at the beginning of this chapter, and Section 6.2.

It is usually easier to solve a problem by dividing it into small pieces or tasks. When using a computer to solve a problem, this is particularly true. Good programs are usually divided up into small modules. These modules can be made into separate segments by defining them as PROCEDUREs.

An effective and efficient method of developing a program is through the top-down process. When developing top-down programs, the "highest" level modules are first identified by function. For example,

x.1   define variables and constants
x.2   print titles
x.3   read, print numbers

At this point, the first level of program development can be written. Writing a program in a top-down manner by using stubs enables the programmer to get part of the program working before having to grapple with all the details. This can be accomplished even though we do not know very many of the details. In the following example, how much data there is to be read and the data TYPE(s) involved are initially undefined or unknown, but the program structure can be written.

This can be done by inserting *stubs* for statements that have yet to be written. For example,

```
PROGRAM SALARY(INPUT,OUTPUT);
   (* THIS PRINTS AGE AND SALARY INFORMATION *)
   (* VARIABLES TO BE DEFINED WHEN KNOWN *)
(* ================================================================= *)
PROCEDURE TITLES;
BEGIN (* TITLES STUB *)
    WRITELN('STUB: TITLES')
END;  (* PROCEDURE TITLES *)
(* ================================================================= *)
PROCEDURE READPRINT;
BEGIN  (* READPRINT STUB *)
    WRITELN('STUB: READ AND PRINT (READPRINT)')
END;  (* PROCEDURE READPRINT *)
(* ================================================================= *)
BEGIN  (* MAIN PART OF PROGRAM *)
   TITLES;
   READPRINT
END.  (* SALARY *)
```

This would result in the printout of

```
    STUB: TITLES
    STUB: READ AND PRINT
```

when more detail is known or developed, one stub at a time can be expanded. For example, the previous program SALARY can be further developed by expanding the READPRINT stub as follows.

```
PROGRAM SALARY(INPUT,OUTPUT);
   (* THIS PRINTS AGE AND SALARY INFORMATION *)
VAR
   AGE: INTEGER;
   SALARY: REAL;
(* ================================================================= *)
PROCEDURE TITLES;
BEGIN (* TITLES STUB *)
    WRITELN('STUB: TITLES')
END;  (* PROCEDURE TITLES *)
(* ================================================================= *)
PROCEDURE READPRINT;
BEGIN  (* READING AND PRINTING *)
   READ(AGE,SALARY);
   WRITE('AGE IS:',AGE:4);
   WRITELN(' -- SALARY IS: ',SALARY:8:2)
END;  (* PROCEDURE READPRINT *)
(* ================================================================= *)
BEGIN  (* MAIN PART OF PROGRAM *)
   TITLES;
   READPRINT
END.  (* SALARY *)
```

If the input data was

```
23 645.36
```

the results would be

```
STUB: TITLES
AGE IS:  23 -- SALARY IS   645.36
```

As the program is developed, additional stubs may be required in the lower level modules.

In summary, using stubs enables the programmer to solve a problem in a structured, top-down fashion. The program can be broken up into easily handled pieces or tasks. The details of the tasks do not have to be defined before the decision structure of the program has been analyzed, understood, and programmed. The pieces of the problem can be solved one by one. This makes the solution process easier, simpler, and clearer.

6.3 FUNCTIONS

Objectives
Identify what a FUNCTION produces, discuss why a FUNCTION might be used, and specify how a function is declared.

Suggested Background
Introductory material at the beginning of this chapter. Notice that Section 6.2 is specifically not required as Sections 6.2 and 6.3 can be interchanged.

FUNCTIONs can be used to accomplish some of the same things as PROCE-DUREs. PROCEDUREs are best used when you want to replace a group of statements with a single statement. FUNCTIONs are best used when a group of statements or a complex single statement results in a single value. A FUNCTION enables a programmer to gain this value in a readable and modularized form.

A FUNCTION is an independent program unit. It can have its own declarations for LABELs, constants, TYPEs, and variables, as well as for other FUNC-TIONs and PROCEDUREs. Pascal has several predefined FUNCTIONs. They are often referred to as *built-in* as they are built into the language. The use of two of these predefined FUNCTIONs, ROUND and TRUNC, has already been discussed.

In a Pascal program, FUNCTIONs are defined after the constant and variable declarations, but before the main part of the program. (An earlier chapter describes the order in which all the possible parts of a Pascal program are to be defined.) The form of a Pascal program containing a FUNCTION is

```
PROGRAM <program name>(<external file names>);
VAR
   <variable definitions>
FUNCTION <function name>: <type>;
BEGIN
   <function statements>
END; (* <function name> *)
BEGIN  (* MAIN PART OF PROGRAM *)
   <main program statements>
END. (* <program name> *)
```

The data TYPE for each FUNCTION is specified because a scalar value is associated with the FUNCTION name. The line beginning with FUNCTION and ending with the semicolon is called the *FUNCTION heading*. The complete FUNCTION declaration terminates with the END delimiter that is paired with the BEGIN of the FUNCTION. All FUNCTIONs must have a BEGIN-END pair.

If a program has several FUNCTIONs, they can be all placed in the same area of the program, one after the other. If the program also has PROCEDURE definitions (PROCEDUREs are discussed in another section of this chapter), they can be mixed up with the FUNCTION definitions. Either FUNCTION or PROCEDURE definitions may come first. FUNCTIONs and PROCEDUREs may also be defined within FUNCTIONs and PROCEDUREs. This chapter does not explicitly discuss the definition of FUNCTIONs and PROCEDUREs within other FUNCTIONs and PROCEDUREs; the topic is discussed in another chapter. However, when this happens, these definitions are placed in the same way in FUNCTIONs and PROCEDUREs as they are placed in a Pascal program.

The statements within a FUNCTION can be thought of as a separate program that supplies a single value. FUNCTIONs are not executed until they are invoked. FUNCTIONs are invoked by the appearance of the FUNCTION name within a statement that uses the value supplied by the FUNCTION. This could happen within an expression or an output statement. For example,

```
TOTAL := TOTAL + <function name>
```

or

```
WRITELN(<function name>)
```

Looking Ahead: If desired, variables and constants can be defined within the FUNCTION we well as for the main part of the program. Variables that are defined "outside" of a FUNCTION can be used within the FUNCTION. Variables defined inside the FUNCTION cannot be used outside the FUNCTION in which they are defined. Variables and constants that are defined within a FUNCTION are considered to be "locally" defined and are discussed in a later chapter. This chapter only presents examples that do not use locally defined variables and constants.

6.3.1 Using Functions for Segmentation

Objective
Illustrate how a FUNCTION can be used to accomplish modularization.

Suggested Background
The introductory material at the beginning of this chapter and Sections 6.1 and 6.3. Notice that Section 6.2 is not required.

FUNCTIONs can be best used to achieve segmentation and modularization when the result of the modularized group of statements is a single value. For example, in the program

```
PROGRAM SPENDING(INPUT,OUTPUT);
   (* FOR AN ITEM, READ: COST, COUNT, AND PRICE AND CALCULATE
      THE TOTAL CHARGE TO THE CUSTOMER                        *)
CONST
   SALESTAX = 0.05;
VAR
   COST: REAL;
   COUNT: INTEGER;
   PRICE: REAL;
   DISCOUNT: REAL;
   NETPRICE: REAL;
   TAX: REAL;
   CHARGE: REAL;
BEGIN (* MAIN PART OF PROGRAM *)
   READ(COST,COUNT,PRICE);
   WRITELN('COST=',COST:5:2,' * COUNT=',COUNT:4,' * PRICE=',PRICE:5:2);
   PRICE := COST * COUNT;
   DISCOUNT := 0.17 * PRICE;
   NETPRICE := PRICE - DISCOUNT;
   TAX := SALESTAX * NETPRICE;
   CHARGE := NETPRICE + TAX;
   WRITE(' * THE CHARGE IS: ',CHARGE:7:2)
END.   (* SPENDING *)
```

the result of the charge calculations is a single value. The program SPENDING can be rewritten and modularized as shown below in the program CHARGES. (The comments with "... ==== ..." are not required by Pascal. They have been used to make it easier for a reader to separate the FUNCTIONs from the rest of the program.)

```
PROGRAM CHARGES(INPUT,OUTPUT);
    (* FOR AN ITEM, READ: COST, COUNT, AND PRICE AND CALCULATE
       THE TOTAL CHARGE TO THE CUSTOMER                          *)
CONST
    SALESTAX = 0.05;
VAR
    COST: REAL;
    COUNT: INTEGER;
    PRICE: REAL;
    DISCOUNT: REAL;
    NETPRICE: REAL;
    TAX: REAL;
    CHARGE: REAL;
(* ============================================================== *)
FUNCTION NETCHARGE:REAL;
BEGIN
    PRICE := COST * COUNT;
    DISCOUNT := 0.17 * PRICE;
    NETPRICE := PRICE - DISCOUNT;
    TAX := SALESTAX * NETPRICE;
    NETCHARGE := NETPRICE + TAX
END;  (* FUNCTION NETCHARGE *)
(* ============================================================== *)
BEGIN  (* MAIN PART OF PROGRAM *)
    READ(COST,COUNT,PRICE);
    WRITELN('COST=',COST:5:2,' * COUNT=',COUNT:4,' * PRICE=',PRICE:5:2);
    CHARGE := NETCHARGE;
    WRITE(' * THE CHARGE IS: ',CHARGE:7:2)
END.  (* CHARGES *)
```

In this way, the part of the program that communicates by reading and writing is separated from the part that does the calculations.

This program could be further simplified by combining the FUNCTION invocation and WRITE statement as shown in the following program.

```
PROGRAM CHARGES(INPUT,OUTPUT);
    (* FOR AN ITEM, READ: COST, COUNT, AND PRICE AND CALCULATE
       THE TOTAL CHARGE TO THE CUSTOMER                          *)
CONST
    SALESTAX = 0.05;
VAR
    COST: REAL;
    COUNT: INTEGER;
    PRICE: REAL;
    DISCOUNT: REAL;
    NETPRICE: REAL;
    TAX: REAL;
(* ================================================================ *)
FUNCTION NETCHARGE:REAL;
BEGIN
    PRICE := COST * COUNT;
    DISCOUNT := 0.17 * PRICE;
    NETPRICE := PRICE - DISCOUNT;
    TAX := SALESTAX * NETPRICE;
    NETCHARGE := NETPRICE + TAX
END;  (* FUNCTION NETCHARGE *)
(* ================================================================ *)
BEGIN  (* MAIN PART OF PROGRAM *)
    READ(COST,COUNT,PRICE);
    WRITELN('COST=',COST:5:2,' * COUNT=',COUNT:4,' * PRICE=',PRICE:5:2);
    WRITE(' * THE CHARGE IS: ',NETCHARGE:7:2)
END.  (* CHARGES *)
```

6.3.2 Replacing Multiple Occurrences of the Same Statements

Objective
Illustrate how FUNCTIONs can be used to replace multiple occurrences of the same statement(s) in the same program.

Suggested Background
The introductory material at the beginning of this chapter and Sections 6.1.3 and 6.3.

FUNCTIONs can be used to replace one or more statements that occur at more than one place in a program. A FUNCTION is best used if it is desirable to produce a single value when the statement is invoked.

6.3.2.1 Replacing Complex Single Statements

Objectives
Discuss why it might be useful to replace a complex single statement
with a FUNCTION and provide an illustration.

Suggested Background
The introductory material at the beginning of this chapter and Sections
6.1.3, 6.3, and 6.3.2.

A complex statement may be usefully replaced with a FUNCTION statement.
For example, in the following program a complex calculation for calculating a frog
farm's profit is specified three times.

frog farm profits
1   define variables and constants
2   print fixed costs
3   print titles
4   calculate profits for different volumes
   4.1   first frog volume
      4.1.1   read price and volume
      4.1.2   print price and volume
      4.1.3   calculate expected profit
      4.1.4   print expected profit
   4.2   second frog volume
      4.2.1   read price and volume
      4.2.2   print price and volume
      4.2.3   calculate expected profit
      4.2.4   print expected profit
   4.3   third frog volume
      4.3.1   read price and volume
      4.3.2   print price and volume
      4.3.3   calculate expected profit
      4.3.4   print expected profit
5   finish processing

```
PROGRAM FROGS(INPUT,OUTPUT);
    (* THIS CALCULATES THE EXPECTED PROFITS FOR A FROG FARMER.
       ONE VARIETY OF FROGS IS RAISED, ONLY ONE SIZE IS SOLD.
       ALL FROGS SOLD AT ONE TIME ARE SOLD FOR THE SAME PRICE.
       HOW MANY FROGS ARE SOLD IS DEPENDENT ON THE PRICE CHARGED  *)
CONST  (* FIXED MONTHLY COSTS *)
    COST = 1.73;            (* DIRECT COST OF GROWING ONE FROG *)
    COMMISSION = 0.10;      (* SALES COMMISION PAID TO CHILD *)
    CRANES = 43;            (* NUMBER OF FROGS CONSUMED BY CRANES *)
    UTILITIES = 123.42;     (* ELECTRICITY, PROPANE *)
    MORTGAGE = 638.92;      (* TO NANDI SAVINGS AND LOAN *)
    ADVERTISING = 41.56;    (* CLASSIFIED ADS *)
    PROPERTYTAX = 23.74;    (* MONTHLY PROPERTY TAX PAYMENT *)
VAR
    PROFIT: REAL;  (* PROFIT MADE ON FROG SALES *)
    PRICE: REAL;   (* PRICE CHARGED FOR A SINGLE FROG *)
    NUMBERSOLD: INTEGER;  (* FROGS SOLD AT A GIVEN PRICE *)
BEGIN  (* TRYING TO FIND THE BEST PRICE TO SELL FROGS AT *)
    (* FIXED COSTS *)
    WRITELN('THE COST OF PRODUCING ONE FROG IS: ',COST:5:2);
    WRITELN('PROBABLE NUMBER OF FROGS CONSUMED BY CRANES: ',CRANES:3);
    WRITELN('UTILITIES ARE: ',UTILITIES:6:2);
    WRITELN('MORTGAGE PAYMENT: ',MORTGAGE:6:2);
    WRITELN('ADVERTISING COST: ',ADVERTISING:5:2);
    WRITELN('MONTHLY PROPERTY TAX: ',PROPERTYTAX:6:2);
    (* TITLES *)
    WRITELN;  (* A BLANK LINE BEFORE THE PRICE/PROFIT TABLE *)
    WRITELN('PRICE EXPECTED VOLUME   PROFIT');  (* RESULTS TITLE *)
    WRITELN('----- --------------- --------');
    (* START TO PROCESS DATA *)
    READ(PRICE,NUMBERSOLD);  (* FIRST PRICE AND RESULTING VOLUME *)
    WRITE(PRICE:5:2,NUMBERSOLD:11);  (* ECHO PRINT *)
    PROFIT := NUMBERSOLD * (PRICE - COST) - PRICE*COMMISSION
              - CRANES*COST - UTILITIES - MORTGAGE - ADVERTISING
              - PROPERTYTAX;
    WRITELN(PROFIT:15:2);  (* PROFIT FROM FIRST SET OF DATA *)
    READ(PRICE,NUMBERSOLD);  (* SECOND PRICE AND RESULTING VOLUME *)
    WRITE(PRICE:5:2,NUMBERSOLD:11);  (* ECHO PRINT *)
    PROFIT := NUMBERSOLD * (PRICE - COST) - PRICE*COMMISSION
              - CRANES*COST - UTILITIES - MORTGAGE - ADVERTISING
              - PROPERTYTAX;
    WRITELN(PROFIT:15:2);  (* PROFIT FROM SECOND SET OF DATA *)
    READ(PRICE,NUMBERSOLD);  (* THIRD PRICE AND RESULTING VOLUME *)
    WRITE(PRICE:5:2,NUMBERSOLD:11);  (* ECHOPRINT *)
    PROFIT := NUMBERSOLD * (PRICE - COST) - PRICE*COMMISSION
              - CRANES*COST - UTILITIES - MORTGAGE - ADVERTISING
              - PROPERTYTAX;
    WRITELN(PROFIT:15:2)
END.  (* FROGS *)
```

If the data for this program is

```
3.36    963
1.98   2076
2.98   1452
```

the results will be

```
THE COST OF PRODUCING ONE FROG IS:  1.73
PROBABLE NUMBER OF FROGS CONSUMED BY CRANES:  43
UTILITIES ARE: 123.42
MORTGAGE PAYMENT: 638.92
ADVERTISING COST: 41.56
MONTHLY PROPERTY TAX:  23.74

PRICE EXPECTED VOLUME    PROFIT
----- ----------------  --------
3.36            963       667.32
1.98           2076      -383.23
2.98           1452       912.67
```

Notice that the resulting PRICE/VOLUME table was constructed by two separate output statements. The first was a WRITE statement that echo prints the PRICE and expected number of frogs that will be sold at that price. The second output statement was a WRITELN that prints the expected profits for that sales volume. (Recall that one result of using the WRITELN statement is that the machine is instructed to place the output from the *next* output statement on a new output line.)

The preceding program can be more efficiently written, made more readable, and modularized by using a FUNCTION as illustrated in the following program.

```
PROGRAM FROGS(INPUT,OUTPUT);
    (* THIS CALCULATES THE EXPECTED PROFITS FOR A FROG FARMER.
       ONE VARIETY OF FROGS IS RAISED, THEY ARE ONLY SOLD AT MATURITY.
       ALL FROGS SOLD AT ONE TIME ARE SOLD FOR THE SAME PRICE.
       HOW MANY FROGS ARE SOLD IS DEPENDENT ON THE PRICE CHARGED      *)
CONST  (* FIXED MONTHLY COSTS *)
    COST = 1.73;           (* DIRECT COST OF GROWING ONE FROG *)
    COMMISSION = 0.10;     (* SALES COMMISION PAID TO CHILD *)
    CRANES = 43;           (* NUMBER OF FROGS CONSUMED BY CRANES *)
    UTILITIES = 123.42;    (* ELECTRICITY, PROPANE *)
    MORTGAGE = 638.92;     (* TO NANDI SAVINGS AND LOAN *)
    ADVERTISING = 41.56;   (* CLASSIFIED ADS *)
    PROPERTYTAX = 23.74;   (* MONTHLY PROPERTY TAX PAYMENT *)
VAR
    PRICE: REAL;     (* PRICE CHARGED FOR A SINGLE FROG *)
    NUMBERSOLD: INTEGER;   (* FROGS SOLD AT A GIVEN PRICE *)
(* ================================================================= *)
FUNCTION PROFIT: REAL;   (* FUNCTION TO CALCULATE FROG PROFITS *)
BEGIN  (* FUNCTION TO CALCULATE PROFITS *)
    PROFIT := NUMBERSOLD * (PRICE - COST) - PRICE*COMMISSION
              - CRANES*COST - UTILITIES - MORTGAGE - ADVERTISING
              - PROPERTYTAX
END;  (* FUNCTION PROFIT *)
(* ================================================================= *)
BEGIN  (* TRYING TO FIND THE BEST PRICE TO SELL FROGS AT *)
    (* FIXED COSTS *)
    WRITELN('THE COST OF PRODUCING ONE FROG IS: ',COST:5:2);
    WRITELN('PROBABLE NUMBER OF FROGS CONSUMED BY CRANES: ',CRANES:3);
    WRITELN('UTILITIES ARE: ',UTILITIES:6:2);
    WRITELN('MORTGAGE PAYMENT: ',MORTGAGE:6:2);
    WRITELN('ADVERTISING COST: ',ADVERTISING:5:2);
    WRITELN('MONTHLY PROPERTY TAX: ',PROPERTYTAX:6:2);
    (* TITLES *)
    WRITELN;  (* A BLANK LINE BEFORE THE PRICE/PROFIT TABLE *)
    WRITELN('PRICE EXPECTED VOLUME   PROFIT');  (* RESULTS TITLE *)
    WRITELN('-----  --------------  --------');
    (* START TO PROCESS PRICES *)
    READ(PRICE,NUMBERSOLD);  (* FIRST PRICE AND RESULTING VOLUME *)
    WRITE(PRICE:5:2,NUMBERSOLD:11);  (* ECHO PRINT *)
    WRITELN(PROFIT:15:2);  (* PROFIT FROM FIRST SET OF DATA *)
    READ(PRICE,NUMBERSOLD);  (* SECOND PRICE AND RESULTING VOLUME *)
    WRITE(PRICE:5:2,NUMBERSOLD:11);  (* ECHO PRINT *)
    WRITELN(PROFIT:15:2);  (* PROFIT FROM SECOND SET OF DATA *)
    READ(PRICE,NUMBERSOLD);  (* THIRD PRICE AND RESULTING VOLUME *)
    WRITE(PRICE:5:2,NUMBERSOLD:11);  (* ECHOPRINT *)
    WRITELN(PROFIT:15:2)
END.  (* FROGS *)
```

If the data was the same as supplied for the previous program, the results will be the same.

6.3.2.2 Replacing Groups of Statements with FUNCTIONS

Objectives
Discuss why it might be useful to replace a group of statements that results in a single value and provide an illustration.

Suggested Background
The introductory material at the beginning of this chapter, and Sections 6.3, 6.3.2, and 6.3.2.1.

A FUNCTION can be used to replace groups of statements. It is best to use a FUNCTION when a single value results from the execution of the group of statements. A FUNCTION can perform several tasks, such as READ and WRITE, as well as calculating a value. However, unless the single value that results from the invocation of the FUNCTION is useful, it would make more sense to define the statements as a PROCEDURE. The following program MONEYNEEDED illustrates the use of a FUNCTION that contains several statements that are to be executed when the FUNCTION is invoked.

```
PROGRAM MONEYNEEDED(INPUT,OUTPUT);
   (* FOR AN ITEM, READ: COST, COUNT, AND PRICE AND CALCULATE
      THE TOTAL CHARGE TO THE CUSTOMER                          *)
CONST
   SALESTAX = 0.05;
VAR
   COST: REAL;
   COUNT: INTEGER;
   PRICE: REAL;
   DISCOUNT: REAL;
   NETPRICE: REAL;
   TAX: REAL;
(* ================================================================ *)
FUNCTION NETCHARGE:REAL;
BEGIN
   PRICE := COST * COUNT;
   DISCOUNT := 0.17 * PRICE;
   NETPRICE := PRICE - DISCOUNT;
   TAX := SALESTAX * NETPRICE;
   NETCHARGE := NETPRICE + TAX
END;  (* FUNCTION NETCHARGE *)
(* ================================================================ *)
BEGIN  (* MAIN PART OF PROGRAM *)
   READ(COST,COUNT,PRICE);  (* FIRST PRICE INFORMATION *)
   WRITELN('COST=',COST:5:2,' * COUNT=',COUNT:4,' * PRICE=',PRICE:5:2,
           ' * THE NET CHARGE=',NETCHARGE:7:2);
   READ(COST,COUNT,PRICE);  (* SECOND PRICE INFORMATION *)
   WRITELN('COST=',COST:5:2,' * COUNT=',COUNT:4,' * PRICE=',PRICE:5:2,
           ' * THE NET CHARGE=',NETCHARGE:7:2);
   READ(COST,COUNT,PRICE);  (* THIRD PRICE INFORMATION *)
   WRITELN('COST=',COST:5:2,' * COUNT=',COUNT:4,' * PRICE=',PRICE:5:2,
           ' * THE NET CHARGE=',NETCHARGE:7:2)
END.  (* MONEYNEEDED *)
```

The program MONEYNEEDED uses the FUNCTION that was first developed in the example program CHARGES in Section 6.3.1. The two differences between MONEYNEEDED and CHARGES are that (a) the FUNCTION identified NET-CHARGE is invoked three times in MONEYNEEDED and was invoked only once in CHARGES and (b) the invocation is part of a WRITELN statement that also echo prints the input data. The echo print will be completed before NETCHARGE is invoked as the actions in the WRITELN will be sequentially performed, left to right.

6.4 QUESTIONS

6.1   How does a PROCEDURE differ from a FUNCTION? In what ways are they the same?
6.2   What is a segment?
6.3   What is a stub?
6.4   When is it desirable to use a FUNCTION instead of a procedure?
6.5   When might it be desirable to use a PROCEDURE instead of a FUNCTION? Why?

6.5 PROBLEMS

6.1. Prepare a one-page report of your college life consisting of
  (a) courses that you have taken and those you are presently taking,
  (b) where you live, and
  (c) any extracurricula activities that you are involved in (include work).
Display this report using a different PROCEDURE for each part.

6.2. Joe Josephson of the Pittsburgh Pirates is currently negotiating his contract for next year. He needs to know how well he performed last season in comparison with the entire team (excluding his performance). You should use separate PROCEDUREs to display the titles, his individual performance, and the team's performance. The report should have the form:

```
JOE JOSEPHSON'S PERFORMANCE
---------------------------
      hits - xxx
      at bats - xxxxx
      batting average - .xxx

PITTSBURG PIRATE'S PERFORMANCE
------------------------------
      hits - xx
      at bats - xxxx
      batting average - .xxx
```

Test your program with the following data.

For Joe:	150 hits for 600 at bats
For the team:	1000 hits for 3987 at bats

6.3. Every three years Janet Murphy replaces her current car with a new one. This time she has decided to look into whether it would be cheaper to lease a car for three years or to buy a new one. Using a separate subprogram for each module, design and write the stubs for a program that will input the monthly payment for leasing the car and then calculate the total price of buying a new car. Your program should have at least five modules. The program should report the module name represented by the stub when each module is to be executed.

6.4. Using a separate subprogram for each module, design and write the stub structure for a program that will input a traveling salesman's expenses for the day and then report the expense report displayed below. The total spent by the salesman is to be calculated and subsequently presented at the end of the expense report.

```
                        DAILY EXPENSE REPORT
         ITEMS                                    EXPENSE AMOUNT

         BREAKFAST                                     x.xx
         LUNCH                                        xx.xx
         DINNER                                       xx.xx
         HOTEL                                        xx.xx
         TIPS AND MISC.                               xx.xx
         LAUNDRY AND VALET                            xx.xx
         TELEPHONE AND POSTAGE                       xxx.xx
         AIR, TRAIN, BUS TRANSPORTATION             xxxx.xx
         LOCAL TRANSPORTATION                        xxx.xx
         CAR RENTAL                                  xxx.xx
         GAS AND OIL                                  xx.xx
         PARKING, TOLLS                               xx.xx
         CAR WASH                                     xx.xx
         REPAIRS, PARTS, ETC.                       xxxx.xx
         ENTERTAINMENT                               xxx.xx

         TOTAL ----------------------------- xxxxxx.xx
```

Your program should report the module name represented by the stub when each module is to be executed.

6.5. Using a separate subprogram for each module, design and write the stub structure for a program that will input three grades for a student, calculate a final grade, and assign the student a letter grade. Each of the three input grades has a maximum of 100 points. The first grade or homework grade is 40% of the final score. The second or midterm test grade is 25% and the final test or third grade is worth 35%.

Assign letter grades as follows:

A for a final score of 90 or better
B for a final score of 80, but less than 90
C for a final score of 70, but less than 80
D for a final score of 60, but less than 70
F for a final score below 60

Your program should report the module name represented by the stub when each module is to be executed.

6.6. Katrina decides to keep a log of all her school expenses. Her incentive is that her father has told her that he will help her by paying 75% of each month's total expenses.

Using a separate subprogram from each module, design and write the stub structure for a program that will input Katrina's individual school expenses (in dollars and cents), report each expense in a journal (output report), and at the end of the month (when there are no more expenses to input), calculate 75% of the total expenses. Then display the dollar amount paid by Katrina's father and the amount paid by Katrina.

The journal report should look as follows:

```
                MONTHLY EXPENSES JOURNAL

          EXPENSE                    AMOUNT
             1                       xxx.xx
             2                       xxx.xx
             .                         .
             .                         .
             .                         .
    MONTHLY TOTAL                    xxxx.xx
    AMOUNT PAID BY DAD:              xxxxxx.xx
    AMOUNT PAID BY JANE:             xxxxxx.xx
```

Your program should report the module name represented by the stub when each module is to be executed.

6.7.   Write a modularized program using PROCEDUREs to display a profile of yourself, consisting of:

   (a)   A section of general information about yourself; specifically include:

phone number
street address
city
state
zip code

   (b)   A section that lists the subjects presently enrolled in at the university.
   (c)   A section that lists the area(s) of study that interest you as an individual.
   (d)   A section that describes your physical attributes:

height
eye color
hair color
sex

Each and every one of these sections should be reported by a different PROCEDURE. If you desire, the information can be fictitious.

6.8.   Karim eats at his favorite restaurant three times a day, five days a week. Each day that he eats there, he spends exactly $10.50. Karim feels that he must tighten his budget, so to plan properly he must first find out how much he spends in a week, in a month, and finally in a year.
   Your job is to write a program to calculate his expenses and then make a financial report to Karim. The report should include the following.
   (a)   How much he spends weekly.
   (b)   How much he spends monthly.
   (c)   How much he spends yearly.
   The calculations are to be done in one PROCEDURE and the report displayed in another PROCEDURE.

6.9.   Santa Claus needs your help to keep track of what everyone wants for Christmas. The work has been divided among several people. Your task is to generate lists for the following people.

> Mary: diamonds, pearls, rubies, sapphires
> Tom: toy cars, trucks, motorcycles
> John: train set, teddy bear
> Julie: doll house, dolls, jump rope
> Martha: microwave oven, blender, mixer
> George: saw, hammer, axe

You are to create a PROCEDURE for each of these people and then invoke each in the main program. This report is to be given to Santa in a neat, orderly form.

6.10. Your brother seems to have a fever. You wish to measure his temperature but you only have a Celsius thermometer in the house. Since you don't know what the normal body temperature is in Celsius and therefore cannot tell if his temperature is higher than normal, you decide to write a program that will convert the Celsius temperature to Fahrenheit. Your brother's temperature is 37 degrees Celsius. [*Hint:* The formula you need is (9/5*C)+32=F.] Display the temperature in Fahrenheit. Use a FUNCTION to calculate the temperature in Fahrenheit.

6.11. Blue, little Johnny's basset hound, is 6 human years old. Blue isn't quite as playful as he was as a pup. Johnny wants to find out just how old Blue is in dog years. Knowing that the first dog year is equal to one human year, the second is equal to 6 human years, and every dog year after that is equal to 7 human years, calculate how old Blue is in dog years. Input Blue's age and display a title, his age in dog years, and his age in human years. Calculate Blue's age by the use of a FUNCTION.

6.12. There are six students in a small chemistry class. You are to calculate and display the average IQ of the students in the class. The following formula can be used to calculate the average.

$$\text{Average IQ} = \frac{\text{Sum of the IQs}}{\text{Number of IQs}}$$

Display each IQ as it is input and then calculate and display the average IQ. Supply meaningful titles. Test your program with the following data.

> 101   94   130   145   110   107

Use a FUNCTION to calculate the average.

6.13. Display a poem, either original or borrowed. The poem should be displayed in the following sequence.

> Title
> Author
> Poem

These separate parts should be displayed by using separate PROCEDUREs that are invoked in the main part of the program.

Chapter 7

CONTROL STRUCTURES: COMPOUNDING, DECISIONS, REPETITION

Objectives
Describe how statements can be grouped together and how repetitive execution of statements can be specified and controlled.

Suggested Background
The core chapters on Pascal (3, 4, 5). Some people might prefer to cover the chapter on selection (Chapter 8) before this one. This can be done. The first two sections of this chapter are common material for this and Chapter 8. The material in this chapter discussing how repetitive statement execution is accomplished (starts with Section 7.3) can be delayed until after the material in Chapter 8 is covered. The problems and questions at the end of Chapters 7 and 8 do not require a knowledge of the material from the other chapter.

When solving problems, we often find that there is more to do than just follow a list of instructions, one by one. It is often necessary to group things together that are related or that are to be done at the same time. Often, there is a need to select among different courses of action. Sometimes, tasks are repeated while something is true or until some condition is met. Tasks may have to be repeated a specified number of times. The process of grouping, selection, and repetition can be used to provide control over the solution of a problem. This is the case whether or not a computer is being used to implement the solution.

A day's activities can have all of these control elements. For example, there might be (a) a group of wake-up activities that are always performed; (b) a set of activities that are done if a visit is made to the hair stylist, later in the day; (c) a choice that is to be made between shopping and fishing; and lastly (d) sleep. A organized plan could be

plan of a day's activities
1   wake-up activities
    1.1   get up out of bed
    1.2   wash
    1.3   eat
2   IF visit the hair stylist, THEN
    2.1   have hair shampooed
    2.2   have hair cut
        2.2.1   choose style
        2.2.2   watch work performed
    2.3   pay stylist
3   select the day's major activity
    3.1   IF shopping, THEN BEGIN
        3.1.1   find the store
        3.1.2   identify desired items
        3.1.3   IF money available, THEN buy desired items
    3.2   ELSE BEGIN fishing
        3.2.1   find the lake
        3.2.2   WHILE trying to catch fish
            3.2.2.1   IF hook needs bait, THEN put bait on hook
            3.2.2.2   throw baited hook in water
            3.2.2.3   IF fish grabs hook and bait, THEN
                3.2.2.3.1   jerk line
                3.2.2.3.2   IF fish caught, THEN unhook and keep
    3.2.3   return home
    3.2.4   IF fish were caught, clean them
4   sleep

Some of these activities (groups 1 and 4) are always done and are grouped together as they represent activities done together. Another activity (group 2) is selected to be either done or not done. Another set of activities (group 3) includes a selection between doing one thing (shopping: 3.1) or another (fishing: 3.2).

The organization of a problem's solution is called the *structure* of the solution. The tools that are used to organize the problem's solution can be called the *control structures*.

Pascal has several very powerful tools or statements to provide control structures for programs. These capabilities help the programmer to write highly structured, effective problem solutions.

7.1 BEGIN-END

Objectives
Discuss why statements may have to be compounded together in a
Pascal program and specify how it can be done.

Suggested Background
The previous material in this chapter.

Statements in a Pascal program can be grouped together between the reserved
delimiters BEGIN and END. The grouped statements form what is known as a
compound statement. The general form of a compound statement is

```
BEGIN
    <statement>;
    <statement>;
    .
    .
    .
    <statement>
END;
```

For example,

```
BEGIN
    READ(FARMNUMBER,APPLES,PEARS);
    PRODUCE := APPLES + PEARS;
    WRITELN(FARMNUMBER,APPLES,PEARS,PRODUCE)
END;
WRITELN('PRODUCE TOTAL CALCULATED');
```

tells the computer to consider the statements between the BEGIN and END delimiters
to be a single compound statement and to execute them as a sequential group. This
ensures that the entire group is handled as a single activity.

The need for a compound statement may not be clear at this point. However,
later in this chapter it will be seen that certain control statements can only be used to
cause the execution of single statements. The compound statement provides this
capability so that choices can be made among doing different groups of statements,
each of which is treated as a single statement.

Notice that the semicolon (";") is used only to separate successive Pascal
statements. A semicolon is not part of a Pascal statement. Likewise notice that
BEGIN and END are not Pascal statements and only serve as delimiters to indicate
which statements should be compounded together. Consequently, a semicolon does
not follow the BEGIN. In the previous example, the semicolon following the END

serves to separate the compound statement delimited by the BEGIN and END from the next statement, which is

```
WRITELN('PRODUCE TOTAL CALCULATED')
```

7.2 DECISION EXPRESSIONS

Objective
Describe how Pascal's decision structures are controlled.

Suggested Background
The previous material in this chapter.

Most of the control structures in Pascal utilize a boolean expression as a means of deciding what to do. A boolean expression often reflects a logical test that is performed someplace in the program. Within a given statement, the boolean value that results from the evaluation of a boolean expression can be supplied

(a) as the value resulting from the evaluation of an explicitly stated logical test, or
(b) as the value of a boolean variable, or
(c) by the returned value of a FUNCTION, or
(d) explicitly as a boolean value of either "TRUE" or "FALSE."

In Section 5.3 the logical operators and their uses in logical or relational tests were discussed. It was pointed out that the result of a logical test is a value of either "TRUE" or "FALSE". The resulting value can be used directly or indirectly in a control statement. For example, in the program fragment

```
VAR
    TESTRESULT: BOOLEAN;
    APPLECOUNT: INTEGER;
    .
    .
    .
BEGIN
    .
    .
    .
    TESTRESULT := APPLECOUNT > 5;
```

the value of TESTRESULT after the evaluation of

```
APPLECOUNT > 5
```

will be "TRUE" if the value of APPLECOUNT is greater than "5" and "FALSE" otherwise. A control statement could use either the complex boolean expression

```
APPLECOUNT > 5
```

or the simple boolean expression of a single boolean variable

```
TESTRESULT
```

as the decision control specification.

7.3 REPETITIVE CONTROL

Objectives
Discuss why some problems need repetitive control of statements and describe how Pascal can be used to do this.

Suggested Background
The previous material in this chapter. Starting with this section, the remaining material in this chapter may be delayed until after Chapter 8.

Sometimes, the solution to a problem requires that a task be repeated one or more times. For example, a person digging a hole will repeat the task of removing dirt from the hole until the hole is big enough.

Pascal provides the problem solver with several different ways of controlling repetitive execution of a statement or a group of statements. These control structures are one of the important ways that Pascal helps a problem solver in the problem solution task.

The technical term for repetition is *iteration*. Pascal provides tools to control both general and specific iteration. General iteration includes repetitively doing something while a specified condition exists or until a specified condition happens. A more specific form of iteration, involving counting between a starting and a finishing value, is also provided.

7.3.1 WHILE

The WHILE control instruction provides a natural, top-down way of directing the flow of iterative program execution. For example, a person might say "WHILE fishing, this should be done, that should be done, and this should be done."
The form of the WHILE control structure is

```
WHILE <boolean expression> DO
    <statement>;
```

Most commonly, the statement controlled by a WHILE is a compound statement, so the most common form of the WHILE control structure is

```
WHILE <boolean expression> DO BEGIN
    <statement>;
    <statement>;
    .
    .
    .
    <statement>
END
```

As long as the boolean value resulting from the evaluation of the controlling boolean expression is "TRUE" at the time the WHILE is examined, the statements compounded together will be executed sequentially. The controlling boolean expression is evaluated immediately before executing the first statement following the DO. After the last statement in the group is executed, the boolean expression associated with the WHILE will be evaluated again. If the expression has the value "TRUE", the compounded statement following the DO will be executed again. If the expression has the value "FALSE", the statements compounded together that follow the DO will be skipped.

It is a common mistake of people learning Pascal to think that as soon as any variable that appears in the controlling boolean expression is changed anywhere within the controlled statement that the controlling expression is retested to see if controlled iteration should continue. This is not so. The controlling expression for a

WHILE expression is evaluated only before executing the first statement after the DO. This is done once for every possible repetition of the controlled statement.

The following COUNTDOWN example illustrates how the WHILE can be used.

Example: COUNTDOWN

Count down to zero from an integer number that is supplied by an input statement.

count down to zero from a starting value
1   define variables
2   establish starting value
   2.1   read starting number
   2.2   set count to starting number
3   while the count is greater than or equal to zero
   3.1   print the count
   3.2   decrease the count by 1
4   print the message that the count down is finished
5   end of problem

```
PROGRAM COUNTDOWN(INPUT,OUTPUT);
   (* THIS PROGRAM COUNTS DOWN TO ZERO FROM AN EXTERNALLY
      SUPPLIED STARTING VALUE                              *)
VAR
   START: INTEGER;
   COUNT: INTEGER;
BEGIN (* PROGRAM TO COUNT DOWN FROM A SUPPLIED NUMBER TO ZERO *)
   READ(START);  (* READ STARTING NUMBER *)
   WRITELN('.....COUNT DOWN WILL START WITH THE NUMBER',START:4);
   COUNT := START;
   WHILE COUNT >= 0 DO BEGIN  (* COUNT DOWN TO ZERO *)
      WRITELN('THE COUNT IS',COUNT:4);
      COUNT := COUNT - 1
   END; (* COUNT DOWN *)
   WRITELN('.....COUNT DOWN FINISHED')
END.  (* PROGRAM TO COUNT DOWN *)
```

If the value of "6" is read in as data, the result will be

```
.....COUNT DOWN WILL START WITH THE NUMBER   6
THE COUNT IS   6
THE COUNT IS   5
THE COUNT IS   4
THE COUNT IS   3
THE COUNT IS   2
THE COUNT IS   1
THE COUNT IS   0
.....COUNT DOWN FINISHED
```

The WHILE structure can also be used to control a group of statements where repetition is to be continued while a given threshold has not been reached. This is illustrated by the following example PICKAPPLES.

Example: PICKAPPLES

A certain university has its own apple orchard. If one of the university's food service workers has unused time, the worker will take the apple picking basket and pick apples. Picking stops for the day when at least 144 apples are harvested. Each time some apples are picked, the identification number of the apple picker and the count of apples picked are recorded. While the minimum number of apples has yet to be picked, a Pascal program is needed to record the apple picking data and then total how many apples have been picked so far.

keep track of apples picked
1   define constants and variables
    1.1   establish constant minimum count of apples to be picked
    1.2   define variables
2   initialize
    2.1   set total count of apples picked so far to zero
    2.2   print titles
3   while the total number of apples is less than the minimum required
    3.1   read in the apple picker's identification number, apple count
    3.2   add count of apples picked this time to total of all apples picked
    3.3   print the apple picker's identification number, count of apples picked this time, and the total count of apples picked so far
4   print that the minimum count of apples has been picked
5   end of problem

```
PROGRAM PICKAPPLES(INPUT,OUTPUT);
    (* READS IN THE NUMBER OF APPLES PICKED
        WHILE THE MINIMUM NUMBER OF APPLES
        HAS YET TO BE PICKED                     *)
CONST
    MINIMUMAPPLES = 144;
VAR
    APPLESPICKED: INTEGER;
    APPLEPICKER: INTEGER;
    APPLETOTAL: INTEGER;
BEGIN  (* APPLE PICKING *)
    APPLETOTAL := O;  (* INITIALIZE APPLE COUNT *)
    WRITELN('APPLE     APPLES  *  TOTAL');   (* OUTPUT *)
    WRITELN('PICKER    PICKED  *  PICKED');  (* TITLE *)
    WRITELN('-----------------*--------');  (* LINES *)
    WHILE APPLETOTAL <= MINIMUMAPPLES DO BEGIN  (* READ APPLES PICKED *)
        READ(APPLEPICKER,APPLESPICKED);
        APPLETOTAL := APPLETOTAL + APPLESPICKED;  (* TOTAL PICKED *)
        WRITELN(APPLEPICKER:4,APPLESPICKED:9,'   *   ',APPLETOTAL:4)
    END;  (* READING APPLES PICKED *)
    WRITELN('-----------------*--------');
    WRITELN('HAVE PICKED THE MINIMUM NUMBER OF ',MINIMUMAPPLES:3,
            ' APPLES.');
END. (* APPLEPICKER *)
```

If the input data are

```
                    1 23
                    2 24
                    1 12
                    4 14
                    3 26
                    2 18
                    1 18
                    4 13
                    3 11
```

then the resulting output will be

```
        APPLE     APPLES  *  TOTAL
        PICKER    PICKED  *  PICKED
        -----------------*--------
          1          23   *    23
          2          24   *    47
          1          12   *    59
          4          14   *    73
          3          26   *    99
          2          18   *   117
          1          18   *   135
          4          13   *   148
        -----------------*--------
        HAVE PICKED THE MINIMUM OF 144 APPLES.
```

Sometimes a group of actions is to be repeated while a certain condition is true. For example, a child might continue to eat candy while there is any remaining. There are similar cases in computing. A common need is to keep reading data while there are more to be read. This is illustrated by the following program SUM.

Example: SUM

A customer may choose to purchase any amount of goods. The goods purchased are to be counted, the price listed, and the total price computed. A Pascal program is to print the item count and price while there may be more items to be considered. When all the items have been considered, the total price is to be reported.

count, print, sum purchases
1   define variables
2   initialize
    2.1   set count of items to zero
    2.2   set total of prices so far to zero
    2.3   print titles
3   print prices
    3.1   try to read a price for a first item
    3.2   while there may be another item price to be read
        3.2.1   add to the count of prices read so far
        3.2.2   print the count and item price
        3.2.3   add the price to the total of all prices read so far
        3.2.4   try to read another item price
4   print the final titles
5   end of problem

```
PROGRAM SUM(INPUT,OUTPUT);
    (* READS AND SUMS A LIST OF PRICES OF ITEMS WHERE
        THE COUNT OF ITEMS IS UNKNOWN                    *)
VAR
    COUNT: INTEGER;   (* COUNT OF THE PRICES READ *)
    PRICE: REAL;
    TOTALPRICE: REAL;  (* TOTAL OF ALL PRICES READ *)
BEGIN  (* READING AND SUMMING PRICES *)
    COUNT := 0;
    TOTALPRICE := 0;
    WRITELN(' ITEM *');  (* OUTPUT *)
    WRITELN('COUNT * PRICE');  (* TITLE *)
    WRITELN('------*------');  (* LINES *)
    READ(PRICE);  (* TRY TO READ FIRST PRICE *)
    WHILE NOT EOF DO BEGIN  (* AS LONG AS LAST READ WAS SUCCESSFUL *)
        COUNT := COUNT + 1;  (* COUNT NUMBER OF PRICES READ SO FAR *)
        WRITELN(COUNT:4,'  * ',PRICE:5:2);  (* PRINT LAST PRICE READ *)
        TOTALPRICE := TOTALPRICE + PRICE;
        READ(PRICE)  (* ALL READING AFTER FIRST READ *)
    END;  (* READING *)
    WRITELN('------*------');
    WRITELN('TOTAL PRICE IS',TOTALPRICE:7:2)
END.  (* READING AND SUMMING PRICES *)
```

If the input data are

$$23.59$$
$$0.16$$
$$84.23$$
$$54.0$$
$$32.45$$

then the resulting output will be

```
 ITEM *
COUNT * PRICE
------*------
    1  * 23.59
    2  *  0.16
    3  * 84.23
    4  * 54.00
    5  * 32.45
------*------
TOTAL PRICE IS 194.43
```

Notice that two READ statements have been used. This handles the case where there isn't an initial input data value. The absence of any input data can also be handled by using nested control structures. Nested control structures are discussed in Chapter 9.

An alternate way of handling the input cycle could be

```
      .
      .
      .
WHILE NOT EOF DO BEGIN
   READLN(PRICE);  (* READ A PRICE *)
      .
      .
      .
END;  (* READING *)
      .
      .
      .
```

This form would only require a single read because EOF has a TRUE value if the file is initially empty. However, the problem with this approach is that it assumes that data will be coming in on separate records and that the only desired data items on each record will be the first one. The first approach shown will work as long as every item of available input data is desired. Only a single READ statement is used in the nested control structured reading discussed in Chapter 9.

7.3.2 REPEAT-UNTIL

Objectives
Discuss and specify the REPEAT-UNTIL control structure. The effect of this control structure is similar to that of WHILE.

Suggested Background
The introductory material at the beginning of this chapter, and Sections 7.1 and 7.2. Section 7.3.1 is not required. This means that this section may be done before Section 7.3.1.

The REPEAT-UNTIL iterative control structure is similar to the WHILE structure. Either can be used to control the repeated execution of a group of statements. They differ in that the statements controlled by a WHILE are repeated as long as something is true (i.e., while it is true), as opposed to the REPEAT-UNTIL where the controlled statements are repeated UNTIL something is true.

The form of the REPEAT-UNTIL control structure is

```
REPEAT
   <statement>;
   <statement>;
      .
      .
      .
   <statement>
UNTIL <boolean expression>
```

The statements controlled by the REPEAT-UNTIL are executed until the evaluation of the boolean expression produces a "TRUE" value. The boolean expression associated with the UNTIL is evaluated each time after the controlled statements have been executed and the UNTIL has been reached. Consequently, every REPEAT-UNTIL group will be executed at least once. This differs from the WHILE structure, which evaluates its controlling boolean expression each time before the controlled statements are executed. Thus, the controlled statement in a REPEAT-UNTIL will be executed at least once in contrast with the WHILE controlled statement, which may not be executed at all.

Notice that the REPEAT-UNTIL control structure does not need a BEGIN-END to bracket more than one statement. The REPEAT-UNTIL structure itself compounds statements. REPEAT and UNTIL are delimiters and are not statements. The REPEAT-UNTIL control structure includes the controlling boolean expression after the UNTIL. Consequently, a semicolon does not follow either the REPEAT or the UNTIL delimiters. When separating a REPEAT-UNTIL structure from another statement, the semicolon is placed after the controlling boolean expression.

It is a common mistake of people learning Pascal to think that as soon as any variable that appears in the controlling boolean expression is changed anywhere within the controlled statement, the controlling expression is retested to see if controlled iteration should continue. This is not so. The controlling expression for a REPEAT-UNTIL expression is evaluated only as part of the UNTIL. This is done once for every possible repetition of the controlled statement.

The following COUNTDOWN program illustrates the use of REPEAT-UNTIL regularly to decrease a value by a constant.

Example: COUNTDOWN
Count down to zero from an integer number that is supplied by an input statement. This assumes that the input value is greater than zero.

count down to zero from a starting value
1   define variables
2   establish starting value
   2.1   read starting number
   2.2   set count to starting number
3   repeat until the count is less than zero
   3.1   print the count
   3.2   decrease the count by 1
4   print the message that the count down is finished
5   end of problem

```
PROGRAM COUNTDOWN(INPUT,OUTPUT);
   (* THIS PROGRAM COUNTS DOWN TO ZERO FROM AN EXTERNALLY
      SUPPLIED STARTING VALUE                              *)
VAR
   START: INTEGER;
   COUNT: INTEGER;
BEGIN (* COUNTING DOWN FROM A SUPPLIED NUMBER TO ZERO *)
   READ(START);  (* READ STARTING NUMBER *)
   WRITELN('.....COUNT DOWN WILL START WITH THE NUMBER',START:4);
   COUNT := START;
   REPEAT  (* COUNT DOWN UNTIL PAST ZERO  *)
      WRITELN('THE COUNT IS',COUNT:4);
      COUNT := COUNT - 1
   UNTIL COUNT < O; (* COUNT DOWN FINISHED *)
   WRITELN('.....COUNT DOWN FINISHED')
END.  (* PROGRAM TO COUNT DOWN *)
```

If the value of 6 is the input to the program, the result will be

```
.....COUNT DOWN WILL START WITH THE NUMBER   6
THE COUNT IS   6
THE COUNT IS   5
THE COUNT IS   4
THE COUNT IS   3
THE COUNT IS   2
THE COUNT IS   1
THE COUNT IS   O
.....COUNT DOWN FINISHED
```

The REPEAT-UNTIL structure can also be used to control a group of statements when it is desired to terminate their repetition after a given threshold is reached. This is illustrated by the following program PICKAPPLES.

Example: PICKAPPLES

A certain university has its own apple orchard. If one of the university's food service workers has unused time, the worker will take the apple picking basket and pick apples. Picking stops for the day when at least 144 apples are harvested. Each time some apples are picked, the identification number of the apple picker and the count of apples picked are recorded. Until the minimum number of apples is picked, a Pascal program is needed to record the apple picking data and compute the total count of all apples picked so far.

keep track of apples picked
1   define constants and variables
    1.1   establish constant minimum count of apples to be picked
    1.2   define variables
2   initialize
    2.1   set total count of apples picked so far to zero
    2.2   print titles

3   repeat until the total number of apples is greater than the minimum required

     3.1   read in the apple picker's identification number, apple count

     3.2   add count of apples picked this time to total of all apples picked

     3.3   print the apple picker's identification number, count of apples picked this time, and the total count of apples picked so far

4   print that the minimum count of apples has been picked

5   end of problem

```
PROGRAM PICKAPPLES(INPUT,OUTPUT);
   (* READS IN THE NUMBER OF APPLES PICKED
       UNTIL THE MINIMUM NUMBER OF APPLES IS PICKED *)
CONST
   MINIMUMAPPLES = 144;
VAR
   APPLESPICKED: INTEGER;
   APPLEPICKER: INTEGER;
   APPLETOTAL: INTEGER;
BEGIN  (* APPLE PICKING *)
   APPLETOTAL := O;  (* INITIALIZE APPLE COUNT *)
   WRITELN('APPLE    APPLES *  TOTAL');   (* OUTPUT *)
   WRITELN('PICKER   PICKED *  PICKED');  (* TITLE *)
   WRITELN('-----------------*--------');  (* LINES *)
   REPEAT  (* READING APPLES PICKED *)
       READ(APPLEPICKER,APPLESPICKED);
       APPLETOTAL := APPLETOTAL + APPLESPICKED;  (* TOTAL PICKED *)
       WRITELN(APPLEPICKER:4,APPLESPICKED:9,'   *  ',APPLETOTAL:4)
   UNTIL APPLETOTAL >= MINIMUMAPPLES;  (* READING APPLES PICKED *)
   WRITELN('-----------------*--------');
   WRITELN('HAVE PICKED THE MINIMUM NUMBER OF ',MINIMUMAPPLES:3,
       ' APPLES.');
END. (* APPLEPICKER *)
```

If the input data are

```
                             1 23
                             2 24
                             1 12
                             4 14
                             3 26
                             2 18
                             1 18
                             4 13
                             3 11
```

then the resulting output will be

```
APPLE     APPLES   *   TOTAL
PICKER    PICKED   *   PICKED
------------------*--------
    1        23    *      23
    2        24    *      47
    1        12    *      59
    4        14    *      73
    3        26    *      99
    2        18    *     117
    1        18    *     135
    4        13    *     148
------------------*--------
HAVE PICKED THE MINIMUM OF 144 APPLES.
```

Sometimes a group of actions is to be repeated until a given condition occurs. For example, a person might keep pulling dandelions from a lawn until there are no more in the lawn. There are similar cases in computing. A common need is to keep reading and processing until all the data has been read. This is illustrated by the following example.

Example: SUM

A customer may choose to purchase any amount of goods. The goods purchased are to be counted, the prices listed, and the total price computed. A Pascal program is to print the item count and price until there are no more items to be considered. When all the items have been considered, the total price is to be reported.

count, print, sum purchases
1   define variables
2   initialize
    2.1   set count of items to zero
    2.2   set total of prices so far to zero
    2.3   print titles
3   print prices
    3.1   try to read a price for a first item
    3.2   repeat until there are no other item prices to be read
        3.2.1   add to the count of prices read so far
        3.2.2   print the count and item price
        3.2.3   add the price to the total of all prices read so far
        3.2.4   try to read another item price
4   print the final titles
5   end of problem

The following program SUM follows this plan.

```
PROGRAM SUM(INPUT,OUTPUT);
    (* READS AND SUMS A LIST OF PRICES FOR ITEMS WHERE
        THE COUNT OF ITEMS IS UNKNOWN                    *)
VAR
    COUNT: INTEGER;
    PRICE: REAL;
    TOTALPRICE: REAL;
BEGIN  (* READING AND SUMMING PRICES *)
    COUNT := 0;
    TOTALPRICE := 0;
    WRITELN(' ITEM *');  (* OUTPUT *)
    WRITELN('COUNT * PRICE');   (* TITLE *)
    WRITELN('------*------');   (* LINES *)
    READ(PRICE);  (* TRY TO READ FIRST PRICE *)
    REPEAT  (* AS LONG AS LAST READ WAS SUCCESSFUL *)
        COUNT := COUNT + 1;  (* COUNT NUMBER OF PRICES READ SO FAR *)
        WRITELN(COUNT:4,' * ',PRICE:5:2);  (* PRINT LAST PRICE READ *)
        TOTALPRICE := TOTALPRICE + PRICE;
        READ(PRICE)  (* ALL READING AFTER FIRST READ *)
    UNTIL EOF;
    WRITELN('------*------');
    WRITELN('TOTAL PRICE IS',TOTALPRICE:7:2)
END.  (* READING AND SUMMING PRICES *)
```

If the input data are

```
23.59
 0.16
84.23
54.0
32.45
```

then the resulting output will be

```
 ITEM *
COUNT * PRICE
------*------
    1 * 23.59
    2 *  0.16
    3 * 84.23
    4 * 54.00
    5 * 32.45
------*------
TOTAL PRICE IS 194.43
```

Notice that two READ statements have been used. The two READ statements were necessary to handle the case where there isn't an initial input data value. The absence of an initial data value can also be handled by using nested control structures. Nested control structures are discussed in Chapter 9.

7.3.3 FOR

Objectives
Develop an awareness of why it might be necessary to repeat a task a specified number of times and describe how Pascal accomplishes this through the use of the FOR statement. The FOR statement can often be replaced by the use of a WHILE or REPEAT-UNTIL control structure combined with a counter. Some people prefer to minimize the use of the FOR statement.

Suggested Background
The introductory material at the beginning of this chapter and Sections 7.1 and 7.2. Neither Section 7.3.1 nor 7.3.2 is required. Either or both of them may be done before or after this section.

The solution of some problems requires that tasks be repeated an exactly specified number of times. Sometimes a value is to be regularly increased or decreased by a specified amount. An example of a job that requires repetitive action is opening ten eggs and frying them.

fry ten eggs
e.1   open egg carton
e.2   FOR ten eggs, DO the following
     e.2.1   select an egg
     e.2.2   crack the egg on the edge of the frying pan
     e.2.3   open the egg over the frying pan
     e.2.4   drop the egg into the frying pan
e.3   cook the eggs

Sometimes the solution of a problem also requires the sequential numbering of a group of objects. For example,

acquire seashells for study
e.1   visit the seashore
e.2   FOR seashells numbered 1 to 15
     e.2.1   pick up a seashell
     e.2.2   number the shell
     e.2.3   mark on a map where it was found
     e.2.4   store the numbered shell in the collection box
e.3   store the collection box in the truck

It also may be necessary to generate the numbers in a given sequence because we need to use the numbers themselves. For example, a count down for a rocket launch might need 10,9,8, . . .,0.

This is a restricted form of iteration using counting. In Pascal the FOR iterative control structure provides these capabilities. Counting can also be done with the WHILE or the REPEAT-UNTIL control structures. People sometimes choose to use the FOR structure instead because it offers a means for explicitly setting the range of iteration.

The form of the FOR structure is either

```
FOR <control variable> := <initial value> TO <final value> DO
    <statement>
```

which is used when the final value is to be greater than or equal to the initial value, or

```
FOR <control variable> := <initial value> DOWNTO <final value> DO
    <statement>
```

if the final value is to be less than or equal to the initial value.

In both cases, the initial and final values can be explicitly specified or the values may be represented by an expression. In the last case, the expression will only be evaluated the first time the FOR statement is executed.

The final value is reached by changing the initial value by 1 each time there is a repetition. Both the initial and final values are integers. If the initial and final values are the same, the controlled statement will be executed once. If the initial value is greater than the final value (in the case of FOR-TO), or if the initial value is less than the final value (in the case of FOR-DOWNTO), the controlled statement will not be executed. The repeated statement should not assign a value to the control variable or to the initial or final value.

The following program NUMBERS illustrates the explicit definition of the initial and final values as well as the control of a single statement.

```
PROGRAM NUMBERS(OUTPUT);
    (* THIS PROGRAM PRINTS THE NUMBERS BETWEEN 8 AND 12 *)
VAR
    NUMBER: INTEGER;
BEGIN  (* PRINTING THE NUMBERS BETWEEN 8 AND 12 *)
    FOR NUMBER := 8 TO 12 DO
        WRITELN('THE NUMBER IS NOW ',NUMBER:2);
    WRITELN('... ALL NUMBERS PRESENTED')
END. (* PRINTING THE NUMBERS BETWEEN 8 AND 12 *)
```

The result is

```
THE NUMBER IS NOW  8
THE NUMBER IS NOW  9
THE NUMBER IS NOW 10
THE NUMBER IS NOW 11
THE NUMBER IS NOW 12
... ALL NUMBERS PRESENTED
```

Notice that the complete FOR statement in the preceding program is

```
FOR NUMBER := 8 TO 12 DO
   WRITELN('THE NUMBER IS NOW',NUMBER:2)
```

and that a semicolon is only used to separate this statement from the output statement

```
WRITELN('... ALL NUMBERS PRESENTED)
```

The output statement is only executed after all the iterations have been completed.

The iterative limits of a FOR statement can come from data that is read in from outside of the program. External iterative limits and the use of DOWNTO to supply a control variable with a decreasing value are illustrated in the following program DOWNCOUNT.

Example: DOWNCOUNT
Count down to zero from an integer number that is supplied by an input statement.

count down to zero from a starting value
1   define variables
2   establish starting value
     2.1   read starting number
     2.2   set count to starting number
3   for count values from start down to zero
     3.1   print the count
4   print the message that the count down is finished
5   end of problem

```
PROGRAM DOWNCOUNT(INPUT,OUTPUT);
   (* THIS PROGRAM COUNTS DOWN FROM AN EXTERNALLY SUPPLIED
      NUMBER TO ZERO *)
VAR
   START: INTEGER;
   COUNT: INTEGER;
BEGIN  (* COUNT DOWN *)
   READ(START);  (* READ STARTING NUMBER *)
   WRITELN('.....COUNT DOWN WILL START WITH THE NUMBER',START:4);
   FOR COUNT := START DOWNTO 0 DO  (* COUNTING DOWN *)
      WRITELN('THE COUNT IS',COUNT:4);
   WRITELN('.....COUNT DOWN FINISHED')
END.  (* DOWNCOUNT *)
```

If the value read for start is "6", the results will be

```
.....COUNT DOWN WILL START WITH THE NUMBER    6
THE COUNT IS    6
THE COUNT IS    5
THE COUNT IS    4
THE COUNT IS    3
THE COUNT IS    2
THE COUNT IS    1
THE COUNT IS    0
.....COUNT DOWN FINISHED
```

When more than one statement is to be controlled by a FOR structure, the statements must be compounded together using the delimiters BEGIN-END. The form is

```
FOR <control variable> := <initial value> TO <final value> DO BEGIN
    <statement>;
    <statement>;
      .
      .
      .
    <statement>
END
```

The following program calculates the total of all the integers between two values (inclusive). It illustrates a FOR controlled compound statement.

Example: ADDUP
Read in two integer values. Print all the integer values from the first value read to the last value read. Include in this list both the first and last values. Calculate and print the sum of the values printed.

print and sum integers between a starting and a finishing value
1   define variables
2   initialize
    2.1   set sum of all values printed to zero
    2.2   acquire the first and last values
        2.2.1   read the first and last values
        2.2.2   print the first and last values
3   for numbers from the first integer value to the last
    3.1   print the number
    3.2   add the number to the total of all values printed so far
4   print the sum
5   end of problem

```
PROGRAM ADDUP(INPUT,OUTPUT);
    (* THIS PROGRAM SUMS ALL THE INTEGERS BETWEEN TWO EXTERNALLY
        SUPPLIED LIMITS *)
VAR
    FIRST: INTEGER;
    LAST: INTEGER;
    SUM: INTEGER;
    NUMBER: INTEGER;
BEGIN  (* SUM OF A SERIES *)
    SUM := O;  (* INITIALIZE SUM OF NUMBERS IN THE SERIES *)
    READ(FIRST,LAST);  (* READ FIRST AND LAST NUMBERS *)
    WRITELN('THE FIRST NUMBER IS TO BE:',FIRST);
    WRITELN('THE LAST NUMBER IS TO BE:',LAST);
    FOR NUMBER := FIRST TO LAST DO BEGIN  (* GENERATING THE NUMBERS *)
        WRITELN(NUMBER,'...');
        SUM := SUM + NUMBER  (* ADD TO SUM OF NUMBERS IN THE SERIES *)
    END;  (* GENERATING AND ADDING TOGETHER AN INTEGER SERIES *)
    WRITELN('THE SUM OF THE SERIES IS:',SUM)
END.  (* ADDUP *)
```

If the data values read are "3" and "7", the results will be

```
THE FIRST NUMBER IS TO BE:          3
THE LAST NUMBER IS TO BE:           7
            3...
            4...
            5...
            6...
            7...
THE SUM OF THE SERIES IS:          25
```

The statements

```
WRITELN('THE FIRST NUMBER IS TO BE:',FIRST);
WRITELN('THE LAST NUMBER IS TO BE:',LAST);
```

which follow the READ statement provide what is known as *echo printing*. It is a good idea to echo print incoming data as this helps someone to verify the results of the program.

7.4 QUESTIONS

7.1   What does a BEGIN-END control structure accomplish? Why is it used?

7.2   Why is it not necessary to place a semicolon between an END and a preceding statement?

7.3   What TYPE of value (INTEGER, REAL, CHAR, BOOLEAN) results from the evaluation of an expression used to make a decision in Pascal?

7.4   What is the minimum number of times that the statement controlled by a WHILE control structure must be executed?

7.5   What is the miniumum number of times that the statement controlled by a REPEAT-UNTIL structure must be executed?

7.6   What is the minimum number of times that the statement controlled by a FOR structure must be executed?

7.7   Given the following program, what will be the results?

```
PROGRAM QUESTION(OUTPUT);
CONST
   TARGET = 15;
VAR
   VALUE: INTEGER;
   COUNT: INTEGER;
BEGIN
   COUNT := 0;
   VALUE := 19;
   REPEAT
      COUNT := COUNT + 1;
      VALUE := VALUE + COUNT;
      WRITELN(' LOOP NUMBER ',COUNT:3,' VALUE IS ',VALUE:3)
   UNTIL VALUE > TARGET;
   WRITELN(' IT TOOK ',COUNT:3,' LOOPS TO REACH THE TARGET')
END. (* QUESTION *)
```

7.8   Given the following program,

```
PROGRAM QUESTION(INPUT,OUTPUT);
VAR
   A: INTEGER;
   B: INTEGER;
   C: INTEGER;
   D: INTEGER;
BEGIN
   A := 0;
   B := 1;
   C := 0;
   D := 3;
   WHILE A < 21 DO BEGIN
      READ(D);
      A := A + D;
      WRITE(A:3,D:3);
      C := C + B
   END;
   WRITE(C:3)
END.  (* QUESTION  *)
```

and if the incoming data is as shown below, what will be displayed as the results?

```
1 2 3
4 5
6
7 8
9 0 9
8 7 6 5
4 3 2 1 0
```

7.9   Given the following program, what will be displayed as the results?

```
PROGRAM QUESTION(OUTPUT);
CONST
    R = -1;
VAR
    NL: INTEGER;
    L: INTEGER;
    F: INTEGER;
    M: INTEGER;
BEGIN
    M := 0;
    NL := 1;
    L := 0;
    REPEAT
        M := M + R;
        F := L + NL;
        NL := L;
        L := F;
        WRITE(F:3)
    UNTIL F > 15;
    WRITE(M:3)
END. (* QUESTION *)
```

7.10   Given the following program, what will be displayed as the results?

```
PROGRAM QUESTION(OUTPUT);
VAR
    A: INTEGER;
    B: INTEGER;
    C: INTEGER;
BEGIN
    A := 3;
    B := 25;
    C := 4;
    REPEAT
        A := B DIV C;
        B := C MOD A
    UNTIL A * B * C = 0;
    WRITE(A:6,B:6,C:6)
END. (* QUESTION *)
```

7.5 PROBLEMS

> ## Required Background
> These problems require arithmetic, input/output, and the use of itera-
> tive control structures. Specifically not required are selection control
> statements. Problems requiring both iterative and selection control
> statements follow Chapter 9. This allows an interchanging of the order
> in which Chapters 7 and 8 are presented.

7.1. Billy Batson has invented a popcorn machine that he hopes will make him a millionaire.
He has formed a company to produce his new machine. The company has a total production
capacity of 10,000 units a day. On the first day, orders for 24 units are received. On each
succeeding day, the number of units ordered triples. Write a program that will calculate and
report how many units will be produced each day until the production capacity is reached. Your
output should have the form

```
DAY        UNITS PRODUCED
 1             24
 2             72
 3            216
 .              .
 .              .
 .              .
```

7.2. In a certain forest, there are 150 trees marked for cutting. A logging firm cuts five trees a
week. Generate a report displaying how many trees are left after each week's cutting. The
report should be in the following form.

```
WEEK NUMBER   HOW MANY TREES CUT DOWN   AMOUNT OF TREES LEFT
-----------   -----------------------   --------------------
     1                   5                       145
     2                  10                       140
     .                   .                        .
     .                   .                        .
```

The only control structure that you can use is a WHILE statement. You are allowed to
do arithmetic.

7.3. You have been given a piece of plywood 1.5 meters wide, 2 meters long, and 0.05 meter
thick. You are to repeat the following steps until a stack of plywood at least 10.3 meters thick is
obtained.
   (a) Cut the width of plywood in half.
   (b) Stack one of the halves on top of the other.
   Your output should be as follows until the minimum width of 10.3 meters is met.

```
CUT          WIDTH          LENGTH          THICKNESS
 0           1.500          2.000            0.05
 1           0.750          2.000            0.10
 2           0.375          2.000            0.20
 .             .              .                .
 .             .              .                .
 .             .              .                .
```

7.4. Suzie Smith, a university student, commutes to school every day. She has observed how many miles she drives every week and this number is 53 miles. She wants help to discover how many months it will take her to drive 1303 more miles. (Her warranty will expire after she drives another 1303 miles.) You are to help Suzie by writing a program using the REPEAT-UNTIL statement. The results should be displayed in the following form.

```
MONTH     MILES DRIVEN
-----     ------------
  1            53
  2           106
  .             .
  .             .
```

7.5. The Purple Passion Wine Company wants to determine how long it will take a leaking barrel to fill a bucket underneath it. The bucket holds 2354 drops of wine. The barrel leaks wine at the rate of 162 drops an hour. At the end of every three hours, the cat drinks 28 drops worth of wine from the bucket. Write a program to calculate how long it will take the bucket to fill. Use a REPEAT-UNTIL control structure to repeat the calculations until the bucket is at last filled. Present the results in an hour-by-hour form as shown below.

```
HOUR     DROPS IN BUCKET
----     ---------------
  0             0
  1            162
  2            324
  3            458
  .             .
  .             .
```

7.6. George works at the campus Burger Queen. He makes hamburgers during the busiest time. Along with his fellow crew members, it takes George 2 minutes to send 12 hamburgers up front to the dispensing people. A busy lunch hour is a common occurrence and the manager wants to know the amount of time it will take George to get at least 600 hamburgers up to the front. Write a program to display the following.

```
HOUR     MINUTE     AMOUNT OF HAMBURGERS
----     ------     --------------------
  0        2                12
  0        4                24
  .        .                 .
  .        .                 .
```

7.7.   You have managed to save $2500 (in the bank) and have always wanted to take off and try writing a book. Zip Publishing Company likes the idea you have for the book and is willing to pay you $300 a month while you're on leave from your present job. After you review all of your possible expenses, you decide you will need $175 a month for rent along with $250 a month for food and your other expenses. The bank pays interest on your account at the rate of 6% a year, paid on the balance in the account at the end of the month. The bank does not pay any fractional pennies for interest. The month that you run out of money, show any uncovered expenses as a negative bank balance.

Write a program to calculate how long your money will last. Your results should have the form of

MONTH	INCOME	EXPENSES	IN BANK AT END OF MONTH	INTEREST	TOTAL IN BANK
0	0	0	2500.00	0.00	2500.00
1	300	425	2375.00	11.87	2386.87
2	300	425	2261.87	11.30	2273.17
.	.	.	.	.	.
.	.	.	.	.	.

7.8.   Bigelow's department store experiences highly seasonal sales. Last year 40% of the year's sales occurred in December. Total sales last year were $310,000. This year sales for all months but December are expected to be 10% lower but December sales are expected to be 5% higher. This pattern is expected to compound and reoccur for the next six years. Bigelow's pays 60% of the selling price of the goods sold and has a $100,000 per year selling and administrative fixed expense. Write a program that reports income statements for this and the next six years for Bigelow's.

7.9.   A space probe goes faster for the same amount of thrust as it consumes its fuel and thereby loses weight. If the distance covered per hour is increased each hour by 6 miles per second and an additional 1 mile per hour for each pound of fuel consumed and fuel is consumed at the rate of 2 pounds per hour, how long will it take the probe to go 10,000 miles? Assume it starts at a speed of 1 and that the speed increases only at the end of each hour as per the above specifications.

7.10.   Golf can be an expensive game. Each time a person plays, it might cost $6.50 for green fees, an average of $3.00 for lost balls, $5.00 for a cart, and $2.00 for refreshments. Write a program that reports a monthly budget for golfing if a person plays twice in April, four times in May, and six times per month after May through September, twice in October, and then not at all until April again. Show the budget by month and by item. Total the categories for the whole season.

7.11.   Write a Pascal program to do the following.
    (a)   Input a list of five names and test scores.
    (b)   Display each name and score immediately after inputting.
    (c)   Calculate the average score and display

THE AVERAGE SCORE IS xx.xx

where xx.xx is the average you have just calculated.
Test your program on the following data.

Rafael Thomas	42
Margot Franks	81
Billy Blue	64
Jack Armstrong	77
Frank Reynolds	92

7.12.   Joan owns a small chocolate chip cookie company. She wants to find out which is her busiest day of the week for sales. For one week, she has kept a record of the sales of her cookies in dozens per day. One week is based on Sunday through Saturday. Program specifications:
   (a)   Input and display the amount of cookies in dozens sold each day for one week.
   (b)   Calculate the amount of single cookies sold each day.
   (c)   Display a message indicating the day with the greatest volume of cookies sold.
   (d)   Report your results in the following form.

```
DAY   DOZENS SOLD   SINGLE COOKIES SOLD
---   -----------   -------------------
 1       94.0              1128
 .        .                  .
 .        .                  .
```

Test your program with the following data.

SUNDAY	94.0
MONDAY	83.5
TUESDAY	79.0
WEDNESDAY	76.5
THURSDAY	1106.0
FRIDAY	113.5
SATURDAY	104.5

7.13.   Jane decides to keep a log of all her school expenses. Her father has told her that he will help her by paying 75% of the total expenses each month.
   Write a program that will input Jane's individual school expenses (in dollars and cents), display each expense in a journal (output report), and at the end of the month (when there are no more expenses to input), calculate 75% of the total expenses. Then display the dollar amount paid by Jane's father and the amount paid by Jane.
   The journal report should look as follows:

```
    MONTHLY EXPENSES                        JOURNAL
        Expense                             Amount
           1                                XXX.XX
           2                                XXX.XX
           .                                   .
           .                                   .
           .                                   .
           N                                XXX.XX
    MONTHLY TOTAL                         $XXXXX.XX

    AMOUNT TO BE PAID BY DAD:      XXXXX.XX
    AMOUNT TO BE PAID BY JANE:     XXXXX.XX
```

Your Pascal program should use the WHILE control structure with the "EOF" end of file indicator.

Use the following data to test your program.

$$
\begin{aligned}
&2.05 \\
&2.05 \\
&2.05 \\
&0.99 \\
&0.99 \\
&0.56 \\
&2.40 \\
&0.24 \\
&0.34 \\
&0.44 \\
&3.00 \\
&2.04
\end{aligned}
$$

7.14. Sally, a farmer's daughter, spends part of her mornings collecting eggs. Each chicken lays a different number of eggs. When she starts to take eggs from a nest, Sally will take all of the eggs out of that nest. Sally collects eggs until she has 48 or more eggs in her basket.

You are to write a program that will input the number of eggs in a nest, echo print the number, and then total them until 48 eggs have been collected. Your output should have the following form.

```
    EGGS IN LAST NEST    TOTAL EGGS SO FAR
    -----------------    -----------------
            3                    3
            4                    7
            .                    .
            .                    .
```

Test your program with the following data. You may not have to input all the data to reach the required minimum total of 48 eggs.

```
    3  4  9  6  5  1  2  4  6  7  8  1
    4  2  3  5  7  7  5  6  4  2  2  3
```

7.15.   Candy Carter has discovered a tropical isle that she can purchase for $120,000. She has decided to work while accumulating enough money to buy the isle. After she has enough money, she plans to buy the isle, quit work, and collect seashells by the seaside.
You must assume that she

(a)   Has an annual salary of $20,000 and that this salary will not change.

(b)   Has fixed yearly expenses of $3628 and that the total of her yearly expenses will not change.

(c)   Is able to save the difference between her yearly salary and her fixed expenses.

(d)   Can avoid the payment of any and all taxes.

(e)   Does not earn any interest on her money because of the way she avoids paying taxes.

(f)   Is paid her salary once a year.

(e)   Pays her expenses once a year (after receiving her salary).

Your task: Write a Pascal program using the WHILE control structure to calculate how many years Candy must work while saving money for her isle.
The form of the results should be

YEAR	STARTING MONEY	SAVED MONEY
1	0	16372
2	16372	32744
3	32744	49116
.	.	.
.	.	.
.	.	.

7.16.   Write a Pascal program to solve the following problem.

Background: Most animal species have a minimum population threshold number. What this means is that if fewer than that number of species exist, the population stops breeding and the species will die out, even if there are still surviving breeding pairs.

Sometimes the population survival threshold is in the thousands, for example, as was the case with the passenger pigeon. Sometimes the threshold is low. It varies with the species. The population survival threshold for the right whale may be about 165. Currently there are about 1500 right whales left in the South Atlantic (near Argentina). Their numbers continue to decrease due to hunting pressure. (The right whale is so named because it floats when killed. This makes it easier to retrieve and the "right" whale to be killed.)

You may assume that

(a)   At the beginning of each year, if breeding took place, the population will increase by 5 percent due to new births.

(b)   No hunting will take place at the start of the year. Therefore the entire population increase will occur if breeding takes place.

(c)   About 17 percent of the population will be killed after the hunting season starts. Include newborns in this total.

(d)   As a simplification, the gestation period can be ignored. (The gestation period is the length of pregnancy.)

(e)   Breeding stops when the population becomes less than 165.

These assumptions are obviously not enough to accurately describe the entire situation. What you are being asked to do is to solve a simplified problem. The solution of problems similar to this is called *simulation*. In simulation a model consisting of statements describing a phenomenon are stated. Then a computer program can be written to simulate the model. Several models have been developed for simulating wildlife populations.

    Your task: Write a Pascal program using the WHILE control structure to calculate when the population ceases breeding and thus dies out. You do not have to input any values. Define the birth percentage, kill percentage, and survival threshold in a CONST section.

    Your display out should be similar to this.

YEAR	ALIVE AT START	NEW BIRTHS	KILLED	ALIVE AT END
1	1500	74	267	1307
2	1307	65	233	1139
3	1139	56	203	992
.	.	.	.	.
.	.	.	.	.
.	.	.	.	.

    In your calculations, do not count fractional births or deaths. For example, 6.3 should be considered to be 6 and 45.8 should be considered to be 45. Do not start a new year if there are less than 165 whales surviving.

    You may need to use TRUNC to assign a REAL result to an INTEGER variable.

7.17. A manager of a baseball team wants to find out the team average for his eight regular players. He also wants to know the average of each individual player. Using the data he gives you, write a program that inputs in the player number, his number of hits, and the number of times he has been up to bat (*Hint:* The player's average is figured by dividing the number of hits by number of times at bat and then multiplying by 1000. Digits to the right of the decimal point are discarded.) At the end display the team's batting average. Test your program with the following data.

1	23	68
2	18	65
3	9	57
4	18	52
5	10	44
6	12	41
7	21	71
8	15	45

7.18. A farmer sells one grade of wheat at $4.20 a bushel and another grade of wheat at $5.50 a bushel. The farmer continues to sell wheat until he has sold at least $8000.00 worth.

    During a business day, customers arrive at the farm to buy wheat. Each customer who buys from this farmer purchases 148 bushels of wheat at the $4.20 price and 37 bushels of wheat at the $5.50 price. For each customer who buys from the farmer, display the following.

    (a) Identify each customer by number. For example, customer 5 would be the fifth customer to buy from the farmer.

    (b) Report for each transaction:

How many bushels of each kind were sold to this customer.
The total price paid for each kind of wheat.
The total spent by the customer.

(c) Show how much the farmer has sold so far.
When the farmer has sold at least $8000.00 worth for the day, he closes up shop. At this time display:

(e) The total count of customers to whom the farmer sold wheat.
(f) The total count of bushels of each kind of wheat sold.
(g) The total sales in dollars for each kind of wheat.
(h) The farmer's total sales.

7.19. Peter has a large pile of old class notes and tests in file folders that he would like to organize and place in file drawers in his office at home. He can buy 12-inch-deep file drawers for $18.00 each, and he would like to know how many he will need to store all his file folders, allowing for 30% future expansion.

Write a Pascal program using the REPEAT control structure that will input the thickness (in inches) of each of Peter's file folders, count the number of folders, display the thickness of each folder as it is input, and calculate the total amount of space currently needed.

After all the folder thickness has been input, display a final report showing:

The total number of folders Peter has now.
The amount of space needed now.
The amount of space for future expansion.
The number of drawers needed (you may disregard any fraction of a drawer since the expansion space was only an estimate).
The total cost for the drawers.

Use constants where appropriate.
Use the following data to test your program but make sure you can handle any number of input items.

Peter's files
1.37
2.86
1.67
4.87
3.75
2.85
2.74
3.75
2.64
1.76
2.89
2.51
1.93
2.39
2.76

```
0.84
1.65
3.65
2.87
1.38
```

Your program must use the REPEAT/UNTIL Pascal control statement.

7.20.   Harriet bought a new car. When she bought the car, it was full of gasoline. When it is full, it holds 20 gallons. Harriet budgets $18 a week for gas. When she has money left over in her budget, she saves it for future gasoline purchases. When she bought the car, gasoline was $1.27 a gallon. Currently the price for gasoline is going up at the rate of $0.01 a gallon a week. She uses 12 gallons per week. How long will it be before she cannot buy her normal amount of gas? Present your results in the following form.

```
WEEK    PRICE OF GASOLINE    EXCESS BUDGET SAVED
----    -----------------    ------------------
```

Chapter 8

CONTROL STRUCTURES: SELECTION

Objectives
Discuss the need for selecting between statements and describe how Pascal accomplishes selection. Pascal selects by (a) choosing one statement over another and (b) jumping from place to another in the program.

Suggested Background
The core Pascal core chapters (3, 4, 5), and Sections 7, 7.1 and 7.2. Notice that the bulk of Chapter 7 (on repetitive control) is not required. This entire chapter can be done immediately after Section 7.2.

Some problems require that choices be made. For example, children are often given a small amount of money to spend. When a child with a small amount of money has the problem of choosing what candy to buy, there is a selection problem.

Often problems that are to be solved on the computer require that choices be made between alternative paths of action. Pascal provides several ways for the problem solver to choose between different actions.

8.1 IF-THEN-ELSE

Objective
Discuss the use of the basic selection control structure IF-THEN-ELSE.

Suggested Background
The previous material in this chapter.

The IF-THEN-ELSE control structure can be used to accomplish two similar tasks. It can be used to select whether or not a single statement is to be executed. The

IF-THEN-ELSE structure can also be used to select between two statements. Selection is usually made by the evaluation of a directly expressed logical test. However, selection can be controlled by any boolean expression.

8.1.1 IF-THEN

Objectives
Describe and illustrate the use of the IF-THEN control structure.

Suggested Background
The previous material in this chapter.

The simple IF-THEN structure provides the capability of executing or not executing a statement. Its form is

```
IF <boolean expression>
   THEN <statement>
```

The statement following the THEN is executed only if the evaluated result of the boolean expression is "TRUE". For example, in the program fragment

```
READ(BUDGET);  (* READ MEAT BUDGET *)
IF STEAKPRICE > BUDGET  (* TEST IF CAN AFFORD STEAK *)
   THEN WRITE('STEAK TOO EXPENSIVE');
WRITELN('MEAT SHOPPING COMPLETED');
```

the WRITE statement will be executed only if the value of STEAKPRICE is greater than that of BUDGET. The statement

```
WRITELN('MEAT SHOPPING COMPLETED')
```

will always be executed.

8.1.2 IF-THEN-ELSE

Objectives
Discuss and illustrate the use of the IF-THEN-ELSE control structure.

Suggested Background
The previous material in this chapter.

Often selection is made between two different activities. The IF-THEN-ELSE structure provides a way to do this. The form of the IF-THEN-ELSE structure is

```
IF <boolean expression>
   THEN <statement1>
   ELSE <statement2>
```

Statement1 is executed if the evaluation of the boolean expression results in a "TRUE" value and statement2 is executed if the resulting value is "FALSE". This is illustrated in the following program fragment.

```
READ(BUDGET);  (* READ MEAT BUDGET *)
IF STEAKPRICE > BUDGET  (* TEST IF CAN AFFORD STEAK *)
   THEN WRITE('STEAK TOO EXPENSIVE ')
   ELSE WRITE('BUY STEAK ');
WRITELN('MEAT SHOPPING COMPLETED');
```

In this case, either one or the other WRITE statement will be executed. The statement

```
WRITELN('MEAT SHOPPING COMPLETED')
```

will always be executed.

Notice that a semicolon does not separate the THEN clause from the ELSE clause. This is so because both the THEN clause and the ELSE clause are considered to be part of the same IF statement. One way of keeping this straight is never to place a semicolon immediately before an ELSE.

More than one IF-THEN-ELSE clause may be used in a single statement to express a complex situation. For example, in the program fragment

```
READ(BUDGET);  (* READ MEAT BUDGET *)
(* BEGIN MAKING BUYING CHOICE *)
IF STEAKPRICE > BUDGET  (* TEST IF CAN AFFORD STEAK *)
   THEN IF HAMBURGERPRICE > BUDGET  (* NO STEAK, TRY HAMBURGER *)
      THEN WRITELN('BOTH STEAK AND HAMBURGER TOO EXPENSIVE')
      ELSE WRITELN('STEAK TOO EXPENSIVE, BUY HAMBURGER')
   ELSE WRITELN('BUY STEAK');  (* CAN AFFORD STEAK *)
(* CHOICE COMPLETE *)
WRITELN('MEAT SHOPPING COMPLETED');
```

the logical test

```
IF HAMBURGERPRICE > BUDGET
```

is said to be at the second level of "nesting" as it is only considered if selected as part of the THEN clause for the first nesting level selection statement containing the test condition

```
STEAKPRICE > BUDGET
```

More than one nested choice can be expressed. For example,

```
READ(BUDGET);  (* READ MEAT BUDGET *)
IF STEAKPRICE > BUDGET  (* TEST IF CAN AFFORD STEAK *)
   THEN IF HAMBURGERPRICE > BUDGET  (* NO STEAK, TRY HAMBURGER *)
      THEN IF HOTDOGPRICE > BUDGET  (* NO HAMBURGER, TRY HOT DOGS *)
         THEN WRITELN('STEAK, HAMBURGER, AND HOTDOGS TOO EXPENSIVE')
         ELSE WRITELN('STEAK AND HAMBURGER TOO EXPENSIVE, BUY HOTDOGS')
      ELSE WRITELN('STEAK TOO EXPENSIVE, BUY HAMBURGER')
   ELSE IF LOBSTERPRICE > BUDGET  (* CAN AFFORD STEAK, TRY LOBSTER *)
      THEN WRITELN('BUY STEAK')  (* CAN AFFORD STEAK, CANNOT LOBSTER *)
      ELSE WRITELN('BUY LOBSTER');
WRITELN('MEAT SHOPPING COMPLETED');
```

Again, notice that the entire IF structure is considered to be one statement.

Collections of nested IF-THEN-ELSEs such as this will execute correctly once they have been correctly written. However, they are sometimes difficult for a programmer to write correctly. They may be even more difficult for someone else to understand. For this reason, complex IF-THEN-ELSE decisions are often replaced by several simpler IF-THEN decision structures with a separate selection statement used for every different combination of conditions. (Examples using combinations of conditions are explored in Chapter 9.)

Developing the pseudo-code for the solution of a problem greatly helps the development of correct, clear solutions. Pseudo-code also can help in understanding what was done. For example, the pseudo-code for the previous program fragment could be

e.1   READ meat budget
e.2   IF steak price greater than meat budget, try the prices of other meat
    e.2.1   THEN IF hamburger price greater than meat budget,
        e.2.1.1   THEN IF hot dog price greater than meat budget,
            e.2.1.1.1   THEN cannot afford meat
            e.2.1.1.2   ELSE buy hot dogs
        e.2.1.2   ELSE buy hamburger
    e.2.2   ELSE can afford steak, test IF lobster price greater than meat budget
        e.2.2.1   THEN buy steak
        e.2.2.2   ELSE buy lobster

This pseudo-code certainly aids in the understanding of how the choices were made and what they were.

8.1.3 IF Controlled Groups

Objectives
Discuss the need to select among different groups of statements, describe how Pascal can be used to choose among groups of statements, and illustrate how it can be done.

Suggested Background
The introductory material at the beginning of Chapter 7, Sections 7.1 and 7.2, and the previous material in this chapter.

Often more than one thing needs to be done as the result of a single decision. For example, after a person has chosen to go to a certain movie, there are still several actions that need to be taken, such as: finding the theater, buying a ticket, selecting a seat, etc.

When solving a problem on the computer, it is also often necessary to select several statements that are to be executed together. This can be accomplished by selecting a compound statement. Recall that a compound statement is a collection of statements that have been grouped together by a BEGIN-END delimiter pair. For example, in

```
READ(BUDGET);
IF STEAKPRICE > BUDGET
    THEN BEGIN
        WRITELN('STEAK PRICE TOO EXPENSIVE');
        SHORT := STEAKPRICE - BUDGET;
        WRITELN('THE EXTRA AMOUNT NEEDED WOULD BE ',SHORT:5:2)
    END;
WRITELN('SHOPPING COMPLETED');
```

all of the statements between the BEGIN and the END are to be executed if the value of STEAKPRICE is greater than BUDGET.

Just as with single statements selected by a control statement, compound statements may be nested. For example, in

```
READ(BUDGET);  (* READ MEAT BUDGET *)
IF STEAKPRICE > BUDGET  (* TEST IF CAN AFFORD STEAK *)
   THEN BEGIN (* CANNOT AFFORD STEAK *)
      WRITELN('STEAK IS TOO EXPENSIVE');
      SHORT := STEAKPRICE - BUDGET;
      WRITELN('THE EXTRA AMOUNT NEEDED WOULD BE',SHORT:5:2)
   END  (* CANNOT AFFORD STEAK *)
   ELSE IF LOBSTERPRICE > BUDGET  (* CAN AFFORD STEAK, CHECK LOBSTER *)
      THEN WRITELN('BUY LOBSTER')  (* CAN AFFORD LOBSTER *)
      ELSE BEGIN (* CAN AFFORD STEAK, BUT NOT LOBSTER *)
         WRITELN('BUY STEAK');
         EXTRA := BUDGET - STEAKPRICE;
         WRITELN('EXTRA MONEY LEFT IN MEAT BUDGET IS',EXTRA:5:2)
      END;  (* CAN AFFORD STEAK, BUT NOT LOBSTER *)
WRITELN('MEAT SHOPPING COMPLETED');
```

there is one set of tasks to be performed if STEAKPRICE > BUDGET and another set of tasks if steak is affordable, but lobster is not. The following pseudo-code for the program reflects the grouped statement structure.

e.1 READ meat price

e.2 IF steak price greater than meat budget,

      e.2.1 THEN BEGIN reporting on extra money needed

            e.2.1.1 write a message indicating that steak is too expensive

            e.2.1.2 calculate how much more money is needed

            e.2.1.3 write a message indicating extra money needed

      e.2.2 ELSE if steak is affordable, see if can also buy lobster

            e.2.2.1 THEN if can afford lobster, buy lobster

            e.2.2.2 ELSE if can only afford steak, buy steak

                  e.2.2.2.1 write a message indicating that steak is to be bought

                  e.2.2.2.2 calculate extra money in meat budget

                  e.2.2.2.3 write a message to report on extra money in the meat budget

e.3 write a message reporting that the meat shopping has been completed

8.2 DIRECTED EXECUTION OF STATEMENTS

Objectives
Discuss why it might be useful directly to reach a group of statements for execution and specify the two different ways that Pascal provides for direct statement execution.

Suggested Background
The introductory material at the beginning of Chapter 7, Sections 7.1 and 7.2, and the introductory material at the beginning of this chapter. Notice that none of the parts of Section 8.1 are required.

Sometimes, we want to choose among several different activities. If we can identify what we want to do, it may be preferable to do it directly. For example, if a girl is at a party and she already has identified the boy with whom she wishes to dance, she would probably prefer to directly approach the desired boy rather than to have to approach others as well.

Pascal has two different ways of directly executing a part of a program: CASE and GOTO. The case structure provides an easy means for using a data value to choose what is to be done next. The GOTO provides the capability to jump from one part of the program to another. In general, use of the GOTO statement leads to unstructured programs, and its use is discouraged.

8.2.1 CASE

Objectives
Discuss the usefulness of the CASE decision structure and illustrate how it can be used. This is a useful decision structure that is natural to the solution of several different problems.

Suggested Background
The introductory material at the beginning of Chapter 7, Sections 7.1 and 7.2, the introductory material at the beginning of this chapter, and Section 8.2. Notice that Section 8.1 is not required.

The CASE statement provides the capability to use a data value to select the next statement that is to be executed. After the statement is executed, no other statements in the CASE control structure are executed. The general form of the CASE structure is

```
CASE <selector expression> OF
   <case label list> : <statement>;
   <case label list> : <statement>;
     .
     .
     .
   <case label list> : <statement>
END
```

Each CASE label list is a list of constants (separated by commas) of the same type as the selector expression because the CASE-END pair acts to delimit the structure from the rest of the program. REAL is not allowed for use as the TYPE of a selector expression. As many constants as desired may be included in an individual CASE label list. A BEGIN-END delimiter pair is not needed to group the statements under the CASE selector expression.

The use of CASE is illustrated in the following program.

```
PROGRAM CLASS(INPUT,OUTPUT);
   (* THIS PROGRAM READS A PERSON'S SEMESTER IN SCHOOL AND REPORTS
      WHAT THE UNDERGRADUATE CLASSIFICATION SHOULD NORMALLY BE      *)
VAR
   SEMESTER: INTEGER;
BEGIN  (* FINDING STUDENT CLASSIFICATION *)
   READ(SEMESTER);  (* READ IN A STUDENT'S SEMESTER IN SCHOOL *)
   WRITELN('THE STUDENTS SEMESTER IN SCHOOL IS ',SEMESTER);
   CASE SEMESTER OF  (* STUDENT CLASSIFICATION ROUTINE *)
      0: WRITELN('THE STUDENT IS AN INCOMING FRESHMAN');
      1,2: WRITELN('THE STUDENT IS A FRESHMAN');
      3,4: WRITELN('THE STUDENT IS A SOPHMORE');
      5,6: WRITELN('THE STUDENT IS A JUNIOR');
      7,8,9: WRITELN('THE STUDENT IS A SENIOR')
   END;  (* ASSIGNING STUDENT CLASSIFICATION *)
   WRITELN('... STUDENT CLASSIFICATION PROGRAM FINISHED');
END.  (* CLASSIFYING STUDENTS *)
```

If the value of the selector expression is not on one of the CASE label lists, the action of the Pascal compiler is undefined. This means that different things may happen with different Pascal compilers. The Waterloo Pascal compiler recognizes that an error has happened and prints the message

```
*** ERROR: NO MATCH FOR THE CURRENT VALUE IN THE CASE SELECTOR
```

A good program that has been designed for repeated use will *edit check* the data. Edit checking examines the data to see if it falls within the desired limits and then prints any necessary error messages. Simple edit checking is illustrated by rewriting the previous program CLASS to check the range validity of the selector expression.

```
PROGRAM CLASS(INPUT,OUTPUT);
   (* THIS PROGRAM READS A PERSON'S SEMESTER IN SCHOOL AND REPORTS
      WHAT THEIR UNDERGRADUATE CLASSIFICATION SHOULD NORMALLY BE
         SEMESTER    0 = INCOMING FRESHMAN
         SEMESTERS 1,2 = FRESHMAN
         SEMESTERS 3,4 = SOPHMORE
         SEMESTERS 5,6 = JUNIOR
         SEMESTERS 7,8 = NORMAL SENIOR
         SEMESTER    9 = EXTRA LONG SENIOR                  *)
VAR
   SEMESTER: INTEGER;
BEGIN  (* FINDING STUDENT CLASSIFICATION *)
   READ(SEMESTER);  (* READ IN A STUDENT'S SEMESTER IN SCHOOL *)
   WRITELN('THE STUDENTS SEMESTER IN SCHOOL IS ',SEMESTER);
   IF SEMESTER < 0  (* SEE IF IMPOSSIBLY LOW *)
      THEN SEMESTER := -1;  (* CHANGE ALL TOO LOW VALUES TO -1 *)
   IF SEMESTER > 9  (* SEE IF SEMESTER GREATER THAN NORMAL *)
      THEN SEMESTER := 10;  (* CHANGE ALL TO HIGH VALUES TO +10 *)
   CASE SEMESTER OF  (* STUDENT CLASSIFICATION ROUTINE *)
      -1: WRITELN('+++ SEMESTER SPECIFIED IS TOO LOW');
      0: WRITELN('THE STUDENT IS AN INCOMING FRESHMAN');
      1,2: WRITELN('THE STUDENT IS A FRESHMAN');
      3,4: WRITELN('THE STUDENT IS A SOPHMORE');
      5,6: WRITELN('THE STUDENT IS A JUNIOR');
      7,8,9: WRITELN('THE STUDENT IS A SENIOR');
      10: WRITELN('+++ SEMESTER SPECIFIED IS TOO HIGH ')
   END;  (* ASSIGNING STUDENT CLASSIFICATION *)
   WRITELN('... STUDENT CLASSIFICATION PROGRAM FINISHED')
END.  (* CLASSIFYING STUDENTS *)
```

Observe that this program also uses a comment section to describe the student classification system. This is an example of documentation that is "internal" to the program.

Groups of statements that have been compounded together can be controlled by CASE. This is illustrated in the following program.

```
PROGRAM LETTERS(INPUT,OUTPUT);
   (* THIS PROGRAM READS IN A LETTER GRADE AND PROVIDES BOTH AN
      EXPLANATION AS TO WHAT THE GRADE MEANS AND A COMMENT AS TO
      THE STUDENTS PROGRESS                                      *)
VAR
   GRADE: CHAR;
BEGIN  (* FINDING GRADE CLASSIFICATIONS *)
   READ(GRADE);  (* READ IN A GRADE *)
   WRITELN('THE GRADE READ IN WAS: ',GRADE);
   IF (GRADE < 'A') OR (GRADE > 'F')  (* IS GRADE VALID? *)
      THEN GRADE := 'E';  (* INVALID GRADE *)
   CASE GRADE OF  (* GRADE EXPLANATION *)
      'A': BEGIN  (* BEST GRADE *)
               WRITELN('---THIS IS THE BEST GRADE');
               WRITELN('CONGRATULATIONS ON YOUR PROGRESS')
           END;  (* BEST GRADE *)
      'B': BEGIN  (* SECOND BEST GRADE *)
               WRITELN('---THIS IS THE SECOND BEST GRADE');
               WRITELN('YOU ARE DOING WELL IN THE COURSE');
               WRITELN('TRY A LITTLE HARDER, PERHAPS YOU CAN DO BETTER')
           END;  (* SECOND BEST GRADE *)
      'C': BEGIN  (* THIRD BEST GRADE *)
               WRITELN('---THIS INDICATES THAT YOUR WORK IS AVERAGE');
               WRITELN('IT IS POSSIBLE TO DO BETTER')
           END;  (* THIRD BEST GRADE *)
      'D': BEGIN  (* FOURTH BEST GRADE *)
               WRITELN('---THIS INDICATES THAT YOU ARE NOT DOING WELL');
               WRITELN('IT IS SUGGESTED THAT YOU FIND TUTORIAL HELP')
           END;  (* FOURTH BEST GRADE *)
      'E': WRITELN('+++THIS IS NOT A VALID GRADE IN OUR SYSTEM');
      'F': BEGIN  (* WORST GRADE *)
               WRITELN('---THIS INDICATES THAT YOU ARE FAILING');
               WRITELN('IT INDICATES THAT YOU ARE NOT DOING ENOUGH');
               WRITELN('YOU SHOULD DROP THE COURSE OR WORK HARDER')
           END  (* WORST GRADE *)
      END  (* GRADE EXPLANATION *)
   END. (* LETTERS *)
```

8.2.2 GOTO

Objectives
Discuss and describe the Pascal GOTO statement and the advantages/disadvantages of using it. It should be noted that structured programming discourages the use of GOTOs. This section is included in the text for the sake of completeness. Some implementations of Pascal do not support the use of GOTO. (The UCSD Pascal requires an instruction to the compiler before GOTO can be used. UCSD Pascal provides the nonstandard EXIT to accomplish some of the same tasks.)

Suggested Background
The introductory material at the beginning of Chapter 7, Section 7.1, the introductory material at the beginning of this chapter, and Section 8.2. Notice that all of Section 8.1 and 8.2.1 are not required.

The GOTO statement allows the program to change execution sequence by jumping from one place in the program to another. This process of moving from one part of the program to another is also called *unconditional branching*. Before modern programming languages were developed, GOTO statements were necessary to program any but the simplest of problems. Modern programming languages have made the use of the GOTO statement almost unnecessary. This is the only section of the text where programs using the GOTO statement are displayed.

The GOTO statement can be useful to handle error and end-of-file conditions. However, most conditions can be handled best by using statements other than GOTOs. The major problem with using GOTOs is that the programs quickly become complex and thus hard to understand, by both the original programmer and anyone else. GOTOs often lead to unstructured programs that cannot be modularized.

8.2.2.1 Statement Labels

Objectives
Describe the need to mark the statements that a program can jump to and illustrate how it is done.

Suggested Background
Introductory material at the beginning of Chapter 7 and Chapter 8, Sections 8.2 and 8.2.2.

Before it is possible to jump or transfer to another part of the program, it is necessary to mark or label the point to which the program can transfer. This is done by LABELing program statements that serve as transfer destinations. The LABELs that are to be used must be declared at the beginning of the program. The LABEL declaration is placed before the CONST and VAR sections. For example,

```
LABEL
    23,29;
CONST
    PI = 3.1459;
    YES = TRUE;
    NO = FALSE;
VAR
    COUNT: INTEGER;
    TOTAL: INTEGER;
    AVERAGE: REAL;
```

Notice that statement LABELs are unsigned integers. How many digits may be in a LABEL varies from Pascal compiler to Pascal compiler. The most common length is four digits. The Pascal standard specifies that LABELs will range from 0 to 9999.

Use of an integer as a LABEL does not prevent it from being used either as a variable value or as a member of a CASE label list.

The statement that is being labeled is marked in the following manner.

```
<label> : <statement>
```

Although this may look much like a CASE label, it is different as the CASE label represents a data value that must be matched in order for the statement to be executed. A statement LABEL, on the other hand, provides a means for marking a statement. For example, in the program fragment

```
    .
    .
    .
COUNT := 0;
263: READLN(AGE);
WRITELN('AGE =',AGE);
    .
    .
    .
```

the statement

```
READLN(AGE)
```

is marked or LABELed by the integer 263.

8.2.2.2 Simple GOTOS

Objectives
Describe and illustrate the simplest form of an unconditional transfer.

Suggested Background
Introductory material at the beginning of Chapter 7 and Chapter 8, Secrtions 8.2, 8.2.2, and 8.2.2.1.

In its simplest form, the GOTO statement is used to transfer unconditionally to another part of the program. For example, in the following program fragment,

```
.
.
.
COUNT := 0;
263: READ(AGE);
WRITELN('AGE =',AGE);
.
.
.

AGETOTAL := AGETOTAL + AGE;
GOTO 263;
.
.
.
```

the GOTO statement causes the program to transfer execution to the READ statement LABELed by "263" after executing the statement

```
AGETOTAL := AGETOTAL + AGE
```

After this statement is executed, the next statement to be executed will be the WRITELN as the normal top-to-bottom flow of statement execution will then resume.

8.2.2.3 Conditional GOTOS

Objective
Describe how direct transfer can be conditionally controlled.

Suggested Background
Introductory material at the beginning of Chapter 7 and Chapter 8,
Sections 8.2, 8.2.2, 8.2.2.1, and 8.2.2.2.

Transferring execution from one place to another in a program can be conditionally controlled by using the IF-THEN-ELSE control structure. The form can be the simple

```
IF <relational test>
   THEN GOTO <label>
```

This is illustrated by

```
COUNT := 0;
263: READ(AGE);
IF AGE > 65
   THEN GOTO 4624;
.
.
.
AGETOTAL := AGETOTAL + AGE;
GOTO 263;
```

The more complex form of conditional transfer can involve both parts of the IF-THEN-ELSE structure in the form of

```
IF <relational expression>
   THEN GOTO <label>
   ELSE GOTO <label>
```

This is illustrated by

```
IF AGE < 65
   THEN GOTO 281
   ELSE GOTO 384
```

Both of these forms can be seen in the following example program AGES.

```
PROGRAM AGES(INPUT,OUTPUT);
    (* THIS PROGRAM CALCULATES THE AVERAGE AGE OF A GROUP OF PEOPLE AND
        COUNTS HOW MANY FALL INTO EACH OF THE FOLLOWING CLASSIFICATIONS:
            CLASS N: NON-VOTERS (LESS THAN 18 YEARS OF AGE)
            CLASS R: VOTERS WHO ARE FROM 18 TO LESS THAN 65
            CLASS S: SENIOR CITIZEN VOTERS                         *)
LABEL
    263,524,4624,281,384,983,101;
CONST
    VOTERAGE = 18;
VAR
    AGE: INTEGER;
    PEOPLECOUNT: INTEGER;
    AGETOTAL: INTEGER;
    AVERAGEAGE: REAL;
    NONVOTERS: INTEGER;
    VOTERS18TO65: INTEGER;
    VOTERS65OVER: INTEGER;
BEGIN  (* CLASSIFYING AND COUNTING POTENTIAL VOTERS *)
    (* INITIALIZE TOTALS *)
    AGETOTAL := 0;  (* TOTAL OF ALL AGES READ *)
    NONVOTERS := 0;  (*  TOTAL OF ALL FOUND TO BE NONVOTERS *)
    VOTERS18TO65 := 0;  (* TOTAL OF ALL VOTERS BETWEEN 18 TO 65 *)
    VOTERS65OVER := 0;  (* TOTAL OF ALL SENIOR CITIZEN VOTERS *)
    PEOPLECOUNT := 0;  (* PEOPLECOUNT OF ALL READ *)
    263: READ(AGE);  (* READ IN PERSON'S AGE *)
    IF EOF  (* CHECK TO SEE IF ALL DATA HAS BEEN READ IN *)
        THEN GOTO 101;  (* ALL DATA HAS BEEN READ, GO TO SUMMARY *)
    WRITELN('AGE = ',AGE:3);
    IF AGE < VOTERAGE
        THEN GOTO 4624
        ELSE IF AGE < 65
            THEN GOTO 281
            ELSE GOTO 384;
    983: PEOPLECOUNT := PEOPLECOUNT + 1;
    AGETOTAL := AGETOTAL + AGE;  (* SUM AGES *)
    GOTO 263;
    101: AVERAGEAGE:= AGETOTAL/PEOPLECOUNT; (* CALCULATE AVERAGE AGE *)
    WRITELN('.................SUMMARY RESULTS...................');
    WRITELN('NUMBER OF NON-VOTERS IS:',NONVOTERS);
    WRITELN('NUMBER OF VOTERS BETWEEN 18 AND 65 IS:',VOTERS18TO65);
    WRITELN('NUMBER OF VOTERS OVER 65 IS:',VOTERS65OVER);
    WRITELN('THE AVERAGE AGE OF EVERYBODY IS:',AVERAGEAGE:6:2);
    GOTO 524;
    4624: NONVOTERS := NONVOTERS + 1;  (* NON VOTER CLASSIFICATION *)
    WRITELN('NOT OF IMPORTANCE TO THIS CAMPAIGN');
    GOTO 983;
    281: VOTERS18TO65 := VOTERS18TO65 + 1;  (* MAIN BLOCK OF VOTERS *)
    WRITELN('SEND TAX REFORM POSITION');
    GOTO 983;
    384: VOTERS65OVER := VOTERS65OVER + 1;  (* SPECIAL INTEREST GROUP *)
    WRITELN('SEND HEALTH CARE POSITION');
    GOTO 983;
    524: WRITELN('... ALL VOTER AGES HAVE BEEN READ AND CLASSIFIED ...')
END.  (* VOTER CLASSIFICATION AND PEOPLECOUNTING *)
```

8.3 QUESTIONS

8.1   In an IF-THEN-ELSE control structure, why is a semicolon not placed after the completion of the THEN clause and before the initiation of the ELSE clause?

8.2   In a CASE control structure, what TYPE may a case label selector have?

8.3   Are there any problems that cannot be solved using a CASE control structure that can be solved using an IF-THEN-ELSE structure? Describe some.

8.4   Discuss the advantages and disadvantages of using a GOTO statement.

8.4 PROBLEMS

Required Background
These problems require arithmetic, input/output, and the use of selection control structures. Specifically not required are iterative control statements. Problems requiring both iterative and selection control statements follow Chapter 9. This allows the order in which Chapters 7 and 8 are presented to be interchanged.

8.1.   Susie is thinking of purchasing a table that she has found in a catolog from Sweden. She wants it to fit between the couch and the doorway. There are only 26 inches of space for the width. The only problem is that she doesn't have a metric measuring stick and the dimensions of the table are given in centimeters. If the table is square and is 98 centimeters on each side, will it fit where she wants to put it?

Write a Pascal program to calculate the available space in centimeters and display the result. If the table will fit where Susie wants to put it, display yes, if it will not, display no. (*Hint*: 1 centimeter is about 0.4 inch.)

8.2.   A Greater Sopwirth Widget sales representative takes orders for class A widgets. At the end of the day, the sales representative takes the amount available from before plus any new production and subtracts the total quantity ordered. If there is not enough to fill the orders, then the sales representative reports to the production manager the additional amount required. Write a program that will input the quantity of widgets available from before, the quantity produced that day, and the quantity ordered by customers. Then display a report that indicates all the old and new totals and also reports a message if additional production is required and how much should be produced. Test your program with the following two sets of data. (Run your program twice, once for each set of data.)

	set 1	set 2
available:	24	62
new orders:	168	179
produced today:	119	132

8.3. Jim Jones is the director of the West Coast division of a large construction supply company. Each year he receives a bonus equal to 1% of his sales level. However, if his sales level exceeds $25 million, then he is not given a bonus, but a promotion. Write a program that will input the sales level and report Jim Jones' bonus or promotion. Run your program two times, testing it with the following data.

first time: 24682196.84
second time: 26432984.19

8.4. Mr. Smith is running for the legislature. He would like to know how the people in his area feel about the new tax bill, the recreation bill, and the pay increase for members of the legislature. He decides to take a survey asking his constituents to state their feelings on the bill, as follows:

assign the number	if the person
1	strongly agrees
2	agrees
3	is undecided
4	disagrees
5	strongly disagrees

Write a program that will input the survey answers, report the number of people in each category, and report the most popular opinion to Mr. Smith. Test your program with the following data.

	taxes	recreation	salary
person 1	2	1	1
person 2	4	3	1
person 3	2	2	5
person 4	4	1	5
person 5	3	3	2
person 6	2	5	4

You only need to read in the values indicating survey response. It is not necessary to read in person number.

8.5. Input pairs of values of x and y. Then display the values for x, y, z. z can be calculated for each x, y pair as follows:

$$\text{If } x > y, z = 3*x+y$$
$$\text{If } x = y, z = 3*x*y-15$$
$$\text{If } x < y, z = 2*(y-x)$$

Use the values:

x	y
19	17
213	213
17	16
217	964
64	17

8.6. Easter (the "Western Easter" and not the Easter of the Eastern Orthodox churches) falls on the first Sunday following the first full moon that occurs on or after March 21. The following algorithm, due to Gauss, will calculate for a given year y (y $>=$ 1583) a number representing the date of Easter as follows: If d $>=$ 31, then Easter is on March d, and otherwise on April f, f = d – 31. The intermediate values C,G,g,c and E occurring in the algorithm can be briefly described as follows: C is the century; G is the "golden number," the number of the year in the "Metonic cycle" and is used to determine the position of the calendar moon; g is the "Gregorian correction" and is the number of years such as 1700, 1800, 1900, etc., when a leap year was not held; c is the "Clavian correction" for the Metonic cycle and amounts to about 8 days every 2500 years; and E is the "Epact", the age of the moon on January 1, and thus may be used to find when the full moon occurs.

STEP 1.   Let C=floor(y/100)+1.
STEP 2.   Let g=floor(3C/4)−12.
STEP 3.   Let G=mod(y,19)+1.
STEP 4.   Let c=floor((8c+5)/25)−5−g.
STEP 5.   Let e=floor(5y/4)−g−10.
STEP 6.   Let E=mod(11G+20+c,30).
STEP 7.   If E=25, then go to Step 9.
STEP 8.   If G>11, then let E=E +1.
STEP 9.   If E=24, then let E=E +1.
STEP 10.   Let d=44−E.
STEP 11.   If d<21, then let d=d+30.
STEP 12.   Let d=d+7−mod(d+e,7).
STEP 13.   Stop

You are to write a program to determine the date of Easter for this year. Your program should be designed to work for any year between 1800 and 2000. Input the year that you are calculating the date of Easter.

8.7. Cynthia needs to know the tuition costs for her college education. She has been presented with two options and would like to choose the cheapest.
Option One
  (a) Four years of school, not including summers.
  (b) Work for three summers.
Option Two
  (a) Go to school year round for three years.
  (b) Do not work during the summers.
    Tuition starts at $1000 a year and increases 16% a year. Summer school tuition is $300 and it also increases 16% a year. Someone working during the summer can expect to have saved

$900 by the end of the summer. Expected savings per summer increase at the rate of 7% a year. Write a program that will
  (a) Calculate the cost of each option.
  (b) Report the results.
  (c) Report a message indicating the cheapest choice.

8.8. The following process will yield the day of the week (Sunday, Monday, . . .) for any date in this century.
  (a) Input a date.
  (b) Divide the last two digits of the year by 4. Discard any remainder. For example, given 1983, the last two digits are "83". Dividing 83 by 4 produces 20.
  (c) Add the value generated in (b) to the last two digits of the year. For example, 83+20 → 103.
  (d) Find the "month number" from the following table.

month	month number
January	1
February	4
March	4
April	0
May	2
June	5
July	0
August	3
September	6
October	1
November	4
December	6

  (e) Add the "month number" to the total computed in step (c).
  (f) Divide the result by 7. Retain only the remainder.
  (g) The result (the remainder) found in step (f) indicates the day according to the following table.

1	→	Sunday
2	→	Monday
3	→	Tuesday
4	→	Wednesday
5	→	Thursday
6	→	Friday
0	→	Saturday

You are to write a Pascal program to read in a date, echo print the date, and then indicate the day of the week to which the date corresponds. Test your program with the date July 18, 1941, as well as the date that your assignment is due.

Chapter 9

MULTIPLE CONTROL STRUCTURES

Objectives
Describe why it might be useful to control decisions by using more than one condition or more than one control structure and provide illustrations.

Suggested Background
The Pascal core chapters 3, 4, and 5, as well as Chapters 7 and 8. Different sections of this chapter will use different control structures previously developed in Chapters 7 and 8.

When performing tasks, people often control decisions by considering several factors. For example, IF a person is hungry AND he has enough MONEY, THEN he will buy a pizza. Additionally, the performance of a given task can require the combination of several different control structures. For example, WHILE fishing a person may REPEAT various actions UNTIL a certain number of fish have been caught.

e.1. WHILE fishing
    e.1.1 sit in boat
    e.1.2 REPEAT fish catching UNTIL five fish are caught
        e.1.2.1 IF hook needs bait, THEN put bait on
        e.1.2.2 IF fish bites, THEN catch fish
e.2 clean fish

In Pascal multiple condition control can be performed by the use of complex relational expressions. Multiple control structure requirements can be met by nesting control structures.

9.1 MULTIPLE CONDITION CONTROL

Objectives
Describe why the execution of a statement might be controlled by a complex logical statement and show how it could be done.

Suggested Background
Chapter 8 and the previous material in this chapter.

Many decisions require that more than one logical test be performed. A single, large IF-THEN-ELSE statement can accomplish this. However, a series of IF-THEN statements controlled by a multiple condition test is often simpler to understand and to write.

The clarity achieved by using multiple condition control statements can be observed by comparing the programs CLASSIFY and IDENTIFY, which follow. A height table might indicate:

gender	short	average	tall
males	under 69 inches	69 to 72 inches	over 72 inches
females	under 62 inches	62 to 66 inches	over 66 inches

Using an IF-THEN-ELSE structure, a person's classification might be determined by the following solution plan.

classify people within different genders by height
1   define variables
2   acquire a person's gender and height
   2.1   read gender and height
   2.2   print gender and height
3   classify the height within gender, if gender is male
   3.1   then if height < 69
      3.1.1   then print that he is short
      3.1.2   else if height <= 72
         3.1.2.1   then print that he is average
         3.1.2.2   else print that he is tall
   3.2   else if gender is female
      3.2.1   then if height < 62
         3.2.1.1   then print that she is short
         3.2.1.2   else if height <= 66
            3.2.1.2.1   then print that she is average
            3.2.1.2.2   else print that she is tall

3.2.2   else print that an invalid gender description code was read

4   print that classification is finished

5   end of problem

The program CLASSIFY follows this solution plan.

```
PROGRAM CLASSIFY(INPUT,OUTPUT);
     (* THIS PROGRAM CLASSIFIES PEOPLE AS TO THEIR RELATIVE TALLNESS
        THE CLASSIFICATION SCHEME IS BASED ON THEIR HEIGHT IN INCHES

        * GENDER *     SHORT     * AVERAGE *     TALL      *
        *_____*_____*_____*_____*
        * MALE   * LESS THAN 69 * 69 TO 72 * MORE THAN 72 *
        *_____*_____*_____*_____*
        * FEMALE * LESS THAN 62 * 62 TO 66 * MORE THAN 66 *
        *_____*_____*_____*_____*        *)
VAR
   GENDER: CHAR;
   HEIGHT: INTEGER;
BEGIN  (* CLASSIFYING BY HEIGHT WITH RESPECT TO GENDER *)
   READLN(GENDER,HEIGHT);  (* READ A PERSONS GENDER AND HEIGHT *)
   WRITELN('GENDER IS: ',GENDER,' HEIGHT IS: ',HEIGHT:2);
   IF GENDER = 'M'  (* TRY TO CLASSIFY MALES HEIGHT FIRST *)
      THEN IF HEIGHT < 69  (* TRY TO IDENTIFY SHORT MALES FIRST *)
         THEN WRITELN('--- HE IS SHORT.')
         ELSE IF HEIGHT <= 72  (* TRY TO CLASSIFY AS AVERAGE *)
            THEN WRITELN('--- HE IS AVERAGE.')  (* IN RANGE *)
            ELSE WRITELN('--- HE IS TALL.')  (* BY DEFAULT *)
      ELSE IF GENDER = 'F'  (* EDIT CHECK ON GENDER *)
         THEN IF HEIGHT < 62  (* TRY TO IDENTIFY SHORT FEMALES FIRST *)
            THEN WRITELN('--- SHE IS SHORT')
            ELSE IF HEIGHT <= 66  (* TRY TO CLASSIFY AS AVERAGE *)
               THEN WRITELN('--- SHE IS AVERAGE.')  (* IN RANGE *)
               ELSE WRITELN('--- SHE IS TALL.')  (* BY DEFAULT *)
         ELSE WRITELN('+++ INVALID GENDER CODE SUPPLIED.');
   WRITELN('... HEIGHT CLASSIFICATION PROGRAM FINISHED ...')
END.  (* CLASSIFY *)
```

Notice that in the program CLASSIFY it is unclear as to which conditions control the printing of any single statement. Then observe how in the use of complex relational expressions the following program IDENTIFY makes it easier to understand and modify. Notice that parentheses are used to control how the boolean expressions are evaluated.

classify people within different genders by height
1   define variables
2   acquire a person's gender and height
   2.1   read gender and height
   2.2   print gender and height
3   classify the height within gender
   3.1   if gender is not male or female
      3.1.1   then print that an invalid gender code has been read
   3.2   classify males
      3.2.1   if gender is male and height < 69
         3.2.1.1   then print that he is short
      3.2.2   if gender is male and height $>= 69$ and height $<= 72$
         3.2.2.1   then print that he is average
      3.2.3   if gender is male and height > 72
         3.2.3.1   then print that he is tall
   3.3   classify females
      3.3.1   if gender is female and height < 62
         3.3.1.1   then print that she is short
      3.3.2   if gender is female and height $>= 62$ and height $<= 66$
         3.3.2.1   then print that she is average
      3.3.3   if gender is female and height > 66
         3.3.3.1   then print that she is tall
4   print that classification is finished
5   end of problem

```
PROGRAM IDENTIFY(INPUT,OUTPUT);
   (* THIS PROGRAM CLASSIFIES PEOPLE AS TO THEIR RELATIVE TALLNESS
      THE CLASSIFICATION SCHEME IS BASED ON THEIR HEIGHT IN INCHES

      * GENDER *    SHORT    * AVERAGE *     TALL      *
      *_____*_____*_____*_____*
      * MALE   * LESS THAN 69 * 69 TO 72 * MORE THAN 72 *
      *_____*_____*_____*_____*
      * FEMALE * LESS THAN 62 * 62 TO 66 * MORE THAN 66 *
      *_____*_____*_____*_____*          *)
VAR
   GENDER: CHAR;
   HEIGHT: INTEGER;
BEGIN  (* IDENTIFYING BY HEIGHT WITH RESPECT TO GENDER *)
   READLN(GENDER,HEIGHT);  (* READ A PERSONS GENDER AND HEIGHT *)
   WRITELN('GENDER IS: ',GENDER,' HEIGHT IS: ',HEIGHT:2);
   IF (GENDER <> 'M') AND (GENDER <> 'F')  (* CHECK IF VALID CODE *)
      THEN WRITELN('+++ INVALID GENDER CODE SUPPLIED');
   (* IDENTIFY MALES *)
   IF (GENDER = 'M') AND (HEIGHT < 69)  (* SHORT *)
      THEN WRITELN('--- HE IS SHORT.');
   IF (GENDER = 'M') AND ((HEIGHT >= 69) AND (HEIGHT <= 72))
      THEN WRITELN('--- HE IS AVERAGE.');
   IF (GENDER = 'M') AND (HEIGHT > 72)  (* TALL *)
      THEN WRITELN('--- HE IS TALL.');
   (* IDENTIFY FEMALES *)
   IF (GENDER = 'F') AND (HEIGHT < 62)  (* SHORT *)
      THEN WRITELN('--- SHE IS SHORT.');
   IF (GENDER = 'F') AND ((HEIGHT >= 62) AND (HEIGHT <= 66))
      THEN WRITELN('--- SHE IS AVERAGE.');
   IF (GENDER = 'F') AND (HEIGHT > 66)  (* TALL *)
      THEN WRITELN('--- SHE IS TALL.');
   WRITELN('... HEIGHT CLASSIFICATION PROGRAM FINISHED ...');
END.  (* IDENTIFY *)
```

There are a few more lines of programming. However, the second program is much simpler and thus is easier to understand. The amount of additional time required to execute the second program is not great. The additional clarity is worth it.

9.2 NESTED CONTROL STRUCTURES

Objectives
Create an awareness of the value of blocking groups of statements together and describe how it can be done in Pascal.

Suggested Background
The introductory material at the beginning of Chapter 7, Sections 7.1 and 7.2, and the previous material in this chapter.

Nested control structures have several advantages. They provide the capability to create *block* structures that group activities together. Nesting control structures also allows several different types of control to be performed. For example, the previous program IDENTIFY is formed into block structures for male and female gender groups in the following program GROUP.

Example: GROUP

What constitutes a short, average, or tall person is partially dependent on gender. A height that might be considered tall for a female might be considered average for a male. This program reads in a person's gender and height and then reports on the person's relative height classification.

classify people within different genders by height
1   define variables
2   acquire a person's gender and height
     2.1   read gender and height
     2.2   print gender and height
3   classify the height within gender
     3.1   if gender is not male or female
          3.1.1   then print that an invalid gender code has been read
     3.2   if gender is male
          3.2.1   then begin to classify male heights
               3.2.1.1   if height < 69
                    3.2.1.1.1   then print that he is short
               3.2.1.2   if height $>= 69$ and height $<= 72$
                    3.2.1.2.1   then print that he is average
               3.2.1.3   if height > 72
                    3.2.1.3.1   then print that he is tall
     3.3   if gender is female
          3.3.1   then begin to classify female heights
               3.3.1.1   if height < 62
                    3.3.1.1.1   then print that she is short
               3.3.1.2   if height $>= 62$ and height $<=66$
                    3.3.1.2.1   then print that she is average
               3.3.1.3   if height > 66
                    3.3.1.3.1   then print that she is tall
4   print that classification is finished
5   end of problem

The following program GROUP follows this plan.

```
PROGRAM GROUP(INPUT,OUTPUT);
   (* THIS PROGRAM CLASSIFIES PEOPLE AS TO THEIR RELATIVE TALLNESS
      THE CLASSIFICATION SCHEME IS BASED ON THEIR HEIGHT IN INCHES

        * GENDER *     SHORT     * AVERAGE *      TALL      *
        *_____*_____*_____*_____*
        * MALE   * LESS THAN 69 * 69 TO 72 * MORE THAN 72 *
        *_____*_____*_____*_____*
        * FEMALE * LESS THAN 62 * 62 TO 66 * MORE THAN 66 *
        *_____*_____*_____*_____*        *)
VAR
   GENDER: CHAR;
   HEIGHT: INTEGER;
BEGIN  (* CLASSIFYING BY HEIGHT WITH RESPECT TO GENDER *)
   READLN(GENDER,HEIGHT);  (* READ A PERSONS GENDER AND HEIGHT *)
   WRITELN('GENDER IS: ',GENDER,' HEIGHT IS: ',HEIGHT:2);
   IF (CODE <> 'M') AND (GENDER <> 'F')  (* CHECK IF VALID GENDER *)
      THEN WRITELN('+++ IMPROPER GENDER CODE SUPPLIED');
   IF GENDER = 'M'
      THEN BEGIN  (* BLOCK CLASSIFYING MALES *)
         IF HEIGHT < 69  (* SHORT *)
            THEN WRITELN('--- HE IS SHORT.');
         IF (HEIGHT >= 69) AND (HEIGHT <= 72)  (* AVERAGE *)
            THEN WRITELN('--- HE IS AVERAGE.');
         IF HEIGHT > 72  (* TALL *)
            THEN WRITELN('--- HE IS TALL.')
      END;  (* CLASSIFY MALES *)
   IF GENDER = 'F'
      THEN BEGIN  (* BLOCK CLASSIFYING FEMALES *)
         IF HEIGHT < 62  (* SHORT *)
            THEN WRITELN('--- SHE IS SHORT.');
         IF (HEIGHT >= 62) AND (HEIGHT <= 66)  (* AVERAGE *)
            THEN WRITELN('--- SHE IS SHORT.');
         IF HEIGHT > 66  (* TALL *)
            THEN WRITELN('--- SHE IS TALL.')
      END;  (* CLASSIFYING FEMALES *)
   WRITELN('... HEIGHT CLASSIFICATION PROGRAM FINISHED ...');
END.  (* GROUP *)
```

Notice that how the classification decisions are made easier to understand because all the decisions for each gender group are clearly defined.

Some tasks can be best handled by combining two control structures. The following program FACTORIAL combines both the FOR and WHILE control structures to compute a series of factorial values.

```
PROGRAM FACTORIAL(OUTPUT);
   (* THIS PROGRAM CALCULATES THE FACTORIALS FOR THE NUMBERS 1 TO 5 *)
VAR
   NUMBER: INTEGER;
   REDUCEDNUMBER: INTEGER;
   FACTORIAL: INTEGER;
BEGIN (* CALCULATING FACTORIALS *)
   WRITELN('NUMBER * FACTORIAL');
   WRITELN('-------*----------');
   FOR NUMBER := 1 TO 5 DO BEGIN
      FACTORIAL := NUMBER;
      REDUCEDNUMBER := NUMBER - 1;
      WHILE REDUCEDNUMBER > O DO BEGIN   (* CALCULATE FACTORIAL *)
         FACTORIAL := FACTORIAL * REDUCEDNUMBER;
         REDUCEDNUMBER := REDUCEDNUMBER - 1
      END;  (* CALCULATING FACTORIAL *)
      WRITELN(NUMBER:4,'   * ',FACTORIAL:6)
   END;  (*  FACTORIAL CALCULATIONS *)
   WRITELN('-------*----------')
END. (* FACTORIAL *)
```

Another example of the use of combined control structures can occur in the reading and processing of data. This is illustrated in the following program TOTAL. Note that this structure allows a single READ to handle the condition where there isn't at least one input value as well as the condition where there is at least one input data item.

Example: TOTAL

A list of prices is to be totaled. The count of how many prices are to be totaled is unknown. It may turn out that there are no prices to be totaled. If there may be more prices to be read, try to read and print prices. When all the prices have been read, print the total of all the prices.

read, print total prices
1   define variables
2   initialize
    2.1   set the total of all prices read so far to zero
    2.2   print titles
3   while there may be a price to be read
    3.1   try to read a price
    3.2   if the end of the input price file has not been found
        3.2.1   then process the price data
            3.2.1.1   print the price
            3.2.1.2   add the price to the total of all prices
        3.2.2   else print the results
            3.2.2.1   print the final title
            3.2.2.2   print the total of the prices
4   print a message indicating that the price totals are complete
5   end of problem

```
PROGRAM TOTAL(INPUT,OUTPUT);
   (* THIS PROGRAM READS, PRINTS AND TOTALS A GROUP OF PRICES WHERE
      THE NUMBER OF PRICES BEING SUMMED IS UNKNOWN *)
VAR
   TOTALPRICE: REAL;
   PRICE: REAL;
BEGIN  (* READING AND SUMMING PRICES *)
   TOTALPRICE := O.O;  (* INITIALIZE TOTAL OF ALL PRICES READ *)
   WRITELN(' PRICE ');  (* TITLE LINE *)
   WRITELN('-------');  (* TITLE LINE *)
   WHILE NOT EOF DO BEGIN  (* READING PRICES *)
      READ(PRICE);  (* TRY TO READ A PRICE *)
      IF NOT EOF  (* CONTINUE IF A PRICE WAS READ IN *)
         THEN BEGIN  (* PROCESSING PRICE DATA *)
            WRITELN(PRICE:6:2);  (* WRITE PRICE JUST READ IN *)
            TOTALPRICE := TOTALPRICE + PRICE  (* TOTAL PRICES *)
         END  (* PROCESSING PRICE DATA *)
         ELSE BEGIN  (* WRITE TOTAL INFORMATION *)
            WRITELN('-------');
            WRITELN(TOTALPRICE:6:2,' --- TOTAL')
         END  (* WRITING TOTAL INFORMATION *)
   END;  (* READING, PRINTING AND TOTALING PRICES *)
   WRITELN('... PRICE TOTALS COMPLETE')
END.  (* TOTAL *)
```

9.3 QUESTIONS

Required Background
These questions require the combination of both iterative and selection statements. Problems requiring both types of control structures were delayed until this point as the person using this book might have chosen to interchange the order in which Chapters 7 and 8 were covered.

9.1   Why might multiple conditions be used to control execution?
9.2   Why might nested control structures be used to control execution?
9.3   Why might a mix of different control structures be used to control execution?
9.4   When a control structure is nested within another control structure, how many semicolons are used? Why?
9.5   Given the following program,

```
PROGRAM QUESTION(INPUT,OUTPUT);
VAR
    A: INTEGER;
    B: INTEGER;
    S: INTEGER;
    Z: INTEGER;
BEGIN
    S := -2;
    A := O;
    B := O;
    WHILE NOT EOF DO BEGIN
        READ(Z);
        IF NOT EOF THEN BEGIN
            IF Z < O
                THEN Z := -1;
            IF Z > O
                THEN Z := 1;
            CASE Z OF
                -1: A := A + S;
                 O: S := S + 1;
                 1: B := B + S;
            END
        END
    END;
    WRITE(A:8,B:8);
END.  (* QUESTION *)
```

if the incoming data is the following what will be displayed as the results?

```
   0   -2
   9   14  -22
  12    6
  -9
  12   13
 -33
  21    9    0
   1    2    3    4
```

9.4 PROBLEMS

9.1.   Sam uses several trucks to deliver customer orders. As an order is filled, it is loaded on the truck. The orders are small in size but are rather heavy. Therefore the limiting factor is not a particular truck's available space but its weight limit. Write a program that will input a particular truck's total weight limit and then start loading the truck with orders. An order can be loaded only if the truck's weight limit is not exceeded by adding the weight of the order. Display the orders loaded on a truck in the following form.

```
TRUCK CAPACITY IS: xxxxx
---------------------------
ORDER            TOTAL
NUMBER   WEIGHT  LOADED
------   ------  ------
  321      16      16
  364     961     977
  281      30    1007
   .        .       .

   .        .       .
   .        .       .
```

Test your program with the following data. The first number represents the truck's weight limit. The subsequent numbers should be input as pairs representing the order number and the weight of the order.

```
2500
321  16
364  961
281  30
682  415
271  891
465  789
641  463
```

9.2. Thirty cannibals begin to eat ten missionaries. It takes an hour to consume the first missionary. After each missionary is eaten, one cannibal steals away into the forest. Each of the remaining cannibals continues to eat at the same rate. However, as there are fewer consumers, fewer missionaries will be consumed in each hour. Fortunately for the missionaries, help is on the way. Tarzan is coming. However, he is 80 miles away. During the day Tarzan travels at seven miles per hour. During the darkness he reduces his speed to 4 miles per hour. Darkness lasts nine hours. When the cannibals start eating, there are only three hours left to darkness. Write a program to calculate and display how many cannibals will be caught and how many missionaries saved. Display your results in the following form.

```
END OF HOUR   MISSIONARIES LEFT   CANNIBALS EATING   TARZAN DISTANCE
-----------   -----------------   ----------------   ---------------
     0               10                  30                80
     1                9                  29                73
     .                .                   .                 .
     .                .                   .                 .
```

Consider that a missionary partially consumed is not a missionary saved.

9.3. A group of nursing students jogged from downtown to the Great Star Discount Center. They started on Saturday morning at 8:00 and arrived at 6:00 in the late afternoon. Occasionally they stopped for a cup of water along the way. Create a program that will

(a) Input the number of cups of water swallowed during the day's jog at each stop.

(b) Display the number of cups of water swallowed during the day's jog, as each stop's total is input.

(c)   Calculate and display the total number of cups of water swallowed.

(d)   Calculate and display the total number of miles jogged if the students averaged 2 miles per cup of water on the jog.

The cups of water used were

$$
\begin{array}{c}
25\\
30\\
31\\
43\\
42\\
40
\end{array}
$$

9.4.   It is the year 2000 B.C. in Egypt. Pharaoh has just dictated to his people that the criminal Herschel shall be banished from Egypt for his crimes. Pharaoh's orders are that Herschel is to be taken into the desert and left there to wander on foot possibly to find the nearest civilization (it is 200 miles away from Egypt). Herschel is also given five days' rations of food and water.

Pharaoh, displaying his compassion, has Herschel taken 50 miles in the correct direction. Herschel then begins walking. Initially he is able to walk 20 miles a day. However, after each day he becomes weaker and his rate decreases by 1 mile a day. Also, he loses 2 miles of those he gains each day due to wind and sandstorms that blow him backward.

Even though Herschel can stretch his rations, he will collapse and move no more on the 13th day of wandering.

Basic information

Setting: Egypt, 2000 B.C.
Initial miles left to civilization = 200 − 50 = 150
Rate = 20 − (day − 1)
Miles gained = rate − 2 miles per day
Miles left to civilization = miles left to civilization − miles gained

Calculate

The day when Herschel collapses or reaches civilization.
The day, rate, and miles he has left to travel after each day.

Display your results in the following form.

DAY	RATE	MILES LEFT TO TRAVEL
1	20	132
2	19	115
.	.	.
.	.	.

9.5.   The Ace Insurance Company uses a computer program to calculate new premiums for new young male drivers who have had their first automobile accident.

The new premium equals the old premium multiplied by a rate. The rate is based on the applicant's age. The premiums are

age	rate
16	0.20
17	0.20
18	0.19
19	0.17
20	0.17
21	0.15
22	0.13

You are to input a driver's number, age, and old premium, and then calculate the new premium. Your output should have the form:

```
DRIVER NUMBER   AGE   OLD PREMIUM   NEW PREMIUM
-------------   ---   -----------   -----------
    2634         16      500.00        600.00
      .           .         .             .
      .           .         .             .
```

Test your program with the following data.

driver number	age	old premium
2634	16	500.00
7854	19	450.94
3659	21	621.19
1097	16	700.01
8688	17	341.58
4545	20	261.78
3907	22	201.89
3412	21	314.24
6589	18	312.98

9.6. Carefully plan your strategy for solving the following problem BEFORE you code it in Pascal using a pseudo-code.

The marketing department of the Heavenly Smoke Company has 10 salespersons. The yearly sales figures have been tabulated and are as follows:

salesperson's ID number	sales for the year
1	$10,000
2	53,000
3	8,000
4	44,000
5	85,000
6	66,000
7	44,000
8	86,000
9	58,000
10	53,000

Write a Pascal program that will find the identification number of the best salesperson (most sales) and the number of the worst salesperson (least sales). Input the data in the sequence shown.

9.7. A list of integer values contains an unspecified number of data values. Write and run a Pascal program to do the following for any number of data values.

(a) Input each data value and display it as soon as it has been input.
(b) Count the total number of values input.
(c) Compute the number of positive integers in the list.
(d) Compute the number of negative integers in the list.
(e) Do not count zero as being either a positive or a negative number.
(f) Compute the total of all the integers.
(g) When the last record has been input, display (with the appropriate titles) the total number of records, the number of positive integers, the number of negative integers, and the numeric total of all the integers input.

Test your program with the following data.

```
      1
  -   4
  -  67
     32
     67
  -  15
  -   1
    284
     39
     55
      0
     19
  -  23
      0
     18
   -289
     12
      0
    164
```

9.8.   Marvin Cramston just started a new job. He works eight hours a day at the Coronado Fig Factory, boxing packages of figs coming off the assembly line at the rate of 35 figs per hour.

When he starts working, there are five figs in his bin left over from his brother Lamont, who was fired because he could never catch up. Marvin begins boxing at a rate of nine figs an hour, and each hour his efficiency increases. Each hour he can box one extra fig, until he can box them at a rate of 39 per hour (which is about as fast as anyone can box figs). Please note that until Marvin can box figs at the rate of 35 per hour, his bin fills up at the rate of (35 – Marvin's rate) per hour.

We are interested in knowing how many DAYS he will have to work until there is no backlog in his bin at the end of the day. (Assume his work station when he arrives in the morning is exactly as it was when he left on the previous evening.)

9.9.   SureFloat makes fishing boats in lengths of 27, 33, 38, 42, 47, and 56 feet. The capacities of fishing boats, in tons, are 2, 4, 6, 10, 16, and 26. The fuel costs per mile of the boats are $10, $15, $23, $29, $32, and $38. The boats cost, in thousands of dollars, $30, $40, $50, $60, $70, and $80. A boat's useful life is six years. Fish are worth $423 a ton.

The fishing grounds are 3 miles away and each boat can travel at a speed of 8 miles per hour. Fixed costs for a crew are $200 for a 12-hour day. The fixed cost of $200 a day is always paid, even if the crew works for less than 12 hours. The crew is also paid 8% of the value of each catch.

A boat owner needs a program to consider all the costs and time spent going to and returning from the fishing grounds, to select which boat should be bought. (The crew will not work overtime, that is, more than 12 hours.) Generate a report showing profits from fishing if it takes ½, 1, 2, 3, 4, or 5 hours to catch a ton of fish. Produce a report for each boat. Indicate, by a message, when a profit would be expected.

9.10.   The copy editor is laying out the classified advertising pages. He has five 1-inch ads, 18 2-inch ads, and 34 4-inch ads. Columns are 15 inches long. How can he lay out the ads in complete columns so as to waste the least space at the bottom of the complete columns? (For example, three 4-inch ads and one 2-inch ad and one 1-inch ad fill up a column exactly—no waste, but three 4-inch ads alone in a column waste 3 inches.) Write a program that will generate different possibilities and then pick the best one.

9.11.   Rebecca makes extra money by typing other students' papers. She can type a page in 15 minutes. However, if there are one to three mathematical formulas, it takes her 30 minutes. For a page with four to seven mathematical formulas, she takes 50 minutes. If there are more than seven formulas on a page, then she needs 80 minutes to type the page.

Write a program that will input for each page to be typed the number of mathematical formulas on it. Display in a report the number of pages that take 15 minutes, 30 minutes, 50 minutes, and 80 minutes. Also display the total time she will need to type the paper.

Test your program with the following data. Each integer represents the number of equations on a page. (Your program should work for any number of pages.)

0   2   0   5   3   8   0   12   11   4   1

9.12.   Florida in the spring is a very busy place for motel owners because many college students visit there. The Sunshine Motel has 200 rooms, each of which can hold four people. On the first day of March, there are 100 people in the motel. Each day after that, 50 more people check in. You are to calculate the day in March that the motel is filled. Your results should have the form:

```
MARCH   PEOPLE IN MOTEL
-----   ---------------
  1           100
  2           150
  .            .
  .            .
```

9.13. At the end of Main Street in the city of Farmville, there is a policewoman who sits in her car behind a bush. Every person going faster than 45 is pulled over and fined. Those traveling 45 miles per hour or less are not stopped. For every person stopped, the policewoman gets $1 for every mile above the speed limit of 45. You are to input the speed data, whether or not the person was fined, and how much the fine was. The results should have the following form.

```
SPEED   FINED   AMOUNT
-----   -----   ------
  27     NO       0
  46     YES      1
   .      .       .
   .      .       .
```

Test your program with the following data.

$$27 \quad 46 \quad 29 \quad 49 \quad 34 \quad 75 \quad 48 \quad 38 \quad 45$$

9.14. Write a Pascal program that will
  (a) Input the digits of your Social Security number, one digit at a time.
  (b) Display each digit immediately after it is input.
  (c) Count how many of the digits were input, how many were odd, and how many were even (consider zero to be even).
  (d) After all the digits have been input, display the total number of digits that were input, how many were odd, and how many were even.
  (e) Calculate and display the average value of the digits that were input and report the result as a REAL value with three digits to the right of the decimal point.
  Your program must
  (a) Use the UNTIL statement to control inputting.
  (b) Have no more than two READ and/or READLN statements.
  (c) Be able to work for any number of input digits. This means that your program cannot be told how many digits are to be input and has to continue to input until all digits available as data are input.

9.15. Write a Pascal program that will solve the following problem.
  The city traffic manager is interested in trying to reduce the rush hour traffic entering the city. She believes that many vehicles entering the city are not filled to capacity. Before it is possible to propose a solution, a study must be conducted. The study will observe people driving past a certain point during the rush hours. The observer will discover to what extent the passing vehicles are filled. The information recorded for each vehicle will be

number of people transported
maximum capacity of vehicle

Your task is to prepare a program to tabulate the data acquired by the observer and report the results. The program will report on

(a) The count of vehicles transporting 1,2,3,4,5,6 or more than 6 people.

(b) The transportation efficiency of each vehicle. The transportation efficiency is calculated by dividing the number of people transported by the maximum capacity of the vehicle. The transportation efficiencies are to be counted in the following groups.

$$
\begin{aligned}
0 \ \text{to} \ \ 20\% \\
20 >= \ \ 40\% \\
40 >= \ \ 60\% \\
60 >= \ \ 80\% \\
80 >= 100\%
\end{aligned}
$$

For example, if the input data was

```
3 4
5 6
3 4
1 2
```

the output could look like (you may design your own output):

```
-- number of people transported --
    1   2   3   4   5   6   >6
   --- --- --- --- --- --- ----
    0   1   2   0   1   0   0 <==== number of vehicles transporting


--- transportation efficiency ----
 0-20  20-40  40-60  60-80  80-100
 ----  -----  -----  -----  ------
   0     0      1      2      1
```

Your program

(a) Must work for any amount of input data.

(b) Use CASE for part 1.

Use the following as data to test your program.

```
 3  4
 5  6
 3  4
 1  2
 2  4
 1  1
13 42
 3  5
 3  6
 1  6
 1  7
 3 43
 2  2
 4  4
```

9.16. A pair of numbers *m* and *n* are called *friendly* (or they are referred to as an *amicable pair*) if the sum of all the divisors of m (excluding m) is equal to the number n and the sum of all the divisors of the number n (excluding n) is equal to m (m<>n). For example, the numbers 220 and 284 are an amicable pair because the only numbers that divide evenly into 220 are ,2,4,10,11,20,22,44,55, and 110, and 1+2+4+5+10+11+20+22+44+55+110=284 (220's friendly number) and the only numbers that divide evenly into 284 are 1,2,4,71, and 142, and 1+2+4+71+142=220 (284's friendly number).

Many pairs of amicable numbers are known; however, only one pair (220, 284) is less than 1000. The next pair is in the range 1000–1500. Write a Pascal program to find this pair.

9.17. A positive integer greater than 1 is called *prime* if it is evenly divisible by no positive integers other than 1 and itself. Thus 2 and 3 are prime, 4 is not prime because it is divisible by 2, 5 is prime, 6 is not prime because it is divisible by both 2 and 3, etc.

To find out if a number is prime, it is necessary only to divide the number by all the integers from 2 to the square root of the number. If any of these integers divide evenly into the number, then the number is not prime.

A conjecture, first made by Goldbach, whose proof has defied all attempts to disprove it, is that "every even number larger than 2 can be written as the sum of two prime numbers." For example, 4=2+2, 6=3+3, 8=3+5, 10=3+7, 100=89+11, etc.

Write a program that determines for every even integer N between 1 and 200, inclusive (1<=N<=200), the two prime numbers P and Q such that N=P+Q.

9.18. In all the integers greater than 1 there are only four that can be represented by the sum of the cubes of their digits. One of these numbers is 153=3+53+33. Write a program to determine the other three. All four numbers lie in the range 150 to 410.

9.19. One of the endangered species is the harp seal. Indiscriminate commercial hunting has brought the number of these seals to a dangerously low level, especially since the pelts of newborn pups are most valuable to the hunters.

The life cycle of the seals can be simply described by the following model. The herd arrives at the whelping grounds where new pups are born. Within six weeks of this birth, the hunters move in for their kill. The remaining adult females are then impregnated by male seals and the herd migrates to northern Canada and Greenland for a year until the next whelping season.

The following assumptions can be made about the harp seals.

(a)　There is a natural mortality rate of 8% applied to all seals.

(b)　The population is equally divided between males and females.

(c)　Each pregnant female produces one pup a year.

(d)　The pregnancy rate is 90%. This is equivalent to applying a pregnancy rate of 45% to the whole population.

(e)　A female may be impregnated when she is one year old. This means that any pup that is not killed the first year and which survives the natural mortality rate is a candidate for impregnation.

Write a program to model the dynamics of the harp seal population of 1,300,000 seals, including 267,000 pups, available for hunting at the start of a hunting season.

How long will it take for the species to become extinct if

(a)　All newborn pups are killed each year?

(b)　200,000 pups are killed each year?

Consider the species to be extinct if the population falls below 25,000.

9.20.　Write a program that will input a word and then display this word in giant letters in the middle of a page. For example, if the word input is *ED*, then the program could produce:

```
EEEEEEEEEEEEEEEEEE    DDDDDDDDD
EEEEEEEEEEEEEEEEEE    DDDDDDDDDDDD
EE                    DD       DDD
EE                    DD        DDD
EE                    DD         DD
EE                    DD         DD
EE                    DD          DD
EE                    DD          DD
EEEEEEEEEEE           DD          DD
EEEEEEEEEEE           DD          DD
EE                    DD          DD
EE                    DD         DD
EE                    DD         DD
EE                    DD        DD
EE                    DD       DDD
EE                    DD      DDD
EEEEEEEEEEEEEEEEEEE   DDDDDDDDDDDD
EEEEEEEEEEEEEEEEEEE   DDDDDDDDD
```

Make your giant A out of a series of A's, your giant B out of a series of B's, etc.

Your solution display should contain examples of all the letters. Your letter matrix must be 18 × 18 characters and be able to handle a message of at least 40 characters. Your program must handle all the letters of the alphabet, commas, periods, minus signs, colons, and blanks.

9.21.　In the Land of Zack the money exists in denominations of 1, 2, 3, 5, 7, 11, 13 and 17 zk (1 zk = 0.816 U.S. dollar). The people in this land are exceedingly efficient, so each individual tries to carry around as few zk as possible. As Zack is an advanced society, each citizen owns a compact computer.

You are to write a program that will calculate the minimum number of bills of each denomination that are necessary for any amount between 1 and 1000 zk. Test your program on the following data.

                              Total zk

                                15
                               267
                                19
                                78
                               112
                               988
                               642
                               362
                               437
                               783

Your output should be of the form:

```
TOTAL AMOUNT    AMOUNT OF BILLS IN THE FOLLOWING DENOMINATIONS
------------    ----------------------------------------------
     21                              17-1
                                     13-0
                                     11-0
                                      7-0
                                      5-0
                                      3-1
                                      2-0
                                      1-1
```

Chapter 10

ADDITIONAL DATA DEFINITIONS: RESTRICTION, ENUMERATION, AND SETS

Objectives
Develop an awareness of the use of a variety of user defined data types, of the usefulness of restricting data values, and of how Pascal can be used to accomplish these things.

Suggested Background
The Pascal core chapters 3, 4, and 5. Some of the sections will require a knowledge of the control structures presented in Chapters 7 and 8 in order to understand the programming examples. However, if the complete program examples are ignored, this chapter may be done immediately after Chapter 3. There is significant value in doing so.

Some problems need to use only a limited range of values, such as 1, 2, 3 for first, second, and third prize. Or perhaps the terms "FIRST", "SECOND", "THIRD" would be the best data values to use to express the data in the problem. Often it is useful to define a nonstandard data type or to restrict the way in which a standard data TYPE may be used. For example, normally the set of INTEGERs includes . . . ,–3,–2,–1,0,1,2,3,4,5, ... By using the TYPE specification in Pascal, a new kind of variable can be defined that includes only the INTEGER values of 1,2,3,4,5.

Besides restricting an existing data TYPE, a programmer defined data TYPE can be used to construct tables (arrays or matrices), collections of multiple data items called *records,* and data items connected to each other by a *pointer* structure.

There are two different types of programmer defined data TYPEs: static and dynamic. The form and construction of a static data TYPE are predetermined. Dynamic TYPEs have the capability to vary their form and structure. This chapter is concerned with static data TYPEs. Dynamic structures are discussed in a later chapter.

10.1 PROGRAMMER DEFINED RESTRICTIONS

Objectives
Describe why restricting data values might be useful to solve a problem and demonstrate how Pascal can be used to do this.

Suggested Background
The previous material in this chapter.

Some problems need to restrict the data values that can be used for a particular variable value. Data values not in this list will be considered to be in error. For example, the values for a variable representing a prize that was awarded could be restricted to the values of 1,2,3 for first, second, and third, respectively, for a race that awards only first, second, and third prizes. Or a problem might need to store only the values MALE and FEMALE if gender values are being stored.

10.1.1 Range of Values

Objective
Describe how Pascal can be used to restrict the range of values that a variable can take on. All of Section 10.1.1 could be profitably covered immediately after Chapter 3.

Suggested Background
The previous material in this chapter.

A range of values can be specified by the use of the subrange TYPE. The form is

```
TYPE
   <subrange> = <first value>..<last value>;
VAR
   <variable name>: <subrange>;
```

For example,

```
TYPE
   PLACES = 1..5;
   POSSIBLETEMPERATURES = -100..125;
   GRADES = 0..100;
VAR
   AWARDS: PLACES;
   TEMPERATURE: POSSIBLETEMPERATURES;
   TESTVALUE: GRADES;
   HOMEWORKVALUE: GRADES;
```

An attempt to assign a value to a variable outside of its specified subrange will cause an error to happen when the program is executed.

The TYPE and VAR definitions can be combined. For example, the declaration

```
VAR
   AWARDS: 1..5;
   TEMPERATURE: -100..125;
   GRADEVALUE: 0..100;
   HOMEWORKVALUE: 0..100;
```

eliminates the need for a separate TYPE definition. This text encourages the programmer to define the TYPE structure separately, so that there is a clear, simple, and distinct description of the nature of the data. A subrange must be of an existing scalar data TYPE or a previously defined user data TYPE. A subrange of REAL values is not allowed.

10.1.2 Enumerated Data Values

Objectives
Describe the usefulness of being able to enumerate data values and illustrate how Pascal can be used in this way.

Suggested Background
The sections on BEGIN-END, IF-THEN, CASE, and the previous material in this chapter. If the complete program examples are ignored, this section can be covered immediately after Chapter 3.

If lists of nonstandard data values are desired, they can be specified or enumerated by using the TYPE statement in combination with the VAR statement. The general form of the statement is

```
TYPE
   <programmer defined type> = ( <value>,<value>,...,<value> );
VAR
   <variable name>: <programmer defined type>;
```

The variable can take on only data values from the specified range. For example,

```
TYPE
   GENDER = ( MALE,FEMALE );
   COLOUR = ( RED,ORANGE,YELLOW,BLUE,GREEN,VIOLET );
VAR
   SEX: GENDER;
   PARTCOLOUR: COLOUR;
   HOUSECOLOUR: COLOUR;
```

This defines a variable named SEX whose possible values are limited to MALE or FEMALE. It also provides a restricted list of colours for attachment to a variable. Notice that the same enumeration can be attached to more than one variable. In the case of the preceding example, COLOUR is attached to both PARTCOLOUR and HOUSECOLOUR.

The TYPE enumeration can be included in the VAR section. For example,

```
VAR
   SEX: ( MALE,FEMALE );
   PARTCOLOUR: ( RED,ORANGE,YELLOW,BLUE,GREEN,VIOLET );
```

An attempt to assign a value that was not enumerated to a variable with an enumerated range of values will cause an error when the program is executed. The enumeration also establishes how the variable's values are to be ordered; that is, which one will be considered the greatest value. The ordering resulting from the preceding example is

```
MALE < FEMALE
RED < ORANGE < YELLOW < BLUE < GREEN < VIOLET
```

If a programmer wants to change the ordering of values in an enumerated data TYPE, this can be done in a TYPE definition.

An enumerated value may not belong to more than one enumerated TYPE. The following is not allowed because VIOLET is specified in both TYPE declarations.

```
TYPE
   COLOUR = ( RED,ORANGE,YELLOW,BLUE,GREEN,VIOLET );
   FLOWER = ( ROSE,VIOLET,SWEATPEA,PETUNIA )
```

A misunderstanding that people sometimes have when they first use enumerated data types is that they believe that an enumerated data value can be read in as data. This is not so. Enumerated data values cannot be read in as data. This is because the enumerated values represent new CONSTants whose values cannot be changed. They can only be generated internally in a program. The following example program SURVEY illustrates a simple use of an enumerated data TYPE definition.

Example: Survey

A grade school teacher surveys his class to see what type of pets they have and the age of each pet. It turns out that they have dogs, cats, and fish. Knowing that dogs are considered old after 7 years of age, cats after 5 years, and fish after 2 years, he decides to count how many of each pet type there are and how many of the pets can be classified as old or young. As the class is large, he decides to write a program to do the counting. Each input record consists of the pet's age followed by the pet type code (1 = dog, 2 = cat, 3 = fish).

class survey
1   define data
   1.1   enumerated data TYPE
   1.2   standard data TYPEs
2   initialize counters
   2.1   pet counts
   2.2   young/old counts
3   process pet data
   3.1   while there may be more pet data
      3.1.1   try to read a pet's data
      3.1.2   if age for a pet was found, then begin to process it
         3.1.2.1   read pet code
         3.1.2.2   echo print pet's age, pet code
         3.1.2.3   convert pet code to enumerated data type
            3.1.2.3.1   if pet code is 1,
               3.1.2.3.1.1   then pet is a dog
            3.1.2.3.2   if pet code is 2,
               3.1.2.3.2.1   then pet is a cat
            3.1.2.3.3   if pet code is 3,
               3.1.2.3.3.1   then pet is a fish
         3.1.2.4   add to pet type count
            3.1.2.4.1   if pet is a dog,
               3.1.2.4.1.1   then add to the count of dogs
            3.1.2.4.2   if pet is a cat,
               3.1.2.4.2.1   then add to the count of cats
            3.1.2.4.3   if pet is a fish,
               3.1.2.4.3.1   then add to the count of fish
         3.1.2.5   add to young counts
            3.1.2.5.1   if pet is a dog and older than 7
               3.1.2.5.1.1   then add to count of old
            3.1.2.5.2   if pet is a cat and older than 5
               3.1.2.5.2.1   then add to count of old
            3.1.2.5.3   if pet is a fish and older than 2
               3.1.2.5.3.1   then add to count of old
   3.2   print results
      3.2.1   pet counts: dogs, cats, fish
      3.2.2   old/young counts
4   finish processing

The Pascal program for this plan follows.

```
PROGRAM SURVEY(INPUT,OUTPUT);
   (* THIS PROVIDES THE RESULTS OF A CLASS SURVEY ON PETS *)
TYPE
   CREATURES = ( DOG,CAT,FISH );
VAR
   PET: CREATURES;
   TOTALPETS: INTEGER;
   DOGCOUNT: INTEGER;
   CATCOUNT: INTEGER;
   FISHCOUNT: INTEGER;
   OLDPETS: INTEGER;
   YOUNGPETS: INTEGER;
   AGE: INTEGER;
   PETCODE: INTEGER;
BEGIN  (* PROCESSING THE CLASS SURVEY DATA *)
   (* INITIALIZE COUNTS *)
   TOTALPETS := 0;
   DOGCOUNT := 0;
   CATCOUNT := 0;
   FISHCOUNT := 0;
   OLDPETS := 0;
   YOUNGPETS := 0;
   WHILE NOT EOF DO BEGIN  (* READING AND PROCESSING PET DATA *)
      READ(AGE);  (* TRY TO READ A PET'S AGE *)
      IF NOT EOF  (* IF A PET AGE WAS READ *)
         THEN BEGIN  (* PROCESSING THE DATA FOR A PET *)
            READ(PETCODE); (* READ THE CODE IDENTIFYING THE PET TYPE *)
            TOTALPETS := TOTALPETS + 1;  (* ADD TO TOTAL OF ALL PETS *)
            WRITELN('AGE:',AGE:3,'  -- PET CODE IS: ',PETCODE:2);
            (* CONVERT PET'S CODE TO A MORE MEANINGFUL FORM *)
            IF PETCODE = 1
               THEN PET := DOG;
            IF PETCODE = 2
               THEN PET := CAT;
            IF PETCODE = 3
               THEN PET := FISH;
            CASE PET OF  (* ADD TO COUNT OF SPECIFIC PET TYPES *)
               DOG: DOGCOUNT := DOGCOUNT + 1;
               CAT: CATCOUNT := CATCOUNT + 1;
               FISH: FISHCOUNT := FISHCOUNT + 1
            END;  (* COUNTING HOW MANY OF EACH PET TYPE *)
            (* ADD TO THE COUNT OF OLD AND YOUNG PETS *)
            IF (PET = DOG) AND (AGE > 7)
               THEN OLDPETS := OLDPETS + 1;
            IF (PET = CAT) AND (AGE > 5)
               THEN OLDPETS := OLDPETS + 1;
            IF (PET = FISH) AND (AGE > 2)
               THEN OLDPETS := OLDPETS + 1
         END  (* PROCESSING PET DATA *)
   END;  (* TRYING TO READ PET DATA *)
   YOUNGPETS := TOTALPETS - OLDPETS;
   WRITELN('DOGS=',DOGCOUNT:3,' -- CATS=',CATCOUNT:3,' -- FISH=',
           FISHCOUNT:3);
   WRITELN('OLD PETS=',OLDPETS:5,' -- YOUNG PETS=',YOUNGPETS:5)
END.  (* SURVEY *)
```

10.2 SETS

Objective
Describe how Pascal manipulates sets.

Suggested Background
Section 8. The material in the 8.1 sections is not required. In order to increase flexibility, the material on sets is not referenced outside of this chapter. This means that the sections on sets may be skipped if desired.

Sets are basic components of mathematics. Simply stated, sets are collections of data of the same TYPE. In a set, each unique value is represented only once.

The Pascal standard states that square brackets are to be used to specify a value that is a member of a set. However, many computers do not have square brackets as part of their output capability. Therefore, alternate bracket symbols have been established to indicate set membership. They are "(." and ".)". Most versions of Pascal will accept these alternate symbols. (The Waterloo Pascal compiler uses only the alternate symbols.) This text uses only the alternate bracket symbols to indicate set membership. Appendix C includes a list of both the Pascal standard symbols and the designated alternate symbols.

10.2.1 Set Definition

Objectives
Describe set membership and illustrate how it is achieved in Pascal.

Suggested Background
The introductory material at the beginning of this chapter and Section 10.2.

A set is a collection of objects of the same TYPE. An object of the same TYPE as the objects in the set is either a member of the set or it is not a member of the set. A set may contain any scalar data type, except for REAL. For example, a set may consist of the passing grades for a course: 'A', 'B', 'C', 'D'. (The grades 'E' and 'F' are not members of the set of passing grades.)

The form of a SET definition is

```
TYPE
   <programmer defined base type> = <first value>..<last value>;
   <set description> = SET OF <programmer defined base type>;
VAR
   <set name>: <set description>;
```

The base type specifies all possible values that a given set can have. Standard scalar TYPEs can be used or the programmer can define a base TYPE. A set description declares that there can be a SET with the base type values that were defined in the base type declaration. The SET described name specified in the VAR section labels and creates memory space for the SET described. Note that the set does not contain any members until members are assigned to it. For example, consider the following declaration.

```
TYPE
   PASS = 'A'..'D';
   PASSING = SET OF PASS;
VAR
   PASSCOURSE: PASSING;
   GRADEDESIRED: PASS;
```

In this example, the set PASSCOURSE is a SET that can contain only the subrange values: 'A', 'B', 'C' 'D'. This SET may contain all of these values, some of them, or none of them. A set containing no values is known as an *empty set*.

If desired, the entire definition of the set can be compressed into a single VAR statement. The form is

```
VAR
   <set name>: SET OF <base type>
```

For example,

```
VAR
   PASSCOURSE: SET OF 'A'..'D';
```

The compressed form is not used in this text since it does not provide a separate description of the data structure.

The values of a SET can be specified by an enumerated data TYPE. The last example could be modified to include all possible grades as shown in the following example.

```
TYPE
   ALLGRADES = ( 'A'..'D','F' );
   POSSIBLEGRADES = SET OF ALLGRADES;
VAR
   GRADESGIVEN: POSSIBLEGRADES;
   GRADEAWARDED: GRADES;
```

The last two examples could be further combined as shown in the following example.

```
TYPE
    PASS = 'A'..'D';
    ALLGRADES = ( PASS,'F' );
    PASSING = SET OF PASS;
    POSSIBLEGRADES = SET OF ALLGRADES;
VAR
    GRADESGIVEN: POSSIBLEGRADES;
    ALLGRADESAWARDED: GRADES;
    GRADESDESIRED: PASSING;
```

10.2.2 Operations on Sets

Objectives
Describe and demonstrate the operations that Pascal can perform on sets.

Suggested Background
The introductory material at the beginning of this chapter and Sections 10.2 and 10.2.1. All parts of Section 10.2.2 should be done sequentially.

Sets may have members assigned to them, they may be manipulated, and they may be compared. Sets may be manipulated by combining them, finding the difference between them, and finding what is held in common between them.

10.2.2.1 Assignment

Objects may be added to a set by using the assignment statement. When doing so, the objects to be added are placed in brackets. If they were not, then the operation would be invalid because mixed TYPEs would be present. For example, if the SET of possible grades were to be defined as before, the set of passing grades actually awarded in the course could be initialized to the empty set by

```
PASSCOURSE := (..)
```

If a passing grade would be read in by a read statement such as

```
READ(GRADEAWARDED)
```

the only grade that could be assigned as the object in the set by

```
PASSCOURSE := (. GRADEAWARDED .)
```

The brackets around GRADEAWARDED indicate that it is an object in a SET. Because of the TYPE definitions, the program recognizes that PASSCOURSE is a SET. As mixed TYPE assignments are not permitted, the object being assigned to PASSCOURSE must be identifiable as a set object.

10.2.2.2 Union

Sets are combined using the operation of union. The union operator is "+". The union of two sets is a set containing the objects in both sets. For example,

```
(. 3,5,7 .) + (. 8,6,4 .)
```

will produce the set

```
(. 3,5,7,8,6,4 .)
```

If the same object occurs in both sets, the object will only occur once in the union of the sets. For example,

```
(. 6,12,4 .) + (. 7,6,4,13 .)
```

produces the set

```
(. 6,12,4,7,13 .)
```

Using the SET PASSCOURSE as defined before, an object GRADEAWARDED representing a passing grade can be incorporated into the set by

```
PASSCOURSE := PASSCOURSE + (. GRADEAWARDED .)
```

To avoid an error due to a mixed TYPE operation, GRADEAWARDED must be placed in brackets.

10.2.2.3 Intersection

The intersection of two sets produces a set containing all the objects that are members of both sets. The operation of intersection is indicated by "*". For example,

    (. 6,12,4 .) * (. 7,6,4,13 .)

produces

    (. 6,4 .)

while

    (. 3,5,7 .) * (. 8,6,4 .)

produces the empty set

    (..)

because there are no objects in common between the two sets.

10.2.2.4 Difference

The difference of two sets produces a set containing all the objects of the first set that are not members of the second set. The set difference operator is "–". For example,

    (. 'C','G','A','F' .) - (. 'G','F' .)

produces the set

    (. 'C','A' .)

If an object is in the second set, but is not in the first set, the object does not appear in the resulting set. For example,

    (. 'C','G','A','F' .) - (. 'G','F','H' .)

produces the set

    (. 'C','A' .)

10.2.3 Set Comparisons

Relational operators are available to compare sets. The available relational set operators are

=	set equality
<>	set unequality
<=	is contained in
>=	contains

For example, the following comparisons will produce a TRUE result.

```
(. 3,7,12 .)   =    (. 12,3,7 .)
   (. 3,12 .)  <>   (. 3,7,12 .)
   (. 3,12 .)  <=   (. 3,7,12 .)
(. 3,7,12 .)   >=   (. 7,12 .)
```

Notice that the ordering of the objects in the set is not important.

10.2.4 Set Membership

It is possible to determine if an object is an object in a SET. The Pascal reserved word IN is used to test SET membership. The expression

```
<object> IN <set name>
```

has a TRUE value if the object is in the SET and FALSE if it is not. For example,

```
'B' IN (.'Z','G','B','K'.)
```

results in a TRUE value, while

```
'F' IN (.'Z','G','B','K'.)
```

results in a FALSE value. Just as other tests resulting in a TRUE or FALSE value, IN can be used in a decision structure. For example,

```
READ(GRADEAWARDED);
IF GRADEAWARDED IN PASSCOURSE
    THEN WRITELN('PASSES THE COURSE');
```

The following illustrates the use of IN. The program reads in characters and counts how many are vowels and how many are consonants.

Example: LETTERS

Read in character data until all available data have been read. Print the characters as they are read. Count the characters that are vowels and the characters that are consonants. Ignore any characters that are not vowels or consonants.

count vowels and consonants
1   define variables
   1.1   specify alphabet as a TYPE
   1.2   declare variables
2   initialize
   2.1   set count of vowels read so far to zero
   2.2   set count of consonants read so far to zero
   2.3   print titles
   2.4   specify set of vowels
   2.5   specify set of consonants
3   repeat reading characters until all characters have been read
   3.1   try to read a character
   3.2   if a character was read
      3.2.1   then begin processing the character
         3.2.1.1   print the character
         3.2.1.2   if character in set of vowels
            3.2.1.2.1   then add to count of vowels found
         3.2.1.3   if character in set of consonants
            3.2.1.3.1   then add to count of consonants found
4   report results
   4.1   print last title line
   4.2   print count of vowels found
   4.3   print count of consonants found
5   end of problem

The following Pascal program LETTERS follows this plan.

```
PROGRAM LETTERS(INPUT,OUTPUT);
    (* THIS PROGRAM READS CHARACTER INPUT UNTIL ALL THE AVAILABLE DATA
       HAVE BEEN READ.  THE INPUT IS ECHO PRINTED.  INPUT CHARACTERS
       BELONGING TO THE ALPHABET ARE COUNTED AS BEING EITHER VOWELS OR
       CONSONANTS.  AFTER ALL THE DATA HAVE BEEN READ, THE VOWEL AND
       CONSONANT COUNTS ARE PRINTED.                                 *)

TYPE
    ALPHABET = 'A'..'Z';
    LETTERS = SET OF ALPHABET;
VAR
    CHARACTER: CHAR;
    VOWELCOUNT: INTEGER;
    CONSONANTCOUNT: INTEGER;
    VOWELS: LETTERS;
    CONSONANTS: LETTERS;
BEGIN  (* COUNTING VOWELS AND CONSONANTS *)
    (* INITIALIZE VARIABLES *)
    VOWELCOUNT := O;  (* COUNT OF ALL VOWELS FOUND *)
    CONSONANTCOUNT := O;  (* COUNT OF ALL CONSONANTS FOUND *)
    VOWELS := (. 'A','E','I','O','U','Y' .);  (* SET OF VOWELS *)
    (* THE SET OF CONSONANTS IS DEFINED BELOW *)
    CONSONANTS:=(. 'B'..'D','F'..'H','J'..'N','P'..'T','V'..'X','Z' .);
    (* ALL DATA INITIALIZED *)
    WRITELN('CHARACTERS READ:');  (* ECHO PRINT TITLE *)
    WRITELN('----------------');
    REPEAT  (* READING IN CHARACTERS *)
        READ(CHARACTER);  (* CHARACTER IS A LETTER IF PART OF ALPHABET *)
        IF NOT EOF  (* TEST TO SEE IF A READ HAPPENED *)
            THEN BEGIN  (* SEEING IF A VOWEL OR CONSONANT *)
                WRITE(CHARACTER);  (* ECHO PRINT INPUT CHARACTER *)
                IF CHARACTER IN VOWELS  (* ADD TO VOWEL COUNT IF IN SET *)
                    THEN VOWELCOUNT := VOWELCOUNT + 1;
                IF CHARACTER IN CONSONANTS  (* ADD TO CONSONANT COUNT *)
                    THEN CONSONANTCOUNT := CONSONANTCOUNT + 1
                    (* IF CHARACTER READ IS NOT EITHER A VOWEL OR CONSONANT, IT
                       IS NOT COUNTED AS IT IS NOT PART OF THE ALPHABET *)
            END  (* SEEING IF LETTER A VOWEL OR CONSONANT *)
    UNTIL EOF;
    WRITELN;
    WRITELN('----------------');
    WRITELN('COUNT OF THE VOWELS FOUND IS:------- ',VOWELCOUNT:3);
    WRITELN('COUNT OF THE CONSONANTS FOUND IS:--- ',CONSONANTCOUNT:3)
END.  (* COUNTING VOWELS AND CONSONANTS *)
```

If the input data to this program is

```
ABE ORDERED: APPLES,
ORANGES,
AND PEACHES.
```

the resulting output will be

```
CHARACTERS READ:
-----------------
ABE ORDERED: APPLES, ORANGES, AND PEACHES.
-----------------
COUNT OF THE VOWELS FOUND IS:-------  14
COUNT OF THE CONSONANTS FOUND IS:---  19
```

10.3 QUESTIONS

10.1   What is the difference between a static and a dynamic data TYPE?

10.2   What are the differences between a programmer defined data TYPE and a Standard Pascal defined data TYPE?

10.3   List the different kinds of restrictions that a programmer might place on a data TYPE.

10.4   Differentiate between enumerating data values and specifying a range of values.

10.5   What is a set?

10.6   Collect the following data into the minimum number of sets necessary to hold all the data.

5   6   7.3   A   B   6   2.07   C   5   F   8.3

10.4 PROBLEMS

10.1.   Jacques Aubert is the owner of the Tropette Swimsuit Shop. In order to serve his customers better, he needs to be aware of the colors they prefer. Acting upon his instructions, his sales force recorded the colors of the suits sold. The colors that Jacques has for sale are red (R), blue (B), green (G), violet (V), purple (P), and white (W).

You are to design and write a Pascal program to prepare a report for Jacques listing how many suits of each color he sold. Use an enumerated data TYPE to represent suit color. Test your program on the following data.

WRGWBVGRGBWGVPVVPGGRRBBBG

10.2.   Jacques, the Tropette Swimsuit Shop owner, had a program written to help him count how many suits of each color were sold. The program worked admirably. However, after awhile his sales staff became sloppy when writing down the colors. Sometimes they would write a letter for a color that Jacques did not sell. When the program found one of the invalid letters, it stopped running as it did not know what to do. He decided to have the program rewritten to "edit check" the data. Your task is to expand Problem 10.1 to include a validity check of the swimsuit color. Do this by placing all the valid colors into a set. Then input a candidate color into an unrestricted character variable. If the color is in the set of valid colors, assign it to the variable representing swimsuit color and proceed as specified in Problem 10.1. Otherwise display a message indicating that an invalid color was input, display the invalid color, and continue processing. Test your program on the following data.

WSGWBQGRHBWFVPWPGGRSBBYG

10.3. Annette Baskur is in charge of the Flab Fighters Farm. Her task is to record and summarize the weights of incoming customers. She knows that the most that a customer can weight is 349 pounds and the least is 100 pounds. Your task is to help her by writing a program to count how many customers arrive and to calculate their average weight. Use a variable with a restricted range to record weights. Test your program on the following data.

     101   148   137   196   229   184   162   302   124   117   123   173   119   155

10.4. Because of the high cost of using police cars to patrol the highways, the highway police department has implemented a policy of selectively patrolling only the "high-speed" sections of the highway system. Periodically a police helicopter is flown to a variety of speed check points. At each check point, a police officer randomly selects automobiles and finds the speed of each by using radar. The collection of automobile speeds is used to provide an estimate of the average speed of automobiles traveling on that particular stretch of the highway system. By comparing the results from different sections of highway, the police are able to select the sections that it would be most profitable for them to patrol. Police cars are dispatched to the most profitable sections. Later the sampling process is repeated and dispatching assignments are altered in accordance with the new data.

   Shown below is data from a sample of automobile speeds observed at a particular check point. Develop an estimate of the average speed of automobiles using this stretch of highway by calculating the average speed for these automobiles.

automobile	speed
1	56
2	57
3	54
4	49
5	62
6	68
7	62
8	58
9	55
10	53
11	60
12	65
13	78
14	46

   As you know that your radar unit cannot register speeds outside of the range 0–120, restrict the range of the variable that you use to represent sampled speed.

10.5. Suppose you have a set of class grades (i.e., integer numbers from 0 to 100, inclusive). You would like to make a list of these numbers and also do some calculations on them, but want to avoid having to do any manual calculations.

   Write a program that lists the grades, leaves a space, and then displays

(a) The number of grades in the list.

(b) The average grade.

(c) The number of students who passed and failed (assume that a grade of 60 is required to pass).

Your program should work for any number of grades. Test your program on the following data.

$$78 \quad 100 \quad 29 \quad 72 \quad 69 \quad 95 \quad 84 \quad 86 \quad 50 \quad 94$$

As you know that the range for a grade is from 0 to 100, restrict the range of the variable used to represent an individual student's grade.

10.6. The Aladdin Market Research Company wishes to form a list of prices that are charged for items in the Mighty Mite Market food store chain. The researchers are not concerned with how often a particular price is charged; they only want a list of the prices that are charged. For example, assuming that they found the prices

$$1.98 \quad 9.42 \quad 6.45$$

you are to solve this problem by reading in the data and constructing a SET of the prices that were charged. After all the data has been input, display the values in the set. Test your program with the following data.

$$1.98 \quad 9.42 \quad 6.42 \quad 9.98 \quad 9.98 \quad 1.98 \quad 5.59 \quad 1.98 \quad 9.98 \quad 1.98 \quad 0.98 \quad 1.98$$

Chapter 11

STRUCTURED DATA TYPES

Objectives
The variable TYPEs examined so far have all been simple. Simple data types have only a single component. Data structures also may be made up of more than one component. These are known as *structured TYPEs*.

There are three different structured data TYPEs: static, files, and dynamic. Static structures include ARRAYs and RECORDs, and these are discussed in this chapter. The other structured data TYPEs are FILEs and *dynamic data structures* (which include pointers and linked lists). These last two topics are discussed in later chapters.

11.1 ARRAYS

Objectives
Describe the usefulness of storing values in arrays and present how Pascal can be used.

Suggested Background
The Pascal core chapters, 3, 4, and 5.

Some problems require the storage of lists of data values of the same type. For example, it may be useful to store the list of prices that were paid on a shopping trip. In some areas of problem solving, such a list of stored items is often called a *vector*. Other problems might require that data be stored in a table. For example, a table might be developed to show the temperatures during the week for every hour in the week for every day in the week. In some areas of problem solving, such a table is called a *matrix*. A single list of data values or a vector can be thought of as a table or matrix with only one column of data. Another name for tables or matrices is *array*. Pascal uses the name ARRAY for data stored in this way.

ARRAYs are used to contain collections of variables of the same TYPE. For example, an array could be used to contain a single column of data values representing a day's temperatures:

temperature

```
46        <=== first hour
47        <=== second hour
49        <=== third hour
53        <=== fourth hour
          .
          .
          .
```

In referring to the temperatures in a list or a table, it is usually most convenient to use a *subscript* to identify which temperature is under consideration. Subscripts are used in many mathematical formulas, and are written a little below the rest of the symbols on the line. (Superscripts, which are written a little above the line, are also sometimes used in formulas.) However, in a programming language statement, all the characters in the statement must be on the same line. The subscripts in Pascal statements are placed in brackets. The brackets are used to separate the subscript from the rest of the variable name. Thus, in the table above,

```
TEMPERATURE(.1.) is 46
TEMPERATURE(.2.) is 47
TEMPERATURE(.3.) is 49
TEMPERATURE(.4.) is 53
```

Subscript values are also known as *index* values.

Other collections of data require tables with both rows and columns. For example, if several students were to take more than one test, a table would be required to store the results. For example,

	test 1	test 2	test 3
student 1	64	67	65
student 2	92	91	93
student 3	84	89	100
student 4	99	88	94
student 5	100	97	96

In this example, subscripts are again useful to identify which number in the table is under consideration. As the table has two dimensions (student number and test number), a subscript must have two values to identify a particular element of the table. In this table, for example, TEST (.1,3.) has the value of 65.

11.1.1 Single Dimension Arrays

Objectives
Discuss the need for ARRAYs having only a single row or column of data values and specify how Pascal can be used to handle them.

Suggested Background
The sections on IF-THEN-ELSE, FOR, and the previous material in this chapter.

Tables or ARRAYs of a single column (or row) are a little simpler to talk about than tables or ARRAYs that have more than one dimension, such as an ARRAY with both columns and rows. In principle, all ARRAYs are defined and treated in the same way. However, in order to introduce the concepts involved, this book discusses the simpler single dimensioned ARRAY in this section and multiply dimensioned ARRAYs in the next section.

Just as for other programmer defined data types, the ARRAY structure can be defined in the TYPE declaration. The definition of an ARRAY structure requires the definition of both the ARRAY structure and the range of index values that will be used. Index values are used to identify which element of the ARRAY is under consideration. For example, if rainfall data are being stored for days 215 through 304, for instance, the range of index values that would be needed to store the data would be 215 to 304. For example,

index value	total rainfall for the day
215	0.00
216	0.06
217	3.62
.	.
.	.
.	.
304	1.62

The base TYPE of the array must be defined. The base TYPE may be either a standard scalar TYPE such as INTEGER, or it may be a programmer defined base TYPE. The form of the array declaration is

```
TYPE
    <programmer defined base type> = <first value>..<last value>;
    <index range> = <first value>..<last value>;
    <array structure> = ARRAY(. <index range> .) OF <base type>;
VAR
    <array name>: <array structure>;
```

For example, a table to store temperatures recorded during the morning hours of 1 to 12 could be defined as

```
TYPE
    MORNINGHOURS = 1..12;
    FREQUENCY = MORNINGHOURS;
    TABLE = ARRAY(.FREQUENCY.) OF REAL;
VAR
    TEMPERATURES: TABLE;
```

The ARRAY structure could be reduced to

```
VAR
    TEMPERATURES: ARRAY(. 1..12 .) OF REAL;
```

In either case, the second temperature is known to Pascal as

```
TEMPERATURES(. 2 .)
```

It is also possible to refer to a given ARRAY element by the use of a variable. For example, if the following declaration is made:

```
TYPE
    MORNINGHOURS = 1..12;
    FREQUENCY = MORNINGHOURS;
    TABLE = ARRAY(. FREQUENCY .);
VAR
    TEMPERATURES: TABLE;
    HOUR: MORNINGHOURS;
```

then if

```
HOUR := 2;
```

the ARRAY reference

```
TEMPERATURES(. HOUR .)
```

would also refer to the second temperature—i.e., 47. Notice that a programmer defined TYPE was used to restrict the values that could be assigned to HOUR.

Example: TEMPERATURE

(1) Read in and store a list of 12 temperatures, (2) calculate their average temperature, (3) display a list of all the temperatures higher than the average temperature, and (4) display a list of all the temperatures at or below the average temperature.

store and group temperature
1   define variables and initialize data
    1.1   define programmer defined data TYPEs
    1.2   define temperature array
    1.3   define simple variables
2   try to read and store 12 temperatures
    2.1   read a temperature
    2.2   write a temperature just read
    2.3   store temperature just read and written
3   if 12 temperatures were read in
    3.1   if 12 temperatures were not read, print an error message
    3.2   if 12 temperatures were read, begin calculations
        3.2.1   calculate average temperature
            3.2.1.1   set total of all temperatures read so far to zero
            3.2.1.2   for hours from 1 to 12,
                3.2.1.2.1   add the temperature for this hour to the total of all temperatures
            3.2.1.3   calculate the average temperature
        3.2.2   display the temperatures higher than the average temperature
            3.2.2.1   print titles
            3.2.2.2   for the morning hours from 1 to 12
                3.2.2.2.1   if the temperature is higher than average, then print the hour and the temperature
        3.2.3   display temperatures at or lower than average temperature
            3.2.3.1   print titles
            3.2.3.2   for the morning hours from 1 to 12
                3.2.3.2.1   if the temperature is at or lower than average, then print hour and temperature
4   end of problem

The program named TEMPERATURES uses this plan.

```
PROGRAM TEMPERATURES(INPUT,OUTPUT);
    (* CALCULATE AVERAGE TEMPERATURE AND THEN DISPLAY SEPARATE LISTS OF
       TEMPERATURES ABOVE AND BELOW THE AVERAGE FOR THE MORNING HOURS *)
TYPE
    MORNINGHOURS = 1..12;
    FREQUENCY = MORNINGHOURS;
    LIST = ARRAY(. FREQUENCY .) OF REAL;
VAR
    INCOMINGTEMPERATURE,TOTALTEMPERATURE,AVERAGETEMPERATURE: REAL;
    TEMPERATURE: LIST;
    HOUR: MORNINGHOURS;
    COUNT: INTEGER;
BEGIN  (* PROCESSING TEMPERATURES *)
    COUNT := 0;  (* COUNT OF ALL TEMPERATURES READ IN SO FAR. *)
    WRITELN('TEMPERATURE');  (* TITLE FOR ECHO PRINT *)
    WRITELN('-----------');
    (* TRY TO INPUT TEMPERATURES WHILE LESS THAN A MORNING'S WORTH *)
    WHILE ( (NOT EOF) AND (COUNT < 12) ) DO BEGIN
        READ(INCOMINGTEMPERATURE);   (* TRY TO READ A TEMPERATURE *)
      IF NOT EOF  (* IF AN INCOMING TEMPERATURE WAS READ, PROCESS IT *)
          THEN BEGIN  (* INSERTING TEMPERATURE INTO STORAGE ARRAY *)
              WRITELN(INCOMINGTEMPERATURE:8:1);  (* ECHO PRINT *)
              COUNT := COUNT + 1;  (* ADD TO COUNT OF TEMPERATURES *)
              TEMPERATURE(. COUNT .) := INCOMINGTEMPERATURE  (* STORE *)
          END  (* INSERTING TEMPERATURE INTO STORAGE ARRAY *)
    END;  (* TRYING TO READ AND STORE 12 TEMPERATURES *)
    IF COUNT < 12  (* SEE IF A MORNING'S WORTH HAS BEEN INPUT *)
        THEN WRITELN('****** ERROR: 12 TEMPERATURES WERE NOT AVAILABLE')
        ELSE BEGIN  (* CALCULATIONS FOR 12 TEMPERATURES *)
          (* CALCULATE AVERAGE TEMPERATURE *)
          TOTALTEMPERATURE := 0;
          FOR HOUR := 1 TO 12 DO  (* ADD UP TEMPERATURES *)
              TOTALTEMPERATURE := TOTALTEMPERATURE + TEMPERATURE(.HOUR.);
          AVERAGETEMPERATURE := TOTALTEMPERATURE / 12;
          WRITELN;  (* INSERT A BLANK OUTPUT LINE *)
          WRITELN('TEMPERATURES ABOVE AVERAGE TEMPERATURE OF ',
                  AVERAGETEMPERATURE:4:1);
          (* LIST THE TEMPERATURES ABOVE THE AVERAGE TEMPERATURE *)
          WRITELN('----------------------------------------------');
          WRITELN('HOUR   TEMPERATURE');
          WRITELN('----   -----------');
          FOR HOUR := 1 TO 12 DO
              IF TEMPERATURE(. HOUR .) > AVERAGETEMPERATURE
                  THEN WRITELN(HOUR:3,TEMPERATURE(.HOUR.):12:1);
          (* LIST TEMPERATURES AT OR BELOW AVERAGE TEMPERATURE *)
          WRITELN;  (* INSERT A BLANK OUTPUT LINE *)
          WRITELN('TEMPERATURES AT OR BELOW AVERAGE TEMPERATURE OF ',
                  AVERAGETEMPERATURE:4:1);
          WRITELN('------------------------------------------------------'
          WRITELN('HOUR   TEMPERATURE');
          WRITELN('----   -----------');
          FOR HOUR := 1 TO 12 DO
              IF TEMPERATURE(. HOUR .) <= AVERAGETEMPERATURE
                  THEN WRITELN(HOUR:3,TEMPERATURE(.HOUR.):12:1)
    END  (* CALCULATIONS FOR 12 TEMPERATURES *)
END.  (* TEMPERATURES *)
```

If the input test data for this program are:	Then the results will be:

```
                              TEMPERATURE
                              -----------
        23.4                     23.4
        25.5                     25.5
        24.6                     24.6
        26.6                     26.6
        27.8                     27.8
        27.8                     27.8
        28.1                     28.1
        28.4                     28.4
        29.3                     29.3
        29.8                     29.8
        30.1                     30.1
        30.0                     30.0
        30.2
        30.4          TEMPERATURES ABOVE AVERAGE TEMPERATURE OF 27.6
        31.2          ----------------------------------------------
        31.3          HOUR    TEMPERATURE
        31.1          ----    -----------
          .              5        27.8
          .              6        27.8
          .              7        28.1
                         8        28.4
                         9        29.3
                        10        29.8
                        11        30.1
                        12        30.0

              TEMPERATURES AT OR BELOW AVERAGE TEMPERATURE OF 27.6
              -----------------------------------------------------

              HOUR    TEMPERATURE
              ----    -----------
                1        23.4
                2        25.5
                3        24.6
                4        26.6
```

Notice that only the 12 temperatures were read in, because only 12 were asked for. Because of this, any data after the first 12 temperatures will not be used.

Many problems that are solved with the aid of a computer handle more than one input data item. Sometimes the count of exactly how many items are to be input is unknown, or the count is expected to vary from time to time. Good programs are designed to handle a variable amount of input data, even if it is believed that the exact count of the input data will always be correctly known.

When the count of how many data items is to be read into an ARRAY is uncertain, it is necessary to make sure to construct an ARRAY large enough to hold any anticipated count of input data items. Generally the ARRAY should be defined to be considerably larger than any expected count of input items. At the same time, it is also a good idea to check to make sure that the actual count does not exceed the maximum expected count.

This process is illustrated in the following example program named PRICES, which reads and stores up to 300 input prices. As the question of interest is how to store a variable count of data items into an ARRAY, a stub has been included to replace whatever other processing the program might be asked to do. Stubs are a useful part of the program development process as they allow a programmer to develop a program in stages.

```
PROGRAM PRICES(INPUT,OUTPUT);
    (* THIS RECORDS PRICES OF GOOD FROM A GROCERY STORE. THIS PROGRAM IS
        INCOMPLETE AS WHAT THE RECORDED PRICES ARE USED FOR NOT SHOWN *)
CONST
    MAXIMUM = 300;  (* MAXIMUM NUMBER OF PRICES THAT CAN BE STORED *)
TYPE
    COUNT = O..MAXIMUM;
    INDEX = COUNT;
    PRICELIST = ARRAY(.INDEX.) OF REAL;
VAR
    PRICECOUNT: COUNT;
    PRICE: PRICELIST;
    INPUTPRICE: REAL;
BEGIN  (* TO READ AND STORE PRICES *)
    PRICECOUNT := O;  (* INITIALIZE COUNT OF PRICES SO FAR TO ZERO *)
    WHILE (NOT EOF) AND (PRICECOUNT < MAXIMUM) DO BEGIN  (* TRY INPUT *)
        READ(INPUTPRICE);  (* TRY TO READ A PRICE WHILE STORAGE SPACE *)
        IF NOT EOF  (* IF A NEW PRICE WAS INPUT, PROCESS IT *)
            THEN BEGIN  (* PROCESS A NEW PRICE *)
                PRICECOUNT := PRICECOUNT + 1;  (* ADD ONE TO PRICE COUNT *)
                WRITELN(INPUTPRICE:6:2);  (* EDCO PRINT PRICE JUST INPUT *)
                PRICE(.PRICECOUNT.) := INPUTPRICE  (* STORE PRICE *)
            END;  (* PROCESSING AN INPUT PRICE *)
        IF PRICECOUNT = MAXIMUM
            THEN WRITELN('*** MAXIMUM ALLOWABLE COUNT OF PRICES FOUND')
        END;  (* TRYING TO INPUT PRICES *)
        WRITELN('COUNT OF PRICES INPUT WAS: ',PRICECOUNT:3);

(* +++++++++++++++++++++++++++++++++++++++++++++++++++++++++++++++++++++++++
    STUB: THE PART OF THE PROGRAM THAT IS TO PROCESS THE STORED PRICES
        GOES HERE
    +++++++++++++++++++++++++++++++++++++++++++++++++++++++++++++++++++++ *)
    WRITELN('STUB: THE PART OF THE PROGRAM TO PROCESS STORED PRICES')
END.
```

11.1.2 Data Directed Storage

> **Objectives**
> Discuss and illustrate how the value of the data can be used to specify
> where the data itself is to be stored in an ARRAY.
>
> **Suggested Background**
> The previous material in this chapter.

Sometimes, when data is stored in a computer, exactly where it is stored is specified by the value of the data itself. Doing this is known by a variety of names, including *data directed storage*. Using the value of the data itself to locate where data has been or is to be stored is an important technique.

How this can work may be seen from the following example. Suppose that a real estate office has six agents and wants to keep track of the value of the total sales of each. Further suppose that the agents are numbered from 1 to 6. One way of doing this is to have a separate variable for the total sales for each agent: that is, TOTALSALESAGENT1, TOTALSALESAGENT2, etc. This may be satisfactory when there are only one or two agents, but it gets progressively worse as the number of agents increases because separate instructions must be developed for each agent. However, an ARRAY can enable the creation of a single set of computation statements that can be used for all agents. This has several advantages: there are fewer lines of programming to write, it is more flexible, and there will be fewer opportunities to make mistakes.

Initially a single dimensioned ARRAY of six elements (one for each agent) can be set to zero to represent the total sales (as in Figure 11.1(a)). The first ARRAY element will be used to store the total sales for the first agent, the second ARRAY element will be used to store the total sales for the second agent, etc.

Then, if the first sale for the month was by agent 3 and it was for $76432.12, the resulting values in the ARRAY will be as shown in Figure 11.1(b). The input data could be represented as

```
3   76432.12
```

If the next sale was by agent 5 and was for $32000.00, the results could be as shown in Figure 11.1(c). If the last sale was also accomplished by agent 5 and was for $42384.98, the resulting ARRAY could be as shown in Figure 11.1(d).

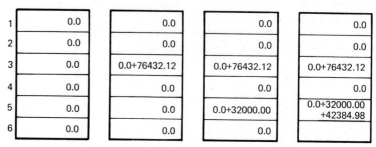

Figure 11.1 Using the input data to direct how and where data is to be summed in an ARRAY. (a) Initialized to zero. (b) Result of agent 3 having a sale of 76432.12. (c) Result of agent 5 having a sale of 32000.00. (d) Result of agent 5 having an additional sale of 42384.98.

The following plan is for the program SALES, which will do this.

record real estate sales
1   define variables
   1.1   CONSTANTS
   1.2   user defined TYPE
   1.3   VARIABLES
2   initialize record of total sales to zero
3   while there may be sales data, try to process it
   3.1   try to read an agent number for a sale
   3.2   if an agent number was input, then record sales data
      3.2.1   read value of the sale
      3.2.2   add value of the sale to the total of agent's sales
4   report total sales greater than 0 for each agent
   4.1   display titles
   4.2   for all possible agent numbers
      4.2.1   if an agent had some sales
         4.2.1.1   then display agent number, total sales for agent
5   end of problem

The following program named SALES follows this plan.

```
PROGRAM SALES(INPUT,OUTPUT);
   (* THIS RECORDS SALES FOR A REAL ESTATE COMPANY. SALES ARE RECORDED
      INDIVIDUALLY BY AGENT NUMBER. *)
CONST
   HIGHESTAGENT = 6;
TYPE
   AGENTNUMBER = 1..HIGHESTAGENT;
   RANGE = AGENTNUMBER;
   SALESRECORD = ARRAY(.RANGE.) OF REAL;
VAR
   TOTALSALES: SALESRECORD;
   AGENT: AGENTNUMBER;
   SALESVALUE: REAL;
BEGIN  (* RECORDING SALES *)
   (* INITIALIZE TOTAL SALES FOR EACH AGENT TO ZERO *)
   FOR AGENT := 1 TO HIGHESTAGENT DO
      TOTALSALES(.AGENT.) := 0.0;
   WHILE NOT EOF DO BEGIN  (* PROCESS ANY AVAILABLE REPORTED SALES *)
      READ(AGENT);  (* TRY TO INPUT THE NUMBER OF AN AGENT *)
      IF NOT EOF  (* IF A AGENT NUMBER FOUND, READ VALUE OF SALE *)
         THEN BEGIN  (* PROCESS SALES DATA *)
            READ(SALESVALUE);  (* VALUE OF THE SALE *)
            (* ADD TO TOTAL SALES FOR THIS AGENT *)
            TOTALSALES(.AGENT.) := TOTALSALES(.AGENT.) + SALESVALUE
         END  (* PROCESSING AN INDIVIDUAL SALE REPORT *)
   END;  (* PROCESSING REPORTED SALES *)
   WRITELN('SUMMARY OF ALL SALES FOR AGENTS SELLING SOMETHING');
   WRITELN('-------------------------------------------------');
   WRITELN('AGENT NUMBER   TOTAL SALES');
   WRITELN('------------   -----------');
   FOR AGENT := 1 TO HIGHESTAGENT DO
      IF TOTALSALES(.AGENT.) > O  (* IF AN AGENT HAD SALES, REPORT *)
         THEN WRITELN(AGENT:7,TOTALSALES(.AGENT.):19:2)  (* TOTAL *)
END.  (* SALES *)
```

If the data for this program are

```
3    76432.12
5    32000.00
5    42384.98
2    52684.00
5    12321.23
2    31005.50
```

the results will be

```
SUMMARY OF ALL SALES FOR AGENTS SELLING SOMETHING
-------------------------------------------------
AGENT NUMBER    TOTAL SALES
------------    -----------
      2          83653.50
      3          76432.12
      5          86707.21
```

11.1.3 Multiple-Dimension Arrays

Objectives
Discuss the usefulness of ARRAYs with multiple dimensions and show how Pascal can be used to manipulate them.

Suggested Background
The sections on IF-THEN-ELSE, FOR, and the previous material in this chapter.

Problem solutions often require the construction of tables with more than one column or more than one row. For example, if three test scores were to be recorded for five students, a table could be used to store the values as follows:

	test 1	test 2	test 3
student 1	64	67	65
student 2	92	91	93
student 3	84	89	100
student 4	99	88	94
student 5	100	97	96

Pascal can have ARRAYs with many different dimensions. The previous table requires a two dimensional array. Other problems may require three, four, five, or more dimensions. The Pascal standard does not specify a maximum number of dimensions that an ARRAY can have.

One form of a multiple dimension ARRAY is an extension of the form of a single dimension ARRAY. It is

```
TYPE
    <programmer defined base type> = <first value>..<last value>;
    <index range 1> = <first value>..<last value>;
    <index range 2> = <first value>..<last value>;
        .
        .
        .
    <index range n> = <first value>..<last value>;
    <array structure name> =
        ARRAY(.<index range 1>,<index range 2>,...,<index range n>.)
        OF <base type>;
VAR
    <variable name>: <array structure name>;
```

Note that any ARRAY, even if it is of more than one dimension, can only contain values of one TYPE. It is not necessary to use programmer defined base TYPEs; the standard scalar TYPEs can be used.

An example of a two dimensional ARRAY is

```
TYPE
    GRADES = 0..100;
    STUDENT = 1..5;
    TEST = 1..3;
    TABLE = ARRAY(. STUDENT,TEST .) OF GRADES;
VAR
    RESULTS: TABLE;
```

This ARRAY is used in the following example.

Example: GRADING

Process student test scores by (1) reading in three test scores for an unknown number of students, (2) calculating the average test score for each student, and (3) calculating the average score for all students for each test. The number of students is assumed to be between 0 and 250.

display test grades
1   define and initialize data
    1.1   define data value ranges
    1.2   specify programmer defined data TYPEs
    1.3   define simple variables
    1.4   initialize count of students found so far
2   while there still may be test score values to be read
    2.1   if test scores were read, count the students, print the scores, calculate the students' average for the tests
        2.2.1   add to the count of students
        2.2.2   print the test scores just read
        2.2.3   total the test scores
        2.2.4   calculate and print the student's average
3   calculate and print average for each test
    3.1   for each test
        3.1.1   set total of scores for this test to zero
        3.1.2   for each student
            3.1.2.1   add to the total of scores for this test
        3.1.3   calculate the average for this test
        3.1.4   print the average
4   end of problem

The following program named GRADING uses this plan.

```
PROGRAM GRADING(INPUT,OUTPUT);
   (* THIS PROGRAM IS DESIGNED TO READ, STORE, AND DISPLAY TEST SCORES
      FOR UP TO 250 STUDENTS.                                         *)
TYPE
   GRADES = 0..100;
   STUDENTS = 0..250;
   TEST = 1..3;
   TABLE = ARRAY(. STUDENTS,TEST .) OF GRADES;
VAR
   RESULTS: TABLE;
   TOTALSTUDENT: INTEGER;
   TOTALSCORE: INTEGER;
   STUDENTCOUNT: STUDENTS;
   SCORE1: INTEGER;
   SCORE2: INTEGER;
   SCORE3: INTEGER;
   STUDENTAVERAGE: REAL;
   SCOREAVERAGE: REAL;
   STUDENTNUMBER: INTEGER;
   TESTNUMBER: INTEGER;
BEGIN  (* PROCESSING TEST SCORES *)
   STUDENTCOUNT := 0;  (* COUNT OF STUDENTS READ SO FAR *)
   WRITELN('=============================');  (* START TITLE LINES *)
   WRITELN('    ---TEST NUMBER---        ');
   WRITELN('    1      2      3    AVE');
   WRITELN('---------------------------');
   (* PROCESS STUDENT SCORES WHILE THERE IS SPACE IN THE TABLE AND
      THERE MAY STILL BE MORE SCORES TO BE READ                     *)
   WHILE ( (STUDENTCOUNT < 250) AND (NOT EOF) ) DO BEGIN
      READ(SCORE1,SCORE2,SCORE3);  (* TRY TO READ STUDENT SCORES *)
         IF NOT EOF  (* IF THREE SCORES WERE READ, PROCESS THEM *)
            THEN BEGIN  (* INSERT THEM INTO THE RESULTS TABLE *)
               STUDENTCOUNT := STUDENTCOUNT + 1;  (* COUNT STUDENTS *)
               WRITE(SCORE1:6,SCORE2:7,SCORE3:7);
               (* INSERT SCORES BELONGING TO A STUDENT INTO RESULTS *)
               RESULTS(. STUDENTCOUNT,1 .) := SCORE1;  (* 1ST SCORE *)
               RESULTS(. STUDENTCOUNT,2 .) := SCORE2;  (* 2ND SCORE *)
               RESULTS(. STUDENTCOUNT,3 .) := SCORE3;  (* 3RD SCORE *)
               TOTALSTUDENT := SCORE1 + SCORE2 + SCORE3;
               STUDENTAVERAGE := TOTALSTUDENT / 3.0;  (* AVERAGE *)
               WRITELN(STUDENTAVERAGE:7:2)
            END;  (* PLACING SCORES INTO RESULT TABLE *)
      READLN  (* MAKE SURE THAT NEXT READ STARTS ON A NEW LINE AND
                  DISCOVER IF THERE IS ANOTHER LINE TO BE READ      *)
   END;  (* READING UP TO 250 DIFFERENT STUDENT SCORES *)
   WRITELN('---------------------------');  (* AFTER ALL SCORES *)
   (* CALCULATE AVERAGE FOR ALL STUDENTS FOR EACH TEST *)
   FOR TESTNUMBER := 1 TO 3 DO BEGIN  (* DO ONE TEST AT A TIME *)
      TOTALSCORE := 0;  (* TOTAL OF ALL SCORES FOR THIS TEST *)
      FOR STUDENTNUMBER := 1 TO STUDENTCOUNT DO  (* EACH TEST SCORE *)
         TOTALSCORE := TOTALSCORE
                          + RESULTS(. STUDENTNUMBER,TESTNUMBER .);
      SCOREAVERAGE := TOTALSCORE / STUDENTCOUNT;
      WRITE(SCOREAVERAGE:7:2)
   END  (* CALCULATING THE AVERAGE FOR EACH TEST *)
END.  (* GRADING *)
```

If the data for this program are

```
 64   67   65
 92   91   93
 84   89  100
 99   88   94
100   97   96
```

the results will be

```
==============================
  ---TEST NUMBER---
    1      2      3    AVE
------------------------------
   64     67     65   65.33
   92     91     93   92.00
   84     89    100   91.00
   99     88     94   93.67
  100     97     96   97.67
------------------------------
 87.80  86.40  89.60
```

11.2 CHARACTER STRINGS

Objectives
Discuss what character strings are and how Pascal reads, stores, and writes them.

Suggested Background
The section on FOR.

The solution to many problems requires the handling of data consisting of one or more characters. These data are known as character *string* data. Some examples of character string data are a person's name, a street address, and a city name.

In Pascal character strings can be handled best by placing them into ARRAYs. Some implementations of Pascal require that CHAR ARRAYs be defined as PACK-ED. This is a more efficient use of space. Character strings stored in PACKED ARRAYs are also easier to manipulate. This is the form used in this text. For example, the declaration

```
TYPE
   SPELLING = PACKED ARRAY(. 1..20 .) OF CHAR;
VAR
   NAME: SPELLING;
```

provides for the storage of names of up to 20 characters in the variable NAME. The length of a character string is equal to the number of characters in the string. For example, the string 'APPLE' is five characters long (the apostrophe marks delimiting the string are not counted).

Character strings may be specified in an assignment statement. For example,

```
SPELLING := 'APPLE'
```

would result in Figure 11.2. Notice that the string is inserted starting at the leftmost available space of the string variable and that blanks are "padded" to the right. This is known as *left justification*.

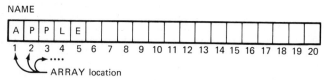

Figure 11.2   Storage of the character string 'APPLE' in the packed string array SPELLING.

The contents of a string variable may be simply written out by specifying the string variable in a WRITE or WRITELN statement. For example,

```
WRITELN(NAME)
```

would result in the entire contents of NAME being written. It is not as easy to read the characters into a string variable. Each character must be read separately. This often is done iteratively. This is illustrated by the following program fragment, which reads in and stores the letters of a name.

```
PROGRAM NAME(INPUT,OUTPUT);
TYPE
   SPELLING = PACKED ARRAY(. 1..20 .) OF CHAR;
VAR
   NAME: SPELLING;
   LETTER: INTEGER;
BEGIN
   FOR LETTER = 1 TO 20 DO BEGIN   (* INPUT LETTERS OF A NAME *)
      READ( NAME(. LETTER .) );
```

This fragment can be used effectively in a program that needs to read and store a person's name. Some implementations of Pascal do not allow direct reading or writing of PACKED structures. This can be handled by first reading an element of the CHAR string into a single CHAR variable and then assigning this variable into the ARRAY. For example,

```
PROGRAM NAME(INPUT,OUTPUT);
TYPE
   SPELLING = PACKED ARRAY(. 1..20 .) OF CHAR;
VAR
   NAME: SPELLING;
   NAMELETTER: CHAR;
   LETTER: INTEGER;
BEGIN
   FOR LETTER = 1 TO 20 DO BEGIN  (* INPUT LETTERS OF A NAME *)
      READ(NAMELETTER);
      NAME(. LETTER .) := NAMELETTER
   END;
```

This technique also has the advantage of having a more positive control of the input data flow. This makes debugging easier.

Example: WEIGHT
Read in a person's name, height, and weight. Echo print this data out and then calculate the person's weight per inch of height.

calculate a person's weight per inch of height
1   define data storage
    1.1   specify constant maximum name length
    1.2   specify array to store the characters of a name
    1.3   define variables
2   print titles
3   repeat reading data until there is no more data to be read
    3.1   try to read a height
    3.2   if a height was read
        3.2.1   then begin to process the rest of a person's data
            3.2.1.1   read weight
            3.2.1.2   read name
            3.2.1.3   try to find the start of another person's data
            3.2.1.4   print the information about current person
                3.2.1.4.1   print weight
                3.2.1.4.2   print height
                3.2.1.4.3   print name
                3.2.1.4.4   report weight per inch
                        3.2.1.4.4.1   calculate weight per inch
                        3.2.1.4.4.2   print weight per inch
4   end of job

The following program named WEIGHT, which uses this plan, is designed to handle data coming in from cards. The distinction between data coming in from cards as opposed to that from a terminal is important because if the input data lines were generated by a terminal, an additional or alternate control structure would have to be added to prevent execution errors from occurring when the input name had a length less than the maximum specified by NAMELENGTH. This could be done by replacing

```
FOR LETTER := 1 TO NAMELENGTH DO BEGIN
   READ(NAMELETTER);
   NAME(. LETTERNUMBER .) := NAMELETTER
END;
```

with the nested control structure of

```
FOR LETTER := 1 TO NAMELENGTH DO BEGIN
   IF NOT EOLN
      THEN BEGIN  (* INPUT LETTERS OF A NAME *)
         READ(NAMELETTER);
         NAME(. LETTERNUMBER .) := NAMELETTER
      END
END;
```

Or an alternate control structure doing its own counting could be used. For example,

```
LETTERNUMBER := O;
WHILE NOT EOLN DO BEGIN
   READ(NAMELETTER);
   IF NOT EOLN
      THEN BEGIN
         LETTERNUMBER := LETTERNUMBER + 1;
         NAME(.LETTERNUMBER.) := NAMELETTER
      END
END;
```

This problem only arises when a CHAR string of variable length is input and when this string is the last data to be input from a particular input line.

```
PROGRAM WEIGHT(INPUT,OUTPUT);
    (* THIS PROGRAM IS DESIGNED TO CALCULATE A PERSON'S
       WEIGHT PER INCH OF HEIGHT. IT DOES THIS BY:
       (A) READING IN A PERSON'S NAME, HEIGHT AND WEIGHT,
       (B) THE PROGRAM THEN ECHO PRINTS THIS DATA BACK OUT, AND
       (C) CALCULATES & PRINTS THE PERSONS WEIGHT PER INCH OF HEIGHT *)
CONST
    NAMELENGTH = 25;
TYPE
    LENGTH = O..NAMELENGTH;
    SPELL = PACKED ARRAY(.LENGTH.) OF CHAR;
VAR
    NAME: SPELL;
    NAMELETTER: CHAR;
    WEIGHT: INTEGER;
    HEIGHT: REAL;
    LETTERNUMBER: INTEGER;
    WEIGHTINCH: REAL;
BEGIN  (* CALCULATING WEIGHT PER INCH OF HEIGHT *)
    WRITELN('HEIGHT WEIGHT   NAME                     WEIGHT/INCH');
    WRITELN('-------------------------------------------------');
    REPEAT  (* UNTIL THERE IS NO MORE DATA TO BE READ *)
        READ(HEIGHT);
        IF NOT EOF  (* IF A HEIGHT WAS READ *)
            THEN BEGIN  (* TO READ THE REST OF A PERSON'S DATA *)
                READ(WEIGHT);
                FOR LETTERNUMBER := 1 TO NAMELENGTH DO BEGIN (* NAME IN *)
                    READ(NAMELETTER);
                    NAME(. LETTERNUMBER .) := NAMELETTER
                END;  (* READING IN A NAME *)
                READLN;  (* MAKE SURE THAT NEXT READ STARTS ON NEW LINE *)
                (* PRINT THE ORIGINAL INPUT *)
                WRITE(WEIGHT:4,HEIGHT:9:1,' ',NAME:NAMELENGTH);
                WEIGHTINCH := WEIGHT / HEIGHT;
                WRITELN(WEIGHTINCH:5:2)
            END;  (* PROCESSING A PERSON'S DATA *)
    UNTIL EOF;  (* READ ALL AVAILABLE DATA *)
END.  (* WEIGHT CALCULATIONS *)
```

If the input data are

```
72 183.8 THOMAS ZARDOK
62 109.5 SALLY ZUCKERMAN
54  98.4 RALPH SMITH
81 198.2 KAREN KAIN
51 105.6 BILLY MURPHY
```

then the results will be

```
HEIGHT WEIGHT  NAME                      WEIGHT/INCH
-----------------------------------------------------
    72   183.8  THOMAS ZARDOK                 0.39
    62   109.5  SALLY ZUCKERMAN               0.57
    54    98.4  RALPH SMITH                   0.55
    81   198.2  KAREN KAIN                    0.41
    51   105.6  BILLY MURPHY                  0.48
```

String variables can be compared. For example, if the TYPE and VAR definitions were

```
TYPE
    STRING: PACKED ARRAY (. 1..20 .);
VAR
    NAME: STRING;
    DESCRIPTION: STRING;
```

the relational test of

```
IF NAME < DESCRIPTION
```

could be made. The string value that is considered to be less in value is the one that would come first if the two strings were sorted. As in a dictionary, the number of characters in the word does not determine which comes first. All of the following would result in a TRUE value.

```
    'A' < 'B'
'ABCD' < 'DA'
 'C5D' > 'C4ARF'
 'DOG' = 'DOG'
'MORK' <= 'MINDY'
 'GRE' <> 'GMAT'
```

11.3 RECORDS

Objectives
Discuss why it may be useful to group data elements of different TYPEs together and illustrate how Pascal does this using RECORDS.

Suggested Background
The sections on BEGIN-END and IF-THEN, the introductory material at the beginning of this chapter, Sections 11.1 and 11.1.1.

Many problems require the collection and storage of different TYPEs of data about the same thing. For example, if a company's payroll were to be calculated, it would be necessary to gather several different TYPEs of data about each person to be paid: name (CHAR), social security number (INTEGER), salary (REAL), etc. The data structure that is used to hold several different TYPEs of data is called a *record*. Records are collected together in *files*.

11.3.1 Defining Records

Objectives
Describe what a RECORD is in Pascal and demonstrate how Pascal defines one.

Suggested Background
Section 11.3.

Records are programmer defined structured variables that may have more than one component. The components may be of different TYPEs. For example, if it is desirable to record information about corn being delivered to a food store, we might want to record the corn's colour (yellow or white), the number of ears, and the price per ear. These data values can be recorded as CHAR, INTEGER, and REAL.

As is true for other programmer specified data TYPEs, the structure of the data TYPE is defined in the TYPE section. The form of the specification is

```
TYPE
   <record type name> =
     RECORD
        <element name>: <type>;
        <element name>: <type>;
          .
          .
          .
        <element name>: <type>
     END;
```

Notice that RECORD and END are Pascal delimiters. They serve to group the data elements in a way similar to the way statements are grouped by BEGIN-END. Any variables using a programmer defined RECORD TYPE are specified in the VAR section. The form of the declaration is

```
VAR
   <variable name>: <record type name>;
```

For example, the RECORD to handle corn deliveries could be defined as

```
TYPE
   DELIVERED =
      RECORD
         COLOUR: CHAR;
         NUMBER: INTEGER;
         PRICE: REAL
      END;
```

Variables using a programmer defined RECORD TYPE are defined in the VAR section. For example,

```
VAR
   CORN: DELIVERED:
```

defines a variable named CORN consisting of the elements: COLOUR, NUMBER, and PRICE. A data value stored in a RECORD is identified by the form:

```
<variable name>.<record element name>
```

For example,

```
CORN.NUMBER := 123;
READLN(CORN.COLOUR);
WRITE(CORN.PRICE);
```

are all examples of references to values in the RECORD of TYPE DELIVERED CORN. Some people use the term *field name* instead of record element name.

Record element names cannot be used by themselves; that is, without a reference to the variable name. The following are examples of references that are NOT allowed.

```
NUMBER := 123;
READLN(COLOUR);
WRITE(PRICE);
```

A shortcut method of supplying the variable name of a record is provided by the use of WITH. WITH can be used to create a block that allows the referencing of a record element without explicitly specifying the variable name. The form of a WITH statement is

```
WITH <variable name> DO BEGIN
   .
   .    reference can be made to element names without referencing
   .    the variable name
   .
END;
```

For example,

```
WITH CORN DO BEGIN  (* PROVIDING ATTACHMENT OF CORN VARIABLE NAME *)
    NUMBER := 123;
    READ(COLOUR);
    WRITE(PRICE)
END;  (* PROVIDING ATTACHMENT OF CORN VARIABLE NAME *)
```

As with any other data TYPE, records can be referenced by other user defined TYPE definitions, including other user defined records. This has the effect of creating a nested record definition. For example,

```
TYPE
    DATE =
        RECORD
            MONTH: PACKED ARRAY(1..8) OF CHAR;
            DAY: 1..31;
            YEAR: 1941..2000
        END;
    DELIVERED =
        RECORD
            COLOUR: CHAR;
            DAYDELIVERED: DATE;
            AMOUNT: INTEGER;
            PRICE: REAL
        END;
```

11.3.2 Files

Objectives
Discuss what a file is and describe how Pascal can be used to define and manipulate one.

Suggested Background
The introductory material at the beginning of this chapter and Sections 11.1, 11.1.1, and 11.3.1.

Records are usually gathered together into collections of records. A collection of records is usually called a *file*. A later chapter discusses how to use files that are stored on a disk. This chapter discusses the use of collections of RECORDs stored as an ARRAY. For example, a table of different TYPE data values about corn purchases could be as follows:

colour	corn delivered number	price
W	100	0.12
W	150	0.06
Y	25	0.07
W	83	0.08
Y	176	0.063
W	42	0.058

This data can be collected into an ARRAY of RECORDs. An ARRAY of RECORDs is equivalent to a file.

The specification for an ARRAY of RECORDS takes the form of

```
TYPE
   <record type name> =
      RECORD
         <element name>: <type>;
         <element name>: <type>;
                 .
                 .
                 .
         <element name>: <type>
      END;
VAR
   <file name>: ARRAY(. <lower index>..<upper index> .)
                OF <record type name>;
```

For example,

```
TYPE
   DELIVERED =
      RECORD
         COLOUR: CHAR;
         AMOUNT: INTEGER;
         PRICE: REAL
      END;
VAR
   CORN: ARRAY(. 1..100 .) OF DELIVERED;
```

Notice that the size of the CORN ARRAY is greater than the number of records presented in the CORN DELIVERED example table. This was done to allow for an increase in the volume of data stored. It is usually a good programming practice to allow for file growth.

Example: CORNDELIVERIES

Read and print a list of corn purchases. Calculate and print the total cost of each transaction, the average amount delivered, and the average amount paid for a piece.

record corn deliveries
1   define data storage
   1.1   specify range for count of deliveries
   1.2   specify delivery record
   1.3   specify variables
2   initialize
   2.1   set count of deliveries to zero
   2.2   set total cost so far to zero
   2.3   print titles
3   while there may be more data to process
   3.1   try to read data on a single corn delivery
      3.1.1   colour of corn delivered
      3.1.2   amount of corn delivered
      3.1.3   piece price of corn delivered
   3.2   if data was read
      3.2.1   then begin to process the data
         3.2.1.1   add to the count of deliveries that were made
         3.2.1.2   print the delivery data
            3.2.1.2.1   delivery count
            3.2.1.2.2   corn colour
            3.2.1.2.3   amount delivered
            3.2.1.2.4   price per piece
         3.2.1.3   store delivered data into a record
         3.2.1.4   calculate delivery cost
         3.2.1.5   print delivery cost
         3.2.1.6   add to total cost of deliveries so far
4   report summary results
   4.1   print last title line
   4.2   initialize summary data
      4.2.1   set total amount delivered to zero
      4.2.2   set total of piece price paid to zero
   4.3   for all the deliveries made
   4.4   calculate averages
      4.4.1   average amount of a delivery
      4.4.2   average piece price of a delivery
      4.4.3   average cost of a delivery
   4.5   print the averages
5   end of problem

The Pascal program CORNDELIVERIES of this plan follows.

```
PROGRAM CORNDELIVERIES(INPUT,OUTPUT);
TYPE
   NUMBERDELIVERIES = 1..100;
   DELIVERY =
      RECORD
         COLOUR: CHAR;
         AMOUNT: INTEGER;
         PIECEPRICE: REAL
      END;  (* END OF DELIVERY RECORD *)
   DELIVERED = ARRAY(. NUMBERDELIVERIES .) OF DELIVERY;
VAR
   CORN: DELIVERED;
   COLOURDELIVERED: CHAR;
   AMOUNTDELIVERED,TOTALAMOUNT,COUNTDELIVERIES: INTEGER;
   DELIVEREDPIECEPRICE,DELIVERYCOST: REAL;
   TOTALCOST,TOTALPIECEPRICE: REAL;
   AVERAGEAMOUNT,AVERAGEPRICE,AVERAGECOST: REAL;
   DELIVERYNUMBER: NUMBERDELIVERIES;
BEGIN  (* RECORDING CORN DELIVERIES *)
   COUNTDELIVERIES := O;  (* COUNT OF ALL DELIVERIES MADE SO FAR *)
   TOTALCOST := O;  (* TOTAL COST OF ALL DELIVERIES MADE SO FAR *)
   WRITELN('================================');  (* OUTPUT TITLES *)
   WRITELN('        ------CORN DELIVERIES-----');
   WRITELN('NUMBER  COLOUR AMOUNT PRICE   COST');
   WRITELN('--------------------------------');
   WHILE NOT EOF DO BEGIN  (* PROCESSING DELIVERY DATA *)
      READ(COLOURDELIVERED,AMOUNTDELIVERED,DELIVEREDPIECEPRICE);
      IF NOT EOF  (* IF THE THREE DATA ITEMS WERE READ *)
         THEN BEGIN  (* PROCESS THE DATA *)
            COUNTDELIVERIES:=COUNTDELIVERIES + 1; (* DELIVERY COUNT *)
            WRITE(COUNTDELIVERIES:4);  (* DELIVERY NUMBER *)
            WRITE(COLOURDELIVERED:7,AMOUNTDELIVERED:9,
                 DELIVEREDPIECEPRICE:7:3);  (* ECHO PRINT *)
            CORN(.COUNTDELIVERIES.).COLOUR := COLOURDELIVERED;
            CORN(.COUNTDELIVERIES.).AMOUNT := AMOUNTDELIVERED;
            CORN(.COUNTDELIVERIES.).PIECEPRICE := DELIVEREDPIECEPRICE;
            DELIVERYCOST := AMOUNTDELIVERED * DELIVEREDPIECEPRICE;
            WRITELN(DELIVERYCOST:7:2);
            TOTALCOST := TOTALCOST + DELIVERYCOST  (* COST SO FAR *)
         END;  (* PROCESSING DATA THAT WAS READ *)
      READLN  (* MAKE SURE THAT NEXT READ STARTS ON A NEW LINE *)
   END;  (* READING DELIVERY DATA *)
   WRITELN('---------------------------------');  (* END OF DETAIL *)
   TOTALAMOUNT := O;  (* TOTAL AMOUNT DELIVERED *)
   TOTALPIECEPRICE := O;  (* TOTAL OF THE TRANSACTION PIECE PRICES *)
   FOR DELIVERYNUMBER := 1 TO COUNTDELIVERIES DO BEGIN  (* TOTALS *)
      TOTALAMOUNT := TOTALAMOUNT + CORN(.DELIVERYNUMBER.).AMOUNT;
      TOTALPIECEPRICE := TOTALPIECEPRICE
                         + CORN(.DELIVERYNUMBER.).PIECEPRICE
   END;  (* CALCULATING OVER ALL TOTALS *)
   AVERAGEAMOUNT:=TOTALAMOUNT / COUNTDELIVERIES;  (* OVERALL AVERAGE *)
   AVERAGEPRICE:=TOTALPIECEPRICE / COUNTDELIVERIES;  (* OVERALL AVE *)
   AVERAGECOST := TOTALCOST / COUNTDELIVERIES;  (* OVERALL AVERAGE *)
   WRITELN('AVERAGE ......',AVERAGEAMOUNT:6:1,AVERAGEPRICE:7:3,
           AVERAGECOST:7:2)  (* PRINT OVER ALL AVERAGES *)
END.  (* CORN DELIVERIES *)
```

If the input data to this program is

```
W 100 0.12
W 150 0.06
Y  25 0.07
W  83 0.08
Y 176 0.063
W  42 0.058
```

then the results will be

```
=====================================
        ------CORN DELIVERIES-----
NUMBER  COLOUR AMOUNT PRICE   COST
-------------------------------------
   1      W     100  0.120  12.00
   2      W     150  0.060   9.00
   3      Y      25  0.070   1.75
   4      W      83  0.080   6.64
   5      Y     176  0.063  11.09
   6      W      42  0.058   2.44
-------------------------------------
AVERAGE ......   96.0  0.075   7.15
```

11.4 RECORD VARIANTS

Objectives
Describe and illustrate how Pascal provides for variably defined records. Record variants are not central to an understanding of Pascal and the topic may be bypassed without substantial loss.

Suggested Background
The sections on CASE and enumerated data types.

So far, all record variables of a predefined TYPE have had the same form and structure. However, it is possible to define record TYPEs that have some elements of the record that are the same for all variables of that TYPE and some elements that may be different. These are called record *variants*. The fixed part of the record that does not change is called the *fixed part* and the part that can change is called the *variant part*.

An example of why record variants might be useful is the case of a farmer keeping track of a variety of produce. For example, the farmer might want to keep track of bushels for corn, and for eggs to keep track of the count of large, medium, and small eggs.

A record variant is always specified with the fixed part first and the variant part last. The form of the specification of a record TYPE with a variant type is

```
<record name> =
   RECORD
      <element name>: <type>;
         .
         .
      <element name>: <type>;
      CASE <tag>: <tag type> OF
         <label>: (<element list>);
            .
            .
         <label>: (<element list>)
   END;
```

That which is grouped under CASE is the variant part. Tag represents the basis of recognizing the difference between the variants. For example, in the following declaration,

```
TYPE
   PRODUCE = (CORN,EGGS,MILK);
   CROPS =
      RECORD
         FARMNUMBER: INTEGER;
         GROSSINCOME: REAL;
         TAXES: REAL;
         CASE PRODUCT: PRODUCE OF
            CORN: (BUSHELS: INTEGER;
                    CORNPRICE: REAL);
            EGGS: (LARGE: INTEGER;
                    LARGEPRICE: REAL;
                    MEDIUM: INTEGER;
                    MEDIUMPRICE: REAL;
                    SMALL: INTEGER;
                    SMALLPRICE: REAL);
            MILK: (GALLONS: INTEGER;
                    MILKPRICE: REAL)
      END;
```

PRODUCT is the tag where the tag TYPE was previously defined as an enumerated TYPE with the values of CORN, EGGS, MILK. It should be noted that instead of CORN, EGGS, MILK, the tag TYPE could have been simply INTEGER with the various products referenced by an INTEGER code. Notice that the elements for each variant are grouped together by a pair of parentheses " (" ")".

Not all programmers agree that it is a good idea to use record variants. Some believe that it is simpler not to use them and simplicity in programming leads to the virtues of easier design and modification and greater readability. This book does not use record variants in other sections.

11.5 QUESTIONS

11.1 How does an ARRAY differ from Standard Pascal scalar data TYPEs?

11.2 In what way does the definition of an ARRAY designed to hold character strings differ from that of an ARRAY designed to hold numeric data?

11.3 In what way can the components of a RECORD differ from the components of an ARRAY?

11.4 Provide three examples where it would be useful to declare a record with a variant part.

11.5 Given the following program,

```
PROGRAM QUESTION(INPUT,OUTPUT);
TYPE
   SCORES = 1..165;
   PEOPLE = 0..200;
   REPORT = ARRAY(.PEOPLE.) OF SCORES;
VAR
   GOLF: REPORT;
   GOLFER: SCORES;
   PERSON: INTEGER;
   INDIVIDUAL: INTEGER;
   MAX: INTEGER;
BEGIN
   MAX := 165;
   PERSON := 0;
   WHILE NOT EOF DO BEGIN
      READ(GOLFER);
      IF NOT EOF THEN BEGIN
         PERSON := PERSON + 1;
         GOLF(.PERSON.) := GOLFER
      END
   END;
   FOR INDIVIDUAL := 1 TO PERSON DO BEGIN;
      IF GOLF(. INDIVIDUAL .) < MAX THEN BEGIN
         MAX := GOLF(. INDIVIDUAL .);
         WRITE( GOLF(.INDIVIDUAL.):4 )
      END
   END;
END.  (* QUESTION *)
```

if the incoming data is the following, what will be displayed as the results?

```
105 108 112
119  97  88 103
105  72  77  92
 69  81  75
 74  66
105
```

11.6 PROBLEMS

11.1. Fanny runs a Flab Fighters Farm For Females franchise. She wants to list her customers' weights according to their classifications: light, normal, heavy. The classification ranges are

> light: 0–100 pounds
> normal: 101–145 pounds
> heavy: over 145 pounds

You are to help Fanny by developing a program that will
(**a**) Input a list of her customers' weights, echo display each as it comes in, and then store each in an ARRAY.
(**b**) Display the three different lists of her customers: light, normal, and heavy.
(**c**) Calculate and display the average weight of all of her customers.
Test your program with the following data.

```
124   245   98   100   157   189   265   181   148   157   96   134   133
142   214   99   178   143   152   203   154   162   124   98   198   162
108   164   89   164   189   177   201   171   138   158   96   143   147
```

Your program should be able to handle up to 150 different customer weights. You should not count the number of weights that are to be input.

11.2. The Bank of Pamplona wishes to know the distribution of the size of its customers' accounts. It wants
(**a**) to know how many accounts are in a specified range and
(**b**) a list of all the accounts in a specific range.
The ranges are (in psetas)

> 0– 1000
> 1001– 10000
> 10001– 50000
> over 50000

Write a program to solve the bank's needs. Assume that the bank will never have more than 200 customers. Do not count how many items are to be input before running the program.
Test your program with the following data.

```
987   10099   23456   123   987   76543   783   2689   5000   6521   6899   56100
```

11.3. The Peach and Pear Grocery Store has five checkout lanes labeled lanes "1", "2", "3", "4", and "5". As a customer is input to checkout, the customer estimates the wait in each of the five lines and will join the line with the smallest time estimate. The length of time for a shopper to check out is estimated by looking for a quick approximation of the amount of groceries in the grocery basket. To do this, baskets can be placed into one of three classes:

S: a small number of items
H: about half full
F: full, or almost full

The time estimate for a basket for each class is

S: 2 minutes
H: 4 minutes
F: 5 minutes

Write a program that will input the following information for the customers waiting in
line.

The lane that the customer is in.
The approximate amount of groceries in the customer's basket.

Store all of the lane data in a two-dimensional ARRAY before doing any reporting or
calculating. Display the lane data and then identify the lane that a new customer should join to
get through checkout as quickly as possible. Accumulate the waiting time for each lane in a
single-dimension ARRAY.

Test your program with the following data. (You should have seven separate input data
records.)

```
---------- lane ---------
 1      2      3      4      5
===    ===    ===    ===    ===
 S      H      S      F      F
 F      H      F      S      H
 S      S      H      H      F
 F      F      F      H      S
 H      S      H      F      H
 H      H      S      H      F
 S      H      F      S      H
```

11.4.   Natasha is the manager of the Greater Mosul Bank. She is considering hiring a person
to come in part time. She would like to know what hour during the day is the busiest (most
customers in the bank) and what hour has the fewest customers. Ralph takes a survey for
Natasha of the number of customers in the bank and tabulates the following results.

work hour	number of customers
1st	33
2nd	82
3rd	125
4th	200
5th	250
6th	50
7th	113
8th	306
9th	158

Write a program that will input these results into an ARRAY and then search and display the ARRAY for the information desired.

11.5. The marketing department for Siege Widget Company has 10 salespersons. The yearly sales figures have been tabulated and are as follows:

salesperson number	sales for the year
1	$10,000
2	53,000
3	8,000
4	44,000
5	85,000
6	66,000
7	44,000
8	86,000
9	58,000
10	153,000

Write a program that will store the sales figures in an ARRAY and then display the data ranked by sales. Your results should have the form:

```
NUMBER     SALES
------     ------
  10      153000
   8       86000
   .          .
   .          .
   .          .
```

11.6. The management of the Flab Fighters Farm has asked Annette Baskur to improve their customer preference statistics. What they want is to know average customer weight when the customers arrive and average customer weight when they leave, as well as histograms displaying how many customers fall into each weight class upon arrival and upon departure.

The weight classes are 00–109, 110–119, . . ., 349–349 pounds. Use a dollar sign "$" to represent each customer in the histogram. For example, if the customer weights were 121, 132, 105, 114, 124, 119, 129, the resulting histogram would be

$$
\begin{array}{ll}
100-109 & \$ \\
110-119 & \$\$ \\
120-129 & \$\$\$ \\
130-139 & \$
\end{array}
$$

Use an ARRAY to record the count of customers in each weight class. Test your program with the following data.

    101   148   137   196   229   184   162   302   124   117   123   173   119   155

11.7.   The local pet store has 35 different bowls with fish in them. The first six have goldfish, the next seven have guppies, the next nine have angel fish, the next eight have goldfish, and the last five hold tiger fish. As the bowls vary in size, the number of fish that are in each bowl at the start of the day also varies. The counts of fish in each bowl are as follows:

$$
\begin{array}{ll}
\text{bowls} \ \ 1- \ 3: & 15 \text{ fish} \\
\text{bowls} \ \ 4- \ 7: & \ 8 \text{ fish} \\
\text{bowl} \qquad \ \ 8: & 19 \text{ fish} \\
\text{bowls} \ \ 9-12: & 16 \text{ fish} \\
\text{bowls} \ 13-22: & 14 \text{ fish} \\
\text{bowls} \ 23-24: & 31 \text{ fish} \\
\text{bowls} \ 25-29: & \ 9 \text{ fish} \\
\text{bowls} \ 30-33: & 26 \text{ fish} \\
\text{bowls} \ 34-35: & \ 8 \text{ fish}
\end{array}
$$

A trained seal finds its way into the store. The seal begins to eat fish in the following manner.

(a) It begins with bowl 1.

(b) It counts four bowls and then eats a fish (the first fish it eats comes from bowl 4 and it is a goldfish.)

(c) It again counts to four, starting with the next available bowl, and eats a fish (the second fish it eats comes from bowl 8 and it is a guppie).

The conditions that control the seal are

(a) If there are no fish left in a bowl, the seal does not count the bowl and skips it.

(b) When the last bowl is reached, the seal starts over with bowl 1 (or bowl 2, etc., if bowl 1 is empty).

(c) the seal continues to eat until 361 fish are consumed.

You are to write a Pascal program that will calculate and report how many of each type of fish remain after the seal has had dinner. Display both how many fish remain in each bowl and the total count of each type remaining.

(*Hint:* You will probably want to use an ARRAY indexed from 1 to 35 to keep track of how many fish are left in each bowl.)

11.8. In arranging dinner parties, it is common to alternate men and women at the table. If your dinner guests are Nicholas, Bill, Sara, Alice, Eugene, and Karen, display all the possible ways the seating could be arranged. Always place a man in chair 1. Your results should have the following form.

```
                              CHAIR NUMBER
     1           2           3           4           5           6
  NICHOLAS     SARA        BILL        ALICE       EUGENE      KAREN
  NICHOLAS     SARA        BILL        KAREN       EUGENE      ALICE
  NICHOLAS     SARA        EUGENE      ALICE       BILL        KAREN

      .           .           .           .           .           .
      .           .           .           .           .           .
      .           .           .           .           .           .
```

11.9 Hussian is starting a new company. He is trying to decide on his paid vacation policy. He needs advice on which plan to choose. His choices are

   (a) North American practice:
      (a.1) No vacation during the first year of employment
      (a.2) One week during the second and third years of employment.
      (a.3) Two weeks during the fourth, fifth, and sixth years of employment.
      (a.4) Three weeks every year of employment after the sixth year of employment.
   (b) French practice:
      (b.1) One week during the first year of employment
      (b.2) Five weeks every year of employment after the first year of employment
   (c) Nonunionized, general labor:
      No paid vacation.

Hussian plans to run his company 50 weeks per year. (Two weeks per year are lost to government mandated paid vacation days—religious holidays, birthdays, the coming of spring, etc). At all times, he needs to have 95 people working for him. When someone is on vacation, he must hire a temporary worker. Temporary workers cost 115% of the cost of a regular worker. His regular workers cost $23,684.12 a year.

Whenever a worker leaves the company (i.e., employee "turnover"), Hussian must spend 35% of the worker's yearly cost to replace the worker. Each vacation policy has a different expected turnover. The percent of expected turnover for each plan is as follows:

year	option A	option B	option C
1	20	18	20
2	24	16	25
3	23	15	30
4	19	14	35
5	18	14	35
6	17	13	35
7	14	12	35
8	13	9	35
over 8	13	7	35

As can be seen, this is a complicated decision. To help Hussian with his decision, write a program to compute and display a table in the following form.

```
            ---------- TOTAL SALARY COST -----------
  YEAR       OPTION A        OPTION B        OPTION C
  ----      ----------      ----------      ----------
    1        xxxxxxx.xx      xxxxxxx.xx      xxxxxxx.xx
    2             .               .               .
    3             .               .               .
    .             .               .               .
    .             .               .               .
    .             .               .               .
    9             .               .               .
```

Note that the total salary cost includes the regular employee's salary, cost of replacement while on vacation, and turnover replacement cost.

11.10. Tom and Anne Jung believe that they are spending too much money. To gain better control over their finances, they decide to list and then study all their expenditures for a week. The expenditures for the week studied were

```
                    12.32
                     0.98
                    45.42
                     5.00
                    29.41
                     0.07
                     0.59
                    11.22
                    34.15
                    28.98
                    15.64
```

To get a better picture of their expenses, they decide to
(a) calculate the average expenditure, and
(b) group expenditures as follows:

```
    0.00 to  0.99      1.00 to  9.99     10.00 to 19.99
   20.00 to 29.99     30.00 to 39.99     40.00 and more
```

You are to write a Pascal program to accomplish this task. Your program is to
(a) Input the data and store it in an ARRAY.
(b) Echo display each price after it has been input.
(c) After all the prices have been input and stored,
    (c.1) calculate the average price, and
    (c.2) display the prices in the desired groups.
Your program must be able to work for any number of prices from 0 to 400. Assume that the maximum price is $99,999.99. It is not, repeat not, necessary to sort the prices.

11.11.   Input 10 numbers into an ARRAY, then rearrange these numbers in descending order (i.e., from largest to smallest) in another ARRAY.

The reordering may be done by a *linear sort*. A linear sort repeatedly scans the input ARRAY for the largest remaining value and stores this value in the next available position in the ordered ARRAY.

Display both ARRAYS side by side. That is, each line of output should contain two numbers. The two columns of numbers resulting from the 10 lines of output depict the original and descending ordering of the numbers respectively.

Test your programs with the following data.

95   24   67   113   78   12   24   205   140   6

11.12.   Banker Metesky has 12 depositors in his bank. He has no idea who his biggest or smallest depositor is. He needs you to give him a list from the smallest to the largest of his depositors. Your program should echo display the data as it is input, and display the smallest to largest depositor. At the end, write a special line to tell banker Metesky which depositor is the smallest and which is the biggest. Test your program with the following data.

1	600
2	84
3	700
4	210
5	98
6	358
7	60
8	550
9	341
10	100

(*Hint:* A two-dimensional ARRAY would be useful.)

11.13.   An automobile racing track prepares a data record for each trial run by cars preparing for a race. The first number is the car number and the next number is the time required to cover one lap in seconds and hundredths of a second. A car may make more than one trial lap.

Your assignment is to do the following.

(a)   Input the data given below in exactly the order shown. Your program must be capable of inputing from 0 to 100 records.

(b)   Count the number of laps covered by each car.

(c)   Calculate the total time spent on the track by each car.

(d)   Assuming the track is 2.3 miles long, calculate the average speed in miles per hour for all runs (Count of laps times 2.3 times 3600 divided by the total time).

(e)   Find and display which car had the highest average speed.

(f)   Display these results as a report in the form shown below. Note that each car number may only appear once in the report.

```
CAR NO.     NO. OF LAPS     TOTAL TIME     AVERAGE SPEED
  143           3            178.42          139.22
   .            .              .                .
   .            .              .                .
   .            .              .                .

CAR XXX HAS THE HIGHEST AVERAGE SPEED
```

Use the following data to test your program.

143	61.32
119	69.01
157	63.82
93	59.90
143	58.08
6	60.00
333	66.10
157	62.25
568	61.11
6	60.08
143	59.01
18	65.93
566	70.59
100	68.44
109	64.41
333	57.20
99	68.42

11.14. The Trust Us Finance Company maintains summary records for its year-end accounting purposes. The company has at most 100 customers. For each customer it prepares a data record showing the balance outstanding at the end of each quarter. The following data record would indicate that the balance for customer 1 was $138.29 at the end of the first quarter. Similarly, the balance for the second quarter was $624.00, etc.

138.29   624.00   58.30   964.95

Interest on the loans is charged annually at the rate of 18% of the average quarterly balance. You are supplied with an unknown number of data records and are required to write a program to do the following.

(a) For each customer, compute the average quarterly balance.
(b) Compute the interest due by each customer (18% of the above amounts).
(c) For each quarter, compute the total balance due by all customers.

You must use a two dimensional ARRAY whose size must be at least 100*4. Your report should be in the following form.

```
                    FLYBYNITE FINANCE COMPANY
                      OUTSTANDING BALANCES

           QUARTER 1   QUARTER 2   QUARTER 3   QUARTER 4    AVE.   INT.
LOAN 1      138.29      624.00       58.30      964.95     446.39   80
LOAN 2      726.48      623.92        ...

   .           .
   .           .
   .           .
AVERAGE     228.57         .           .           .        XXX    XX
```

Test your program on the following data.

138.29	624.00	058.30	964.95
726.48	623.92	555.55	444.44
308.16	112.84	297.88	014.02
200.00	200.00	200.00	200.00
765.43	210.98	891.23	456.78
003.02	005.28	004.95	001.00
024.87	126.62	400.00	050.05

(*Hint:* Don't worry about the appearance—i.e., spacing and headings—of your output until you have a program that produces the correct numbers on the correct lines.)

11.15. The accounting procedure at some computer centers consists of assigning a charge number to each user, which the user must submit with each job.

Suppose at the end of each job, the computer produces a record containing the user's charge number followed by the seconds used. Write a program that inputs these records and calculates the total amount of time used by each user on all jobs the user ran and charges the user at a rate of $0.38 a second. The output should be in columnar fashion with user number, total time used, percent of total, and charge to the user. Test your program with the following data.

40709	1.27
80001	2.34
50200	2.11
40709	4.02
40201	3.11
70207	2.06
50200	3.09
80001	1.02
40709	0.79
70207	3.04

11.16. The equation $16/64 = 1/4$ is a correct result obtained by the "false cancellation" of the 6 in the numerator and denominator. Not all cases of false cancellation will produce the correct result. For example, if the 2's are canceled from 12/26, the incorrect answer of 1/6 is produced.

Write a Pascal program to find all cases in which false cancellation produces the correct result for $AB/BC = A/C$ when A, B and C are integers between 1 and 9 inclusive. Do not consider the special cases of 22/22, 33/33, etc.

11.17.   The theory of partitions is concerned with the number of ways in which a number can be represented as the sum of its parts. For example, the number 4 can be represented as

$$4$$
$$3+1$$
$$2+1+1$$
$$2+2$$
$$1+1+1+1$$

and the number 5 can be represented as

$$5$$
$$4+1$$
$$3+1+1$$
$$2+2+1$$
$$2+1+1+1$$
$$1+1+1+1+1$$

If we denote the number of partitions of a positive integer N by $P(N)$, we have $P(4) = 5$ and $P(5)=7$.

Write a Pascal program to determine $P(N)$ for $N=1, 2 \ldots 12$.

11.18.   Six is a *perfect* number. The Greeks called it "perfect" because it is the sum of all its divisors except itself (the only numbers that divide evenly into 6 are 1, 2, 3, and 6, and $6 = 1+2+3$). The ancient mystics explained that God chose to create the world in 6 days instead of 1 because 6 is a perfect number. In the time since the Greeks, perfect numbers have taken on an aspect more ethical than practical. In the first century A.D. the numbers were rated as "abundant" (such as 12, whose divisors have a sum greater than 12), "deficient" (such as 9, whose divisors have a sum less than 9), or "perfect." The mystics then laid down the moral and ethical properties of each type of number. In the 12th century, the study of perfect numbers was recommended for "healing of souls."

Write a program to list all the numbers 2 to 200, classify each as abundant, deficient, or perfect, and keep track of the number of numbers in each class. As a matter of interest, all known perfect numbers are even; it is unknown whether odd perfect numbers exist.

11.19. Figure P.11.19 illustrates a crate that can hold 36 eggs with two eggs in opposing corners. It is divided into 36 compartments, 6 rows and 6 columns. Twelve eggs can be put in the crate without having more than two eggs in any row, including all the diagonal rows.

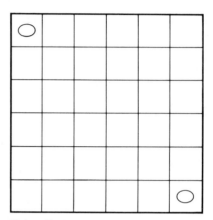

Figure P11.19

Write a program to place the eggs in the carton. Leave the initial two eggs in the corners.

Display your answer showing 1's for eggs and 0's for empty places. For example, the initial carton contents could be displayed as

```
1    0    0    0    0    0
0    0    0    0    0    0
0    0    0    0    0    0
0    0    0    0    0    0
0    0    0    0    0    0
0    0    0    0    0    1
```

11.20. The numerals in the ancient Roman system of a notation are still used for certain limited purposes. The common basic symbols and their decimal equivalents are I=1, V=5, X=10, L=50, C=100, D=500, and M=1000.

Roman integers are written according to the following rules.

(a) If a letter is immediately followed by one of equal or lesser value, its value is added to a cumulative total. Thus XX=20, XV=15, VI=6.

(b) If a letter is immediately followed by one of greater value, its value is subtracted from a cumulative total. Thus IV=4, XL=40, CM=900.

Write a program that will convert an integer written in Roman notation to the equivalent decimal integer. The Roman integer will contain six letters or less.

Your program's results should have the following form.

```
ROMAN          DECIMAL
NUMERAL        INTEGER
MCMXIV          1914
```

Test your program with the following data.

```
MCMXIV
XIV
X
IV
DLIV
CCCIII
```

11.21.   A certain solitaire game can by played on a 6 × 6 corner of a checkerboard. The first cell (top left-hand corner) is empty; all the others contain checkers, chips, beans, etc. The problem is to reduce the checkers to one and finish with the last checker in cell 1. A move is defined as jumping any one checker over one other checker in a single straight-line step (no "bent" paths such as 1–8–9) and then removing the jumped-over checker from the board.

1	2	3	4	5	6
7	8	9	10	11	12
13	14	15	16	17	18
19	20	21	22	23	24
25	26	27	28	29	30
31	32	33	34	35	36

Your output should have the form:

MOVE	FROM	TO	REMOVE
1	1	.	.
2	.	.	.
3	.	.	.
4			
.			
.			
.			

Note: There are three possible first moves:

	3	2
1	15	8
1	13	7

Write a Pascal program to play the game.

11.22.   Mr. Krause runs a hotel with three bars. He has asked you to give him a breakdown of the drinks sold in each bar. As it is July, sales of gin are high and he would like this breakdown first.

You are to prepare a program that will total the number of ounces of gin sold in each bar, and give the average drink size, the weighted average sales for gin per bar, and the standard sales value of a quart of gin.

Mr. Krause has given you the following information.

	type of drink	price	number of ounces	number sold
Bar 1	Dubonnet cocktail	$1.25	¾	18
	Gimlet	1.20	1½	20
	Pink Lady	1.20	1¼	14
	Martini	1.20	2	30
Bar 2	Dubonnet cocktail	$1.25	¾	14
	Gimlet	1.20	1½	16
	Gin (with mix)	1.00	1¼	26
	Jack Daniels	1.50	1¼	17
Bar 3	Gimlet	$1.20	1½	20
	Pink Lady	1.20	1¼	18
	Gin (with mix)	1.00	1¼	22

(1)   There are 32 ounces in a quart of gin.

(2)   All mixed drinks (except gin) are bought premixed.

Reference: "Food and Beverage Cost Planning and Control Procedures," by Carl Albers of the American Hotel and Motel Association, 1974.

11.23.   Develop an algorithm to calculate and display the first 567 digits of pi. A series for the computation of pi is

$$Pi/4 = 1 - 1/3 + 1/5 - 1/7 \ldots$$

Note: The difficult part of the problem is to compute a number with an accuracy of 567 digit places. Normal computer arithmetic is not this accurate.

11.24.   Input the words contained in the first paragraph of the preface to this book into the computer. Then display a list of all the words that you have input, but display each word only once. For example, if the following words were your data.

'THE'

'RED'

'DOG'

'SAT'

'ON'

'THE'

'RED'

'ROCK'

your output would be

```
                          THE
                          RED
                          DOG
                          SAT
                          ON
                          ROCK
```

Note that the second occurrences of the words 'the' and 'red' were ignored.

11.25. Four students take five examinations. They perform as follows:

	exam 1	exam 2	exam 3	exam 4	exam 5
student 1	14.	30.	49.	37.	51.
student 2	52.	40.	66.	74.	58.
student 3	82.	50.	79.	58.	65.
student 4	90.	60.	87.	93.	77.

Assume that there is one data record for each student. Input their marks into a two-dimensional ARRAY. Calculate the average mark for each student, the average score on each exam, and the average for all students on all exams.

Your output should be in the form:

```
                    INPUT DATA                          STUDENT AVERAGES
        XX.X     XX.X     XX.X     XX.X     XX.X              yy.y
        XX.X     XX.X     XX.X     XX.X     XX.X              yy.y
        XX.X     XX.X     XX.X     XX.X     XX.X              yy.y
        XX.X     XX.X     XX.X     XX.X     XX.X              yy.y
 cxam   ZZ.Z     ZZ.Z     ZZ.Z     ZZ.Z     ZZ.Z              aa.a

 average                                                   overall
                                                           average
```

11.26. Use a one-dimensional ARRAY to compute a total for the number of apples, oranges, etc, grown on all the farms in the valley. Each farm's produce should be on one data line. Your result output should include:

Count of farms
Total apples
Total oranges

Display the data for each farm as you input the information. Also calculate and display the average count of apples, oranges, etc., per farm. Appropriate titles must be supplied.

Our program is to count the number of farm data records. The same program should be able to handle from 0 to 100 farms.

The input information is

	apples	oranges	bananas	rabbits	radishes	carrots
farm 1	36	247	30	3	20	768
farm 2	43	416	175	4	38	412
farm 3	93	94	3	5	46	842
farm 4	10	0	46	6	2	662
farm 5	0	26	12	7	30	768
farm 6	76	93	0	8	57	319

11.27. Godel numbers find their origin in information theory. They can be utilized in what is known as *Godelized language*.

A Godelized language is a system of encoding any message of any kind as a single, very large number. The message is first written out in clear language and then encoded as bases and exponents. Each letter of the message is represented in order by the natural order or primes—that is, the first letter is represented by the base 5, then 7, 11, 13, 17, etc. The identity of the letter occupying that position in the message is given by the exponent: Simply, the exponent 1 means that the letter in that position is an A, the letter 2 means that it is a B, 3 a C, etc. The message, as a whole, is then rendered as the product of all the bases and exponents. For example, the word "CAB" can thus be represented as 2*2*2 *3 * 5*5, or 600 (=8 * 3 * 25). The name "ABE" would be represented by the number 56,250, or 2 * 3*3 * 5*5*5*5*5 (=2 * 9 * 3125). The exponent "0" has been reserved for a space and the exponent "27" has been assigned arbitrarily to indicate a period. As can be seen, the Godelized form for even a short message involves a very large number, although such numbers may be transmitted quite compactly in the form of a sum of bases and exponents.

Write a Pascal program to produce the Godel number for the phrases

    CAB
    ABE
    HI NICE MACHINE
    ABANDON HOPE
    VICE
    SAAB
    BE

Consider each line a separate phrase.

(a) Your program must utilize two subprograms. One subprogram is to do all the multiplying that occurs in your program. The other subprogram is to be used whenever your program initializes a variable to one. The mainline program is to specify the numbers that are to be multiplied and then pass these numbers to the appropriate subprogram. The subprogram then is to pass the result back to the mainline program.

(b) Your program must handle all the phrases in one running of the program.

(c) There must be only one phrase per input data record.

(d) The output must be of the form:

THE GODEL NUMBER FOR THE PHRASE 'CAB ' IS: 600

(e)   The Godel number may not have any leading zeros.

(f)   Your program should work for phrases of up to 15 characters and Godel numbers of up to 132 digits.

(g)   Your program should work for a variable number of input phrases.

11.28.   In an attempt to quell an epidemic of obesity, Vic Fanny's Reducing Salon has offered several week-long special exercise sessions. Customers are encouraged to attend more than one session (as required by their "condition"). Whenever a customer completes one of these sessions, a data record is prepared as follows:

Columns 1–10: first name
Columns 11–20: last name
Columns 22–25: number of pounds lost during that week

At the end of each month, the results are to be summarized in a report of the following form, produced by a program of your design:

```
Last Name      First Name      Total Loss      Avg. Loss Per Session
***************************************************************************
Attired        Natily            42.0            14.0
Loader         Frieda            10.2            10.2
   .              .                .               .
   .              .                .               .
   .              .                .               .
```

Note that (i) there is only one line of the report for each last name, and (ii) the names are listed in alphabetical order (by last name). Your program must use at least two-dimensional ARRAY. You may assume:

(a)   There will be no more than 20 data records.

(b)   No two customers have the same last name.

Test your program with the following data.

Natily	Attired	20.0
Lefty	Wright	06.3
Sid	Smith	12.2
Richard	Nixon	00.1
Ali	Money	04.5
Sid	Smith	16.9
Natily	Attired	08.0
Richard	Nixon	00.3
Anne	Thrax	26.7
Frieda	Loader	10.2
Natily	Attired	14.0
Aunty	Sweetums	19.9

Chapter 12

PROCEDURES AND FUNCTIONS

Objective
Discuss PROCEDUREs and FUNCTIONs beyond that given in Chapter 6. If desired, the critical parts of this chapter (12.1, 12.2) can be covered immediately after the first chapter on subprograms (Chapter 6).

Suggested Background
A knowledge of the core chapters 3, 4, and 5. Some sections also require specific knowledge of selection and control statements. The suggested background will be specified when the sections are presented.

PROCEDUREs and FUNCTIONs are subprograms that can be invoked upon demand. Each subprogram is constructed in much the same way as a program. The shell of a subprogram is similar to a program's shell. The chief differences are: (1) the first statements of a program and of a subprogram are different and (2) the END delimiting a program is followed by a period (".") in comparison with the END delimiting a subprogram, which is followed by a semicolon (";") Another way to say this is that a subprogram is a *block* preceded by a subprogram heading and with the separation from the rest of the program marked by a semicolon.

Chapter 6 discussed how PROCEDUREs and FUNCTIONs could be used: to organize programs, to aid in the top-down development process, and to write programs more efficiently. That earlier chapter dealt with the most fundamental subprogram forms, forms that did not contain CONST and VAR sections or additional PROCEDURE or FUNCTION definitions. In this type of subprogram, the value of a given constant or variable is known everywhere in the program.

Often it is desirable to separate the values of variables and constants in a subprogram from those in other parts of the program. It is useful to separate values for three reasons: security, clarity, and ease of program development.

Clarity is important both for writing the program and to aid in correcting any invalid statements (debugging). If the programmer needs to be concerned only with variable values in a small part of a large program, it is much easier to understand clearly what role the variable is to play in solving the problem and what actions are directed toward it.

Controlling the security of a variable means that the circumstances for changing the value of the variable are restricted. When the value of a variable can be changed only in a limited section of the program, it is easier to ensure that it has a valid value and that the variable is only being used for a single purpose. Similarly, isolating the definition and use of a specific variable to a limited section of the entire program helps in the program development process. Different parts of the program can be developed independently by the same or different programmers without concern as to which variables are identified and how they are used in other places in the program.

12.1 SCOPE

Objectives
Discuss why the value of a variable might be restricted to particular places in a program and describe how this restriction can come about.

Suggested Background
The previous material in this chapter.

Variable clarity and control are achieved by limiting the "scope" of a variable. A variable of limited scope is known only within a certain part of the program.

The scope of a variable or any identifier is controlled by the block structure of the program. Recall that a Pascal program consists of a program heading of the form

```
PROGRAM <program name>(<files>)
```

followed by a block, which is the rest of the program. Each subprogram declared within a block also contains a heading and a block. A program can have many blocks declared within it. The program is itself called the *outer* block. Each subprogram is an *inner* block. Just as there may be several Russian dolls nested within each other, there may be several subprograms nested within each other. Data control is accomplished by the basic rule of block structures: all variables declared at the beginning of a block are accessible to all statements that are part of that block—including statements belonging to inner blocks, but to no others.

The identifier of a variable is known only within the program or subprogram in which it is defined. This means that a constant or variable defined for the main program can be known everywhere in the program. Chapter 6 on PROCEDUREs and FUNCTIONs used only constants and variables defined for the main part of the program. Identifiers defined in this way are considered to be *globally* known. A constant or variable defined within a subprogram is known within the subprogram. Variables defined and used in a subprogram are considered to be *locally* known. *Nonlocal* identifiers are identifiers used outside of the subprogram in which they are referenced. The declaration of any subprogram that references a nonlocal identifier must be nested within the subprogram that declares the identifier. In the following program, the variables AGE and WEIGHT are globally known where the variables HEIGHT and GENDER are locally known.

```
PROGRAM PERSON(INPUT,OUTPUT);
    (* THIS READS AND WRITES A PERSONS AGE, WEIGHT, HEIGHT AND GENDER *)
VAR
    AGE: INTEGER;
    WEIGHT: REAL;
(* ============================================================== *)
PROCEDURE REST;
    (* THIS READS AND WRITES HEIGHT AND GENDER *)
VAR
    HEIGHT: REAL;
    GENDER: CHAR;
BEGIN  (* ACTIONS IN REST *)
    READ(HEIGHT,GENDER);
    WRITELN('HEIGHT IS ',HEIGHT:5:1,', GENDER IS ',GENDER)
END;  (* REST PROCEDURE *)
(* ============================================================== *)
BEGIN  (* MAIN PROGRAM: READ AGE,WEIGHT AND REQUEST HEIGHT,GENDER *)
    READ(AGE,WEIGHT);
    WRITELN('AGE IS ',AGE:3,', WEIGHT IS ',WEIGHT:5:1);
    REST  (* INVOKE REST PROCEDURE *)
END.  (* PERSON *)
```

In this program, both WRITELN statements could have been placed in the PROCE-DURE because both AGE and WEIGHT are globally known and can be accessed there. However, both WRITELN statements could not have been placed in the main part of the program because HEIGHT and GENDER are only locally known since they were defined within the REST PROCEDURE.

A graphic way of illustrating this is shown in Figure 12.1.

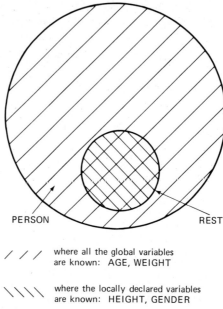

PERSON   REST

/ / /   where all the global variables
          are known: AGE, WEIGHT

\ \ \ \   where the locally declared variables
          are known: HEIGHT, GENDER

Figure 12.1

   When there are several PROCEDUREs and/or FUNCTIONs, some of them either can be defined as "nested" within each other, or they can be separate from each other. How they are defined affects how constant and variable identifiers are known. For example, in the following program,

```
PROGRAM PERSON(INPUT,OUTPUT);
    (* THIS READS AND WRITES: A PERSON'S: AGE,WEIGHT,
                                          HEIGHT,GENDER,
                                          EYE COLOUR
        AND ALSO CALCULATES AND DISPLAYS THEIR RUNNING SPEED   *)
VAR
    AGE: INTEGER;
    WEIGHT: REAL;
(* =============================================================== *)
PROCEDURE REST;
    (* THIS READS AGE,WEIGHT,HEIGHT,GENDER AND CALLS FOR EYE COLOUR *)
VAR
    HEIGHT: REAL;
    GENDER: CHAR;
(* +++++++++++++++++++++++++++++++++++++++++++++++++++++++++++++++++ *)
PROCEDURE EYES;
    (* THIS READS EYE COLOUR *)
VAR
    EYECOLOUR: CHAR;
BEGIN  (* ACTION IN EYES *)
    READ(EYECOLOUR);
    WRITELN('EYECOLOUR IS ',EYECOLOUR)
END;  (* EYES PROCEDURE *)
(* +++++++++++++++++++++++++++++++++++++++++++++++++++++++++++++++++ *)
BEGIN  (* ACTIONS IN REST *)
    EYES;  (* INVOKE EYES PROCEDURE *)
    READ(HEIGHT,GENDER);
    WRITELN('HEIGHT IS ',HEIGHT:5:1,', GENDER IS ',GENDER)
END;  (* REST PROCEDURE *)
(* =============================================================== *)
PROCEDURE RUNNING;
    (* THIS CALCULATES AND DISPLAYS A PERSON'S SPEED *)
VAR
    DISTANCE: REAL;
    TIME: REAL;
    SPEED: REAL;
BEGIN  (* ACTIONS IN SPEED PROCEDURE *)
    READ(DISTANCE,TIME);
    WRITELN('DISTANCE IS ',DISTANCE:4:1,' TIME IS ',TIME:6:2);
    SPEED := DISTANCE/TIME;
    WRITELN('SPEED IS ',SPEED:6:3)
END;  (* RUNNING *)
(* =============================================================== *)
BEGIN  (* MAIN PROGRAM *)
    READ(AGE,WEIGHT);
    WRITELN('AGE IS ',AGE:3,', WEIGHT IS ',WEIGHT:5:1);
    REST;  (* INVOKE REST PROCEDURE *)
    RUNNING
END.  (* PERSON *)
```

The PROCEDURE named EYES is nested within the PROCEDURE named REST. The PROCEDURE identified as RUNNING is separate from the other PROCE-DUREs. A graphic way of illustrating where the different variables are known is shown in Figure 12.2.

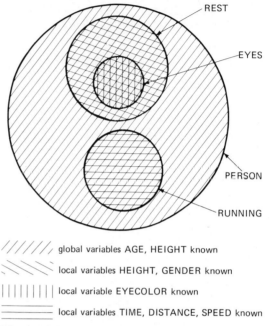

////// global variables AGE, HEIGHT known

local variables HEIGHT, GENDER known

|||||||||| local variable EYECOLOR known

local variables TIME, DISTANCE, SPEED known

Figure 12.2

PROCEDUREs and FUNCTIONs can only be invoked where their identifiers are known. Their identifiers are known in the program or subprogram in which they are defined. For example, in the last program, EYES and SUMMARY cannot be invoked by statements in RUNNING. The PROCEDURE identified as RUNNING cannot be invoked by statements in SUMMARY or in EYES.

It is possible to declare variables with the same identifier in both the main part of the program and in one or more subprograms. The variables may or may not be declared to have the same TYPE. When this happens, the local definition of the variable will be used.

For example, in the following program named SURFACE, AREA is globally accessible while WIDTH and LENGTH are declared in both the main part of the program and in the PROCEDURE. In this case, LENGTH and WIDTH can have different values in the PROCEDURE and elsewhere in the program.

```
PROGRAM SURFACE(INPUT,OUTPUT);
   (* THIS CALCULATES SURFACE AREA *)
VAR
   AREA: REAL;
   LENGTH: INTEGER;
   WIDTH: REAL;
(* =============================================================== *)
PROCEDURE CALCULATE;
VAR
   LENGTH: REAL;
   WIDTH: REAL;
BEGIN  (* ACTIONS IN CALCULATE PROCEDURE *)
   READ(LENGTH,WIDTH);
   WRITELN('LENGTH IS ',LENGTH:5:3,', WIDTH IS ',WIDTH:4:1);
   AREA := LENGTH*WIDTH;
   WRITELN('AREA IS ',AREA:7:4)
END;  (* CALCUALTE PROCEDURE *)
(* =============================================================== *)
BEGIN (* MAIN PART OF PROGRAM *)
   READ(LENGTH,WIDTH);
   CALCULATE;   (* INVOKE CALCULATE PROCEDURE *)
   WRITELN('LENGTH = ',LENGTH:2,', WIDTH = ',WIDTH:5:2);
   AREA := LENGTH*WIDTH;
   WRITELN('AREA = ',AREA:5:2)
END.  (* SURFACE *)
```

If the input data are

```
5  1.29
3.618  0.66
```

the results will be

```
LENGTH IS 3.618, WIDTH IS  0.6
AREA IS  2.1708
LENGTH =  5, WIDTH =  1.29
AREA =  6.45
```

At this point, it might be asked: "Why would the same identifiers be declared in two different places?" The answer is that this can happen quite accidentally while a program is being developed by one person. This is even more likely when more than one person works on the same project. What is needed is some way to allow the problem solver(s) to segment the problem and then to define explicitly what data values are to be passed between the program segments. The following sections discuss how this is accomplished.

12.2 COMMUNICATING WITH SUBPROGRAMS

Objectives
Identify the advantages in controlling what data is passed to a subprogram and specify how this is done in Pascal.

Suggested Background
The previous material in this chapter.

A good way to control the use of variables and constants in a program is to declare every variable and constant that is to be used within a subprogram within that subprogram.

Declaring all the constants and variables that are to be used within a subprogram in the subprogram also makes it easier for a program to be developed by several people. Each person can solve part of the problem and not worry about the identifiers that someone else is using within any particular subprogram. Additionally, it also makes it easier for a single person to develop the pieces of a program as attention need only be given the piece that is under current development. However, if variables and constants are completely declared within each subprogram, there must be some way of communicating values between the parts of the program. This is done by specifying a list of what is to be passed or communicated when a subprogram is invoked. These lists are called *parameter* lists.

Parameter lists are specified as part of an *argument* when a subprogram is invoked. A parameter list is placed between parentheses after the subprogram is invoked or defined. The form of a parameter list specification is

        ⟨procedure identifier⟩(⟨parameter list⟩)

or

        ⟨function identifier⟩(⟨parameter list⟩)

The form of the parameter list is graphically illustrated in Figure 12.3.

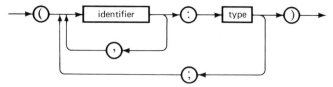

Figure 12.3 Syntax diagram for a parameter list containing only actual parameters.

The form of the specification when the subprogram is defined is

```
PROCEDURE <procedure identifier>(<parameter list>);
    .
    .
    .
END;  (* <procedure identifier> *)
```

or

```
FUNCTION <function identifier>(<parameter list>)<result type>;
    .
    .
    .
END;  (* <function identifier> *)
```

The form of subprograms with parameter lists is graphically illustrated in Figure 12.4.

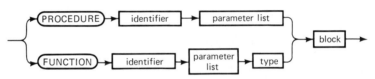

Figure 12.4   Syntax diagram for a subprogram with a parameter list.

When the subprogram is invoked, the identifiers in the subprogram's parameter list are the identifiers that are known in the part of the program where the subprogram is invoked. The declaration of the identifiers in the parameter list serves to declare the identifiers within the subprogram. This means that the identifiers declared within the parameter list of the subprogram definition are not again included in the subprogram's VAR section.

There are the same number of elements in both the invoking parameter list and the parameter list associated with the subprogram's definition. The elements in the parameter lists must correspond to each other in both quantity and TYPE. The elements in the lists are serially paired. This means that the first element in the parameter list for the invoked subprogram is paired with the first identifier in the parameter list of the subprogram's declaration, the second with the second, etc. The paired elements must have the same TYPE.

There are two different ways in which the elements in a parameter list are used: *variable* and *value*. Depending on the use, the elements in the parameter list are declared differently. The difference between variable and value declarations controls the nature of the communication that can take place between the invoking part of the program and the invoked subprogram.

12.2.1 Value Parameters

Objective
Discuss how data can be passed to a Pascal subprogram so that changes in the data in the subprogram will not result in changes in the data values in the part of the program that invoked the subprogram.

Suggested Background
The previous material in this chapter.

Parameters that are used as value parameters allow only one-way communication with a subprogram. The communication is from the invoking statement to the subprogram. What happens is that the value of the variable is passed to the invoked subprogram. This is sometimes also called *pass by value* or *call by value*. The elements in the invoking parameter list can be any element that has an associated value: a specific constant, a variable or constant identifier, or a FUNCTION identifier.

The elements in the parameter list of a subprogram that are used as value parameters are declared as to TYPE. Value parameters create temporary local storage that can be used only within the subprogram. [*Looking Ahead:* A parameter list for a subprogram can contain both value and variable (Section 12.2.2) elements.] These declarations are part of the subprogram. Declarations specified in a parameter list are not repeated within the subprogram. The form of a value parameter list is

```
(<identifier>:<type>; .. ;<identifier>:<type>)
```

For example, the heading for the FUNCTION named AREA defined as

```
FUNCTION AREA(SIDE1:REAL; SIDE2:INTEGER):REAL;
```

will cause the declarations for SIDE1 and SIDE2 to be part of the declarations that are known within the FUNCTION named AREA. Unless declared elsewhere, SIDE1 and SIDE2 will not be known outside of AREA.

In the following program, the values for LENGTH and WIDTH are value parameters that are passed to the FUNCTION identified as AREA. In the FUNCTION identified as AREA, SIDE1 is paired with or corresponds to LENGTH in the invoking statement and SIDE2 is paired with WIDTH. This means that the magnitude that LENGTH has when AREA is invoked is passed to SIDE1 as its actual value and the magnitude that WIDTH has becomes the value of SIDE2.

```
PROGRAM SURFACE(INPUT,OUTPUT);
   (* THIS CALCULATES SURFACE AREA *)
VAR
   LENGTH: REAL;
   WIDTH: INTEGER;
(* ================================================================ *)
FUNCTION AREA(SIDE1:REAL; SIDE2:INTEGER):REAL;
BEGIN  (* ACTIONS IN AREA FUNCTION *)
   AREA := SIDE1 * SIDE2
END;  (* AREA FUNCTION *)
(* ================================================================ *)
BEGIN  (* MAIN PART OF PROGRAM *)
   READ(LENGTH,WIDTH);
   WRITELN('LENGTH IS ',LENGTH:4:1,', WIDTH IS ',WIDTH:2);
   WRITELN('THE AREA IS ',AREA(LENGTH,WIDTH) )
END.  (* SURFACE *)
```

Notice that the variable declaration within the parameter list has the form:

```
(SIDE1:REAL; SIDE2:INTEGER)
```

The semicolon separates the two declarations. If more than one element in a parameter list has the same TYPE, they can be combined in the same way as the
declarations can be combined within a VAR section; that is,

```
(GENDER,EYECOLOUR: CHAR; SPEED,PRICE,DISTANCE: REAL)
```

However, for clarity, this book generally has specified the TYPE for each variable
separately. This practice will be continued for declarations within parameter lists. A
TYPE declaration outside the parentheses delimiting the parameter list declarations is
independent of the declaration within the parameter list. In the previous example
program, the TYPE of the FUNCTION identified as AREA is specified as REAL.

When using value parameters, if the magnitude of a variable that was declared
within the parameter list is changed during the execution of the subprogram, this
change will not be transmitted back to the invoking statement. For example, the new
result for the total of all the ages is not available outside of the PROCEDURE
identified as AVERAGE in the following program named AGES.

Example: AGES
Read in two ages. Print the values. Then calculate and print the average of the
ages.

calculate the average of two ages
1   define variables
2   get the ages
    2.1   read in two ages
    2.2   print the ages
3   find and report the average of the ages
    3.1   add the ages together
    3.2   calculate the average
    3.3   print the average
4   end of the problem

```
PROGRAM AGES(INPUT,OUTPUT);
   (* THIS: READS, PRINTS, TOTALS 2 AGES AND THEN FINDS THE AVERAGE *)
VAR
   FIRSTAGE: INTEGER;
   SECONDAGE: INTEGER;
(* ================================================================ *)
PROCEDURE FINDAVERAGE(AGE1: INTEGER; AGE2: INTEGER);
VAR
   TOTALAGE: INTEGER;
   AVERAGE: REAL;
BEGIN (* ACTIONS IN FINDAVERAGE PROCEDURE *)
   TOTALAGE := AGE1 + AGE2;
   AVERAGE := TOTALAGE/2;
   WRITELN(' -- AVERAGE IS ',AVERAGE:6:2)
END;  (* FINDAVERAGE PROCEDURE *)
(* ================================================================ *)
BEGIN  (* MAIN PROGRAM *)
   READ(FIRSTAGE,SECONDAGE);
   WRITE('THE AGES ARE ',FIRSTAGE:3,' AND ',SECONDAGE:3);
   FINDAVERAGE(FIRSTAGE,SECONDAGE)
END.  (* AGES *)
```

12.2.2 Variable Parameters

Objective
Discuss how data can be passed to a subprogram so that when they are changed in the subprogram, that change is reflected in the part of the program where the subprogram was invoked.

Suggested Background
The previous material in this chapter.

When it is desirable to communicate changes in variable values that happen in the subprogram to the invoking statement, the variables that are to communicate these changes should be declared as variable parameters in the parameter list. As variable parameters also communicate data into the subprogram, they provide a means of two-way communication. Data passed this way are sometimes said to be *passed by reference*. This is because the corresponding elements in both the invoking statement and the parameter list *refer* to the same storage location.

In the invoking statement, the difference between variable and value parameters is that every element that is passed to a variable parameter must have been declared as a variable identifier. When passing actual parameters, the elements in the invoking parameter list may be scalar values or subprogram identifiers, as well as variable identifiers.

Variables that are to be used as variable parameters are preceded by the word VAR in the subprogram declaration. For example, in

```
PROCEDURE AVERAGE(AGE:REAL; VAR TOTAL:REAL)
```

AGE is a value parameter and TOTAL is a variable parameter. Changes to TOTAL will be reflected back to the invoking statement as a change to the magnitude of the element that corresponds to TOTAL in the invoking statement. Changes to AGE in the PROCEDURE identified as AVERAGE will not be reflected back to the invoking statement. There may be more than one variable parameter in a parameter list. For example, in

```
FUNCTION CHARGES(CARDNUMBER:INTEGER; VAR TOTAL:REAL;
                 PRICE:REAL; VAR GALLONS:INTEGER):REAL;
```

the variable parameters are TOTAL and GALLONS while the value parameters are CARDNUMBER and PRICE.

The use of both variable and value parameters is illustrated in the following example program AGES.

```
PROGRAM AGES(INPUT,OUTPUT);
   (* THIS READS, PRINTS AND TOTALS AGES *)
VAR
   AGE: INTEGER;
   AGETOTAL: INTEGER;
(* ================================================================ *)
PROCEDURE TOTAL(YEARS: INTEGER; VAR TOTALYEARS: INTEGER);
BEGIN (* ACTIONS IN TOTAL PROCEDURE *)
   TOTALYEARS := TOTALYEARS + YEARS;
   WRITELN(' -- TOTAL SO FAR IS ',TOTALYEARS:5)
END;   (* TOTAL PROCEDURE *)
(* ================================================================ *)
BEGIN   (* MAIN PROGRAM *)
   AGETOTAL := 0;
   READ(AGE);   (* READ FIRST AGE *)
   WRITE('THE FIRST AGE IS ',AGE:3);   (* ECHO PRINT *)
   TOTAL(AGE,AGETOTAL);   (* ADD FIRST AGE TO TOTAL *)
   READ(AGE);   (* READ SECOND AGE *)
   WRITE('THE SECOND AGE IS ',AGE:3);   (* ECHO PRINT *)
   TOTAL(AGE,AGETOTAL);   (* ADD SECOND AGE TO TOTAL *)
   READ(AGE);   (* READ THIRD AGE *)
   WRITE('THE THIRD AGE IS ',AGE:3);   (* ECHO PRINT *)
   TOTAL(AGE,AGETOTAL)   (* ADD THIRD AGE TO TOTAL *)
END.   (* AGES *)
```

If the data are

```
13 25 12
```

then the results will be

```
THE FIRST AGE IS  13 -- TOTAL SO FAR IS    25
THE SECOND AGE IS 25 -- TOTAL SO FAR IS    38
THE THIRD AGE IS   2 -- TOTAL SO FAR IS    40
```

12.3 USING SUBPROGRAMS WITH CONTROL STRUCTURES

Objectives
Discuss why subprograms and control structures might be combined and illustrate what can be done.

Suggested Background
The previous material in this chapter and the section on WHILE.

Any of the selection and iteration control structures can be combined with a FUNCTION or a PROCEDURE. It is quite normal to do so. The subprogram examples presented up to this point haven't used control structures so that PROCEDUREs and FUNCTIONs could be learned independently from control structures.

The following illustrates how a subprogram could be used with an iterative control structure.

Example: CASTLE

Billy Batson sometimes agrees to help his sister build a sand castle. Each bucket that Billy brings contains 0.36 cubic meter of sand. The size of the castle to be built varies from day to day, but only one bucket is ever used to bring the sand. In order to prepare an accurate construction plan, they need to have a schedule of the following form.

```
CUBIC METERS OF SAND NEEDED =  2.1
BUCKET    SAND        PERCENT OF
NUMBER  DELIVERED   TOTAL NEEDED
------  ---------   -----------
  1       0.36         17.1
  2       0.72         34.3
  3       1.08         51.4
  .         .            .
  .         .            .
  .         .            .
```

collect sand
1 define variables and constants
   1.1   define constant bucket size
   1.2   define variables
2 initialize
   2.1   number of buckets delivered so far
   2.2   total sand delivered so far
   2.3   print titles
3 while total sand delivered is less than the castle size
   3.1   get a bucket of sand
   3.2   add to the count of buckets delivered
   3.3   add to the total of sand delivered so far
4 develop and display results
   4.1   calculate percentage of sand needed delivered so far
   4.2   print the results so far
5 problem completed

Notice that a FUNCTION or PROCEDURE has not been explicitly defined as such within the program plan. Problem tasks that can be conveniently grouped within a subprogram can be identified as a numbered subgroup in the program plan. In the following program CASTLE, 3.1, 3.2, 3.3 will be placed in a subprogram.

```
PROGRAM CASTLE(INPUT,OUTPUT);
   (* THIS REPORTS ON HOW LONG IT WILL TAKE TO ACCUMULATE ENOUGH
      SAND TO BUILD A CASTLE OF A SPECIFIED SIZE              *)
CONST
   BUCKETSIZE = 0.36;
VAR
   CASTLESIZE: REAL;
   BUCKETCOUNT: INTEGER;
   SANDPILE: REAL;
   PERCENTDONE: REAL;
(* ============================================================ *)
PROCEDURE TITLES;
BEGIN  (* ACTIONS IN TITLES PROCEDURE *)
   WRITELN('BUCKET     SAND       PERCENT OF');
   WRITELN('NUMBER   DELIVERED   TOTAL NEEDED');
   WRITELN('------   ---------   ------------')
END;  (* TITLES *)
(* ============================================================ *)
PROCEDURE GETSAND(BUCKETVOLUME: REAL; VAR NUMBERBUCKETS: INTEGER;
                  VAR TOTALSAND: REAL);
BEGIN  (* ACTIONS IN GETSAND PROCEDURE *)
   NUMBERBUCKETS := NUMBERBUCKETS + 1;
   TOTALSAND := TOTALSAND + BUCKETVOLUME
END;  (* GET SAND *)
(* ============================================================ *)
BEGIN  (* MAIN PART OF PROGRAM *)
   READ(CASTLESIZE);
   WRITELN('CUBIC METERS OF SAND NEEDED IS ',CASTLESIZE:5:2);
   TITLES;
   BUCKETCOUNT := 0;  (* INITIALIZE COUNT OF BUCKETS SO FAR *)
   SANDPILE := 0;   (* INITIALIZE SIZE OF SAND PILE SO FAR *)
   WHILE SANDPILE < CASTLESIZE DO BEGIN  (* COLLECT SAND FOR CASTLE *)
      GETSAND(BUCKETSIZE,BUCKETCOUNT,SANDPILE);
      PERCENTDONE := 100.0 * (SANDPILE/CASTLESIZE);
      WRITELN(BUCKETCOUNT:4,SANDPILE:10:2,PERCENTDONE:14:1)
   END  (* COLLECTING SAND *)
END.  (* CASTLE *)
```

12.4 SUBPROGRAMS INVOKING OTHER SUBPROGRAMS

Objective
Describe how subprograms can invoke other subprograms.

Suggested Background
The introductory material at the beginning of this chapter, Sections 12.1, 12.2, 12.2.1, and 12.2.2. Notice that Section 12.3 is not required.

12.4.1 From Within Another Subprogram

Objectives
Discuss and illustrate the way in which Pascal subprograms may be invoked from other subprograms and how a forward reference can be supplied to make subprogram identifiers known to other subprograms when there are sequencing concerns.

Suggested Background
The introductory material at the beginning of this chapter, Sections 12.1, 12.2., and 12.2.1. Notice that Sections 12.2.2 and 12.3 are not required.

A PROCEDURE or a FUNCTION may be invoked from within another subprogram. The identifier of any invoked subprogram must be declared before it can be invoked. Normally the subprogram's identifier is initially declared when the entire subprogram is defined. This is the case when the invoked subprogram is nested within the subprogram that invokes it.

However, if two subprograms are at the same level of nesting, the identifier of the first subprogram is known to the second subprogram because its declaration precedes the second subprogram. However, the identifier of the second subprogram is not known to the first subprogram if the second subprogram is declared in the normal fashion. For example, in

```
PROGRAM EXAMPLE(OUTPUT);
VAR
   .
   .
   .
PROCEDURE COST(PRICE:REAL; COUNT:INTEGER);
VAR
   .
   . .
   .
END;  (* PROCEDURE COST *)
PROCEDURE VOLUME(PRICE:REAL; SALES:INTEGER);
VAR
   .
   .
   .
END;  (* PROCEDURE VOLUME *)
BEGIN  (* MAIN PART OF PROGRAM *)
   .
   .
   .
END.  (* EXAMPLE *)
```

both of the PROCEDUREs identified as COST and VOLUME may be invoked in the main part of the program. Since the declaration of the PROCEDURE identified as COST preceded the declaration of the PROCEDURE identified as VOLUME, COST can be invoked within VOLUME. However, the PROCEDURE identified as VOLUME cannot be invoked within the PROCEDURE identified as COST because the heading VOLUME has yet to be declared.

This problem can be overcome by supplying a FORWARD reference for any subprogram identifier that needs to be known before the subprogram itself is defined. The form of a FORWARD reference is

```
PROCEDURE <procedure identifier>(<parameter list>); FORWARD;
```

or

```
FUNCTION <function identifier>(<parameter list>):TYPE; FORWARD;
```

When a subprogram's identifier has been declared by a FORWARD reference, the parameter list is not repeated when the subprogram itself is fully defined. For example,

```
PROGRAM EXAMPLE(OUTPUT);
VAR
    .
    .
    .
PROCEDURE VOLUME(PRICE:REAL; SALES:INTEGER); FORWARD;
PROCEDURE COST(PRICE:REAL; COUNT:INTEGER);
VAR
    .
    .
    .
END;  (* PROCEDURE COST *)
PROCEDURE VOLUME
VAR
    .
    .
    .
END;  (* PROCEDURE VOLUME *)
BEGIN  (* MAIN PART OF PROGRAM *)
    .
    .
    .
END.  (* EXAMPLE *)
```

12.4.2 Subprogram Identifiers as Parameters

Objective
Describe how subprogram identifiers can be included in a parameter list. This topic may not be immediately useful.

Suggested Background
The introductory material at the beginning of this chapter, Sections 12.1, 12.2, 12.2.1, 12.2.2., and 12.4.1.

FUNCTIONs and PROCEDUREs can be invoked by including them in a parameter list of another subprogram. When this happens, the invoked subprogram should be identified as such in the parameter list. If the invoked subprogram in the parameter list is a FUNCTION, its TYPE should also be specified. The form of the specification of a PROCEDURE as a parameter within another subprogram's parameter list is

```
PROCEDURE <procedure identifier>(<dummy parameter list>)
```

The form of the specification of a FUNCTION within another subprogram's parameter list is

```
FUNCTION <function identifier>(<dummy parameter list>):<result type>
```

A dummy parameter list is required only if the subprogram being invoked has a parameter list. The variable identifiers in the parameter list are not used. They act only as placeholders. The TYPEs specified in the dummy parameter list must correspond with the TYPEs specified in the parameter list of the subprogram's declaration.

Not all PROCEDUREs and FUNCTIONs can be included in a parameter list. The elements in the parameter list of a subprogram that is itself to be included in a parameter list must be value parameters. To see how this works, suppose the following PROCEDUREs were declared.

```
PROCEDURE ESTIMATE(PROCEDURE TOTAL)
PROCEDURE PRICE(WEIGHT:REAL)
PROCEDURE AVERAGE(VAR SUM; GRADE:REAL)
PROCEDURE COST(FUNCTION CHARGES:REAL)
```

A program following these definitions could have

```
ESTIMATE(PRICE)
```

but not

```
        ESTIMATE(AVERAGE)
```

or

```
        ESTIMATE(COST)
```

as AVERAGE has a variable parameter and COST has a FUNCTION parameter.

The following program illustrates the use of subprogram identifiers as elements in a parameter list. Notice that the FUNCTION named AREA was referenced as PART within the FUNCTION named SURFACE. This came about because the FUNCTION was identified as PART in the parameter list for SURFACE. If it had been desired, the name AREA could have been used.

```
PROGRAM BOXES(INPUT,OUTPUT);
    (* THIS CALCULATES THE TOTAL SURFACE AREA OF TWO BOXES *)
VAR
    BOX1LENGTH: INTEGER;
    BOX1WIDTH: INTEGER;
    BOX1HEIGTH: INTEGER;
    BOX2LENGTH: INTEGER;
    BOX2WIDTH: INTEGER;
    BOX2HEIGTH: INTEGER;
    TOTALSURFACE: INTEGER;
(* ============================================================ *)
FUNCTION AREA(SIDE1:INTEGER; SIDE2:INTEGER): INTEGER;
VAR
    EXTENT: INTEGER;
BEGIN  (* ACTIONS IN AREA FUNCTION *)
    EXTENT := SIDE1 * SIDE2;
    WRITELN(SIDE1:4,SIDE2:5,EXTENT:7);
    AREA := EXTENT
END;  (* AREA FUNCTION *)
(* ============================================================ *)
FUNCTION SURFACE(FUNCTION PART(DUMMY1:INTEGER;DUMMY2:INTEGER):INTERGER;
            HEIGTH:INTEGER; WIDTH:INTEGER; LENGTH:INTEGER): INTEGER;
VAR
    BOXSURFACE: INTEGER;
BEGIN  (* ACTIONS IN SURFACE FUNCTION *)
    BOXSURFACE := 2 * (PART(LENGTH,WIDTH) + PART(WIDTH,HEIGTH)
                + PART(LENGTH,HEIGTH) );
    WRITELN('----------------- TOTAL BOX SURFACE IS ',BOXSURFACE:6);
    SURFACE := BOXSURFACE
END;  (* FUNCTION SURFACE *)
(* ============================================================ *)
BEGIN  (* MAIN PART OF PROGRAM *)
    WRITELN('SIDE SIDE  AREA');  (* TITLES *)
    WRITELN('---- ---- ------');
    READ(BOX1LENGTH,BOX1WIDTH,BOX1HEIGTH,
        BOX2LENGTH,BOX2WIDTH,BOX2HEIGTH);
    TOTALSURFACE := SURFACE(AREA,BOX1HEIGTH,BOX1WIDTH,BOX1LENGTH) +
                SURFACE(AREA,BOX2HEIGTH,BOX2WIDTH,BOX2LENGTH);
    WRITELN('THE TOTAL SURFACE AREA IS ',TOTALSURFACE:5)
END.  (* BOXES *)
```

12.5 RECURSION

Recursion is a powerful technique that can be applied to problem solving. Recursion often simplifies the solution to a problem. A recursive routine is one that can invoke itself. Recursive algorithms and definitions play an important part in solving certain problems. Sometimes recursion makes it easier to express a problem's solution because the recursion may be shorter, clearer, or easier to understand. However, a recursive solution may take longer for the computer to execute.

Both PROCEDUREs and FUNCTIONs can be used recursively. They are recursively used when they are invoked by a statement within the subprogram.

Recursion can be used both to continue execution or to perform iterative calculations. For example, the following PROCEDURE reads and prints characters until a blank character is found.

```
PROCEDURE FINDBLANK;
VAR
   LETTER: CHAR;
BEGIN
   READ(LETTER);
   IF LETTER <> ' '
      THEN BEGIN
         WRITE(LETTER);
         FINDBLANK
      END
END;  (* PROCEDURE FINDBLANK *)
```

This also could have been done by using a repetitive control structure. In this case, choosing one over the other is a matter of a programmer's personal style.

Some of the problems that can be successfully solved by recursion are problems that can be expressed as a series of solutions to simpler and simpler versions of the same problem. When doing this, a specific stopping point when the simplest version is reached is described. For example, if the problem is to develop the sum of all the integers between 1 and 5, this can be expressed as

```
1 + 2 + 3 + 4 + 5
```

which then can be made into the simpler problem of

```
(1 + 2 + 3 + 4) + 5
```

and then simplified further as shown below until the simplest case is reached:

```
((1 + 2 + 3) + 4) + 5
(((1 + 2) + 3) + 4) + 5
((((1) + 2) + 3) + 4) + 5
```

This is an example of recursive nesting. The following general program named SERIES will recursively calculate the value of the sum of the integers between any positive integer and 1. The calculations in the program SERIES will proceed precisely as expressed above.

```
PROGRAM SERIES(INPUT,OUTPUT);
   (* THIS READS IN AN INTEGER VALUE AND CALCULATES THE SUM OF THE
      DIGITS FROM 1 TO THE VALUE. THE PROGRAM CHECKS TO SEE IF THE
      VALUE IS AT LEAST ONE *)
VAR
   NUMBER: INTEGER;
(* =============================================================== *)
FUNCTION SUM(DIGIT:INTEGER):INTEGER;
BEGIN  (* ACTIONS IN SUM FUNCTION *)
   IF DIGIT = 1
      THEN SUM := 1
      ELSE SUM := SUM(DIGIT-1) + DIGIT
END;  (* FUNCTION SUM *)
(* =============================================================== *)
BEGIN  (* MAIN PART OF PROGRAM *)
   READ(NUMBER);
   WRITELN('THE VALUE READ WAS ',NUMBER:3);
   IF NUMBER < 1
      THEN WRITELN('THE NUMBER IS NOT ACCEPTABLE, IT IS TOO SMALL')
      ELSE WRITELN('THE SUM OF THE DIGITS BETWEEN 1 AND ',NUMBER:3,
                   ' IS ',SUM(NUMBER):4)
END.  (* SERIES *)
```

Recursive PROCEDUREs are particularly useful when used to perform some kinds of searches. Chapter 13 uses recursive PROCEDUREs to search user designed data structures.

12.6 QUESTIONS

12.1 PROCEDUREs and FUNCTIONs are subprograms that can be invoked by use of the subprogram's name. In what ways is the declaration of a subprogram different from the declaration of a program?

12.2 What is meant by "scope"?

12.3 Why might a Pascal program want to restrict the scope of a variable?

12.4 When is a variable locally known? When is a variable nonlocally known?

12.5 Identify at least two reasons why a variable would not be globally known.

12.6 What is the difference between an actual and a formal parameter?

12.7 In the following heading, what does the TYPE declaration CHAR describe?

FUNCTION SEX(AGE:INTEGER; PRICE:REAL; TRUTH:BOOLEAN):CHAR;

12.8 Describe something that a person might do that is recursive.

12.7 PROBLEMS

12.1. Some tax tables specify that married people pay 30% of their combined salary for the first $10,000 and 32% for any amount over that. The change in rates is at $8000 for single people. Write a program that inputs records that have an "M" or an "S" and a yearly salary figure. ("M" indicates married and "S" indicates single.) The program should report for each record the input data, the amount of tax, and the net salary after tax. Use one PROCEDURE to calculate the taxes for a married couple and another PROCEDURE to calculate the taxes for a single person. Test your program with the following data.

```
M  12364.84
S  12364.32
M   8941.12
M  27683.41
M  96218.19
S  84321.92
S  68440.07
```

12.2. Qrpits have as their goal the invasion of the planet Mprf. They have sent ahead a preinvasion intelligence team of five Qrpit members of the PQIA (Planetary Qrpit Intelligence Agency).

Qrpits have a rather short life cycle (one day). This is usually no problem as at the end of their life cycle they produce a new generation by fusing environmental molecules together and then transfer the group consciousness to the new generation. Usually the population of Qrpits varies from day to day, but does not cease to exist. However, an unknown factor in the Mprf environment sometimes causes progressively fewer Qrpits to be produced.

The equations describing the Qrpit population of Mprf are

(a) If Qrpits > 5
         then next generation Qrpits = Qrpits/2

(b) If 1 < Qrpits <= 5
         then next generation Qrpits = 2*Qrpits + 3 – generation number

(c) If Qrpits <= 1
         then there is no next generation

Note that fractional Qrpits (such as 4.7) cannot exist and TRUNC should be used in the calculations. (4.7 and 4.3 would both be TRUNCated to 4.)

You are to write a Pascal program that will use a recursive PROCEDURE to

(a)   Display the current generation and a PROCEDURE to display one "Q" for every Qrpit existing (the starting generation is generation zero).

(b)   Calculate the count of the next generation and the number of members in it.

(c)   Invoke the PROCEDUREs again if there is a next generation.

(d)   Your program may not use any explicit iterative control statements (WHILE, DO, etc.).

Display your results in the following form.

```
0   QQQQQ
1   QQQQQQQQQQQQQQ
2   QQQQQQ
3   QQQ
4   QQQQQQ
5   QQQ
6   QQQQ
.   .
.   .
.   .
```

where a reported "Q" represents a living Qrpit.

12.3.   Manufacturing companies have both fixed and variable costs. The fixed costs are due to costs such as executive salaries, machinery, purchase prices, et. Variable costs are those that only occur when a product is manufactured, such as labor and materials. Assuming that everything manufactured is sold the same day, a company's daily profits can be calculated by the equation:

```
PROFIT = QUANTITYSOLD*(PRICE-VARIABLECOSTS)-FIXEDCOSTS
```

The Red Dog Balloon Company has a fixed cost of $48.63 each business day. It sells its product for $0.50 an item. The cost for each item is $0.06. You are to produce a daily income statement of the following form.

```
QUALITY
  SOLD        PROFIT
  ----        ------
    15        -42.03
     0        -48.63
   123          5.49
     .            .
     .            .
     .            .
```

After all the data has been input, calculate and report the total quantity sold and the total profit. (*Note:* ARRAYS are not needed.) Calculate the profit using a FUNCTION. The only thing that your FUNCTION is to do is to calculate the profit.

Test your program with the following data.

15
0
123
364
72
95
483
106
269

12.4. A problem often solved recursively is known by numerous names, including the "Tower of Hanoi." According to one version of the problem description, monks in Tibet are said to be playing the game with a stack of 64 pieces. When their game is over, the world is to end.

The game is played with a set of disks; each disk is of a different size. The disks have a hole through them so they can be placed on any one of three shafts (A, B, or C). When the game begins, all the disks are on shaft A, the largest disk on the bottom, the next largest on top of it, etc. When the game ends, all the disks are to have been moved to either shaft B or C, again with the largest on the bottom, the next largest upon it, etc. The player who makes the last move is said to win. The rules governing how the moves may be made are

(a) Only one disk may be moved at a time.

(b) Any smaller disk may be put on top of any larger disk.

(c) No larger disk may ever be put on top of any smaller disk.

(d) Disks may be moved to any shaft.

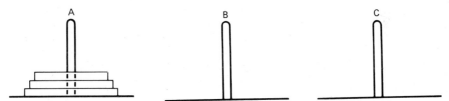

Figure P12.4   Tower of Hanoi starting position for three disks.

For convenience, number the smallest disk 1, the next 2, etc. An example of how a game might proceed for three disks is

```
MOVE DISK 1 TO SHAFT B
MOVE DISK 2 TO SHAFT C
MOVE DISK 1 TO SHAFT C
MOVE DISK 3 TO SHAFT B
MOVE DISK 1 TO SHAFT A
MOVE DISK 2 TO SHAFT C
MOVE DISK 1 TO SHAFT C
```

You are to write a Pascal program that will work for a count of disks from 1 to 64. Your program should input how many disks are on the starting shaft. Test your program using 10 disks. Display all the moves that are made.

12.5.   A vending machine owner sets the prices on his goods so that he makes a minimum expected profit. He does this by charging more for the goods than they cost. In order to set the price properly, he needs to take into account how much the items cost him, the minimum suggested markup (increase in the price of the wholesale price of the goods), and the labor costs associated with putting the goods in the machines. His costs are

(a)   Shipping
      $0.02 an item if more than 100 items are shipped to him
      $0.03 an item if less than 100 items are shipped to him
(b)   Labor
      $5.00 if less than 30 items are to be put into the machines
      $0.1666 an item if 30 or more items are to be put into the machines

His problem is to discover the minimum price that he should charge. He converts the problem into the following pseudo-code problem statement.

setting prices
1   define variables
2   input and display item price, item count, suggested markup
3   calculate the minimum retail price
    3.1   calculate the initial cost
        3.1.1   calculate the shipping cost: if item count > 100,
            3.1.1.1   then shipping cost is $0.02 per item
            3.1.1.2   else shipping cost is $0.03 per item
        3.1.2   item cost is item price plus shipping cost times item count
    3.2   calculate minimum net return required
        3.2.1   calculate labor cost: if item count less than 30
            3.2.1.1   then labor cost is $5.00
            3.2.1.2   else labor cost is item count * $0.1666
        3.2.2   add labor cost to the initial cost increased by suggested markup
    3.3   calculate minimum retail price: net retail return divided by item count
4   display minimum retail price for an item

The vending maching owner decides that this problem should be put on a computer as it will need to be done several times a month. Further, knowing a little about programming, he decides that pseudo-code statements under 3.1 are to be done in a FUNCTION and that the pseudo-code statements under 3.2 are also to be done in a FUNCTION. The FUNCTIONs to accomplish 3.1 and 3.2 are to be different FUNCTIONs. Furthermore, the FUNCTION for 3.1 is to be invoked by its inclusion as an element in a parameter list.

Your task is to write a Pascal program to do the above. Use the following as your test data.

           0.34   72 0.35
           0.14 144 0.47
           0.72   24 0.19

12.6. Billy Batson wishes to keep a running total of all his expenses. Because Billy was frightened by an ARRAY at birth, he will not require the person solving the problem (you) to use one. (However, if you wish to use one, you can.) What Billy wants is an output that looks something like this.

```
   ITEM          PRICE
  COUNT           PAID
------------------------
      1          12.24
      2           5.64
      3           0.59
      4         156.89
------------------------
   TOTAL ...    175.36
```

Because Billy has heard of a concept called modularization, he wants you to
(a) Display the titles in the main part of the program.
(b) Input the prices in the main part of the program.
(c) Count the prices and display them in a FUNCTION or a PROCEDURE.
(d) Total the prices in the main part of the program.
(e) Display the total of the prices in the main part of the program.

12.7 A simple payroll data collection consists of a file of records. Your program is to work for any number of data records between 0 and 100.
The input consists of the following information.

Name (20 characters)
Hours worked (XX.X)
Rate per hour (XX.XX)

You are to produce two reports. Each report contains the name, hours, rate, and amount earned. One report is to be displayed in alphabetic order. The other report is to be displayed in order of decreasing amount earned (i.e., the person who makes the most this week is listed first, second most is listed second, etc.). Time and a half is paid for all hours over 40. As each record is input, display it. The data must be input in the following order. Do the sorts using subprograms.

Smith, Tom	47.6	3.12
Cramden, Ralph	36.2	4.13
Crater, Judge	40.0	13.12
Hunt, Thomas	73.0	0.16
Murphy, Lewis	39.7	1.12
Brandt, Velma	38.0	2.43
Jordan, Carol	19.3	1.45
Worth, Mary	7.2	25.03
Stewart, Kitty	41.3	3.47
Keck, Martin	15.3	0.17
Torpin, Rose	40.0	0.70
Wilson, Anne	3.0	1.14
Vogel, Larry	63.7	1.15

12.8. Write a FUNCTION subprogram defined as SUM (KIND, DATA, N) that returns the sum of squares of the elements in either row N or column N of ARRAY DATA, depending on whether KIND has the value 1 or 2 respectively.

Then write a main program to do the following.

   (a) Input data into an ARRAY named DATA, having 5 rows and 6 columns.

   (b) Then compute the average of the sum of squares for each row and each column of DATA, using the FUNCTION named SUM.

   (c) Finally, display the ARRAY DATA and the average values computed above, according to any aesthetically pleasing format of your choice.

Test your program with the following input data.

11.5	7.3	6.2	8.1	9.0	0.2
2.6	−13.4	12.2	6.6	−1.0	0.8
−5.2	6.9	−3.1	14.2	7.4	0.6
4.8	3.6	−0.4	1.9	13.2	−0.1
3.3	2.7	−2.4	0.0	6.2	0.9

12.9. Write a Pascal program to calculate the factorial values for the numbers 2, 3, . . . , 12 (i.e., 21, 31, . . . , 12!). Use a recursive subprogram. *Hint:*

$$2! = 2*1 = 2$$
$$3! = 3*2*1 = 6$$
$$4! = 4*3*2*1 = 24$$
$$5! = 5*4*3*2*1 = 120$$

12.10. Martin Gardner in the March 1965 issue of *Scientific American* introduced the sliding box puzzle shown in Figure P12.10. The object of the puzzle is to change the pattern on the left to the pattern on the right. the number squares move freely within the box and up until 1965 the best solution on record required 36 moves. This method employed the following moves.

1 2 5 4 3 1 2 3 7 6 1 2 3 7 6 1 2 3 7 5 4 8 1 2 3 6 5 7 6 5 8 4 7 8 5 6

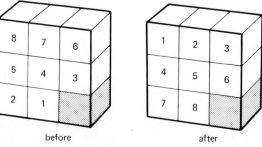

before   after

Figure P12.10 Sliding box puzzle.

Computers were used in the solution to the puzzle and they found 634 methods that required less than 36 moves. There were

10 methods requiring 30 moves
112 methods requiring 32 moves
512 methods requiring 34 moves

Write a program to solve this problem in 38 moves or less. Your first move must be 3 and your second move may not be 3.

12.11. The moving coin game is played on the board shown in Figure P12.11. The board is divided into nine equal squares. At the start of the game, four nickles are placed on the left-most four squares and four dimes are placed on the right-most four squares. The center square is left vacant at the start of a game.

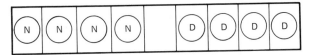

Figure P12.11   Moving coin game.

The object of the game is to move the coins to opposite ends of the board. Coins may move in two ways: They may jump over one of their own coins or one of the other coins and they may move one square at a time toward their goal. However, the coins may not be moved backward. The first four moves of a 24-move solution are

(1)   Move dime left
(2)   Jump nickel right
(3)   Move nickel right
(4)   Jump dime left

Write a program to play this game to a correct final solution. You are advised to try the game prior to writing a program to do so.

12.12. It is possible to place a knight on any square of a chessboard and then in 64 moves have him visit every other square once and only once. This is called a *knight's tour*. Write a program that will attempt to find such a knight's tour.

There are several ways of approaching this problem. One possibility is to use a method involving "backtracking". It turns out that backtracking is quite slow for this particular problem and very careful programming is necessary to produce an acceptable program.

A more efficient method is based on the following rules: For any square x on the chessboard let pi (x) ($i = 1, 2, \ldots$) be the number of squares accessible from x in i moves (not counting squares already visited). Always move the knight to a square x for which P1 (x) is as small as possible. If various choices for x are possible, choose an x for which P2 (x) is also as small as possible.

A method such as the above is called *heuristic:* It is not guaranteed to work in every possible situation; for example, it is not guaranteed to work for a 50 by 50 "chessboard." It has been found to always work for a standard 8 by 8 chessboard. The fact that only the values of P1 (x) and P2 (x) are used is referred to as *double look-ahead* and in other situations a larger look-ahead proves advantageous.

12.13. Two different researchers have gone out into the field and have given IQ tests at random to different subjects. Researchers Jones and Schwartz reported their scores ordered and punched on records. They reported their scores ordered from lowest to highest score.

Their scores were

researcher Jones	researcher Schwartz
15	34
23	45
28	67
47	89
78	111
89	123
92	145
98	169
120	178
123	181
135	
165	
178	

It is your job to produce one list of these scores arranged from high to low. Since the original sets of data were ordered, you will not sort the complete data set. Instead, follow these steps:

(a) Write a PROCEDURE that will reverse the order of the elements in a one-dimensional ARRAY. The item that originally was in the first position should end up in the last position, and vice versa. Therefore, if the ARRAY had been ordered from low to high, this subroutine should change the order so that the ARRAY is now ordered from high to low.

(b) Input each set of data into a separate ARRAY. Display each ARRAY as it is input.

(c) Using the PROCEDURE defined in **(a)**, invert each of the ARRAYs input **(b)**. Note that this means that the subroutine is used twice, once for each ARRAY.

(d) Merge the two ARRAYs into a third ARRAY that will maintain the high to low ordering. If na is the number of items in the first ARRAY and nb is the number of items in the second ARRAY, the length or the merged ARRAY should be na + nb.

(e) Assume that each researcher will collect a maximum of 100 IQs. However, it may sometimes occur that either or both may fail to turn in any data at all. Thus the same program must be capable of accepting anywhere from 0 to 100 data items a data set from either or both of the researchers. This means that your program must do all the necessary counting to compute the number of items in each data set.

(f) Display the final results.

12.14. The 12-month moving average is the first stage of a technique often used in forecasting. Because it is an average, it tends to smooth the influence of trends, cycles, and unpredictable factors in the data. These smoothed results, combined with a seasonal index, can sometimes be used as a valid prediction system.

Programming procedure: Calculate a moving total. The total for the first 12 months (1/83 to 12/83) is entered opposite the seventh month (7/83). For the eighth period moving total, eliminate the first month's data (1/83) from the moving total and add the 13th month's data (1/84). Moving totals for the first 6 and last 5 months' data cannot be computed.

Calculate a moving average for each month by dividing its moving total by 12. The following example shows a sample output.

Example:

```
              FUEL CONSUMPTION (GALLONS)
YEAR-MONTH        CONSUMPTION      12-MONTH TOTAL      12-MONTH AVERAGE
   1983

    1               226.7              0.0                  0.0
    2               208.1              0.0                  0.0
    3               237.1              0.0                  0.0
    4               243.3              0.0                  0.0
    5               248.3              0.0                  0.0
    6               228.4              0.0                  0.0
    7               212.3            2720.2               226.7
    8               217.1            2688.2               224.0
    9               222.7            2656.3               221.4
   10               235.5            2620.9               218.4
   11               222.3            2578.7               214.9
   12               218.4            2527.8               210.6
   1984
    1               194.7            2490.5               207.5
    2               176.2            2453.1               204.4
   ...               ...              ...                  ...
```

Assume the following monthly sales figures for a local grocery store. Write a program to input this data (you do not have to inout the month) and output a table similar to that shown above.

Monthly sales:

month	1983	1984	1985
January	$70410	$71994	$70134
February	68361	71369	72116
March	72192	72246	70319
April	75630	76011	72945
May	78693	77813	76183
June	81042	80099	81369
July	83349	82140	82570
August	82966	84792	86818
September	76831	80119	79314
October	73131	79862	76746
November	68392	70327	72990
December	67165	71416	71852

All moving total averages are to be calculated in a FUNCTION subprogram. The index variation and displaying are to be done in the mainline program.

12.15. Ian Vestor is a partner in Stock and Vestor Securities Ltd. His job involves advising clients as to where to invest their money. A new issue of Fly by Nite Company bonds has just come onto the market. These bonds are being issued in $50, $100, $500, and $1000 denominations. Interest is being paid at 7½% for the first three years, 8% for the next 5 years, and then at 8¼% for the remaining 4 years. The bonds mature after 2 years. If the interest is not collected by the investor after each year, it is added to the face value of the bond. For example, consider a $100 bond:

year	face value	interest	new face value
1	$ 100.00	7½% × $100.00 = $7.50	$107.50
2	$ 107.50	7½% × $107.50 = $8.06	$115.56

So the value of the bond after 2 years will be $115.56.

Mr. Vestor wants a table indicating the value of these bonds, if interest is not collected, at the end of each year until maturity. The form of the table should be

```
             FLY BY NITE BONDS
    YEAR     *
             *                   DENOMINATION
             *       50        100        500       1000
    * * * * * * * * * * * * * * * * * * * * * * * * * * * * * * * *
      1      *        .      107.50        .          .
      2      *        .      115.56        .          .
      .               .         .          .          .
      .                                              
     12               .         .          .          .
```

Write a Pascal program to construct this table. Your program must include a FUNCTION subprogram defined by

```
FUNCTION ANNUALINTEREST (PRINCIPAL,YEAR)
```

which has two arguments PRINCIPAL: principal or face value of bond and YEAR: year (1–12) for which interest is to be computed. The FUNCTION should return the interest for the given principal for that given year. For example, if year is 2 and principal is 107.50, the value returned by annual interest should be $115.56. Note that as the year gets larger, your rate of interest will change.

12.16. The compiler inputs your Pascal program as data and translates every executable statement of your program into machine language. Two of the early stages in this process involve (a) deleting blanks, for which Pascal has no use (edit phase); and (b) checking the validity of your statements (syntax checking phase). This assignment includes writing subproblems for simple cases of each of these two tasks as described below.

(a) Write a subproblem named EDIT that receives as one argument an ARRAY of 80 characters, removes all internal blanks (i.e., all nonblank characters are shifted left, leaving all blanks to the right of the last nonblank character), and returns the result in another 80-character ARRAY.

(b)   Write a subproblem named CHECK that tests Pascal assignment statements for certain types of errors. An assignment statement is received by CHECK in an 80-character ARRAY edited form. The assignment statement is assumed to have one of the forms:

```
result:=operand;
result:=operand+operand;
result:=operand–operand;
result:=operand+operand+operand;
etc.
```

In particular, no parentheses are allowed, and the only operators permitted are "+" and "–". You may assume that the operands (i.e., constants or variable names) are all valid. This means that the only "special symbols" of interest are :, =, +, –, ;, and blank; any intervening sequence of characters is a legitimate constant or variable.

The subprogram should check for the following errors.

1.   An arithmetic operator (+ or –) anywhere to the left of ":=".
2.   An invalid arithmetic expression to the right of the ":=", as indicated by any two consecutive operators of "special symbols," i.e., (:, =, +, –, ;, or blank . Thus, the following forms are invalid:

```
result:=operand++operand . . .
result:= . . . final operand+
```

The subprogram should produce the appropriate error messages:

1.   If arithmetic occurred to the left of the sign, the message is

ARITHMETIC PRECEDES

2.   If two consecutive "special symbols" are discovered, the message is:

INVALID ARITHMETIC

(c)   Write a main program that is to input the executable part of a simple Pascal program that has only assignment statements. The assignment statements are delineated by a BEIN and an END.

Your main program should edit each Pascal statement as it is input and each assignment statement should be checked for validity. After inputting and processing an END statement, your program should stop. The output is produces should resemble the following.

```
ORIGINAL PROGRAM        EDITED PROGRAM          ERRORS
  AGE:=5;                 AGE:=5;
  TOTAL:=5+AGE+;          TOTAL:=5+AGE+;        INVALID ARITHMETIC
```

Use the following Pascal program as input data.

```
BEGIN
  AGE:= 5;
  COST := PRICE - DISCOUNT + 3;
  TOTAL: -5 + AGE+;
  VOLUME+ 23:=17;
  COST:=PRICE+TAX-DISCOUNT
END.
```

12.17. Henry wants to lose 11 pounds by the time of the big dance (in six weeks). He is willing to reduce his calorie intake from his current intake of 2000 to 900 calories a day. However, he would prefer to reduce his intake as little as possible. It takes a 3500 calorie reduction for him to lose one pound. You are to help his plan by showing him the number of days it will take to lose 11 pounds, starting with 100 calories less than his usual intake of 1900 calories and reducing the calorie intake 100 calories until the minimum amount of 900 calories is reached. The output should be in the following form. This is to be done by use of a recursive PROCEDURE.

```
    CURRENT                 DAY TO
    CALORIE                  LOSE
     INTAKE             11  POUNDS
    -------             --------
     1900                     .
       .                      .
       .                      .
       .                      .
      900                     .
```

12.18. Bob Smith is an African Bee keeper. He has just selectively bred a new hybrid queen bee that produces better tasting honey at a faster rate than any other species. The queen produces 5 drone bees every day after her third day of life and another queen bee on every seventh day, in addition to the drones. Each drone bee lives only 20 days and produces 1 gram of honey every day after the second day of life in addition to the honey that it eats itself. Every day the queen consumes 1.5 times as much honey as on the day before. If, on the first day of life, the queen bee consumes 0.5 gram of honey, how long should Bob let the queen bee live? How long will it take for the hive to produce 100 kilograms? Use subprograms to do all calculating and displaying until the 100 kilogram demand of honey is met.

12.19. *Enterameoba coli* is a single celled organism that is currently being used to produce human insulin for diabetic purposes. The human gene that normally produces insulin is implanted into an *E. coli* and functions and divides as the genetic material of the *E. coli* does. The *E. coli* reproduces through binary fission every 20 minutes and produces 1/1000 milliliter during the same period of time. If one *E. coli* is implanted with the human gene, how many generations will it take to produce 1 liter of insulin? How many hours will this take? Display the generation by generation results. Control your calculations by using a recursive PROCE-DURE. Do not use any other iterative control structure.

Chapter 13

DYNAMIC DATA STRUCTURES

Objectives
Define and construct data structures where the extent of the required storage is not clearly known before the program begins execution. The structures are formed of data components that are connected together as required during the program's execution.

Suggested Background
This chapter makes use of portions of all of the preceding chapters. Material used in some sections includes RECORD, WHILE, and IF-THEN-ELSE.

Different tasks may have different storage requirements. Some tasks have very well defined storage requirements, some have storage requirements that are known within loosely defined limits, and others have storage needs that are not very well known at all. Different solution strategies can be used to solve problems with differently defined storage requirements.

Even everyday storage requirements may be known to differing extents. For example, when a person stores jelly beans in a large jar, there is only one storage space involved; sometimes it may have more beans in it than at other times. An example of a less well defined storage requirement is a farmer who needs baskets for the apples she is picking. The nature of the baskets required is well known. However, since the work sometimes progresses faster than at other times, the number of baskets needed will vary. Nonetheless, she does know the maximum number of baskets that will be required at the orchard before starting work. An example of a still more changeable storage requirement is the dynamic customer packaging needs of a discount store. Some customers buy small things and some buy big things. Some things are heavy, some may leak, and some may melt. The mix of bags required changes from day to day and from hour to hour. The store must have a capability to provide a substantially varying amount of customer storage.

So far, when discussing data storage, this book has been concerned with making storage available for objects of data TYPEs with fixed space needs, such as

INTEGERs or RECORDs. The quantity of storage needed for problem solution has been reasonably well known. This chapter is concerned with how to store data where the quantity of data to be stored is uncertain and where the data organization is determined by the nature of the data being stored.

When the quantity of space that is allocated to data storage is fixed and how the data is organized is also predetermined, the data definition is said to be *static*. When the quantity of space that is to be allocated to data storage can change during program execution, the data definition is said to be *dynamic*.

Dynamic data structures can be used in Pascal. A dynamic data variable is created and destroyed dynamically during the execution of the program. The Pascal programmer specifies when space for the variable is to be created and when the space is to be destroyed. A dynamic data structure can be made to expand or contract in size during the program's execution as the data storage requirements change.

13.1 DEFINING DYNAMIC STRUCTURES

Objectives
Introduce the concepts of indirect references, chaining, and pointers.

Suggested Background
The preceding material in this chapter. No specific Pascal knowledge is needed for this conceptual introduction.

Dynamic variables are created on demand by executed statements. This means that statements asking for dynamically provided space do not supply any space until they are actually executed.

Since the existence of a dynamic variable is not known before the statement creating it is executed, the storage space for the variable and the variable name cannot be declared in the VAR section. As a result, dynamic variables cannot be directly referenced by using a variable name. They can only be indirectly referenced through the value of a static variable. The static variable that does the referencing is called a *pointer* and it used to refer to dynamic data values. The collection of all the dynamic data values that are associated with each other is called a *data structure*. A dynamic data structure is composed of *components*. Each component is made up of one or more dynamic variables. Each individual component can be thought of as supplying a single package of related information. For example, if the components are supplying data on people, each component might include age, sex, salary, etc.

The concept of indirect referencing may be new to many readers of this book. Indirect references are essential to using a computer for efficient solution of many problems. Some children's games make use of indirect references. For example, there is the "treasure hunt" game where the players try to follow a trail of messages: the first message tells a player where to find the second message, the second message tells where the third message is, and so forth, until the last message leads to the prize. In this type of chain, each message after the first one is indirectly discovered and is itself an indirect reference. Some computer solved problems use a long chain of indirect references.

13.1.1 Pointers

Objective
Introduce the technique of referencing dynamically stored data by using pointers.

Suggested Background
(a) The preceding sections of this chapter, and (b) the chapter on user defined data, most specifically, the section on RECORDs.

A dynamic variable is referenced indirectly by a pointer. The pointer value is used to access the corresponding dynamic value. The pointer value is stored in an appropriate static variable. A graphic description is shown in Figure 13.1.

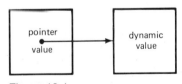

Figure 13.1

A dynamic variable exists until it is explicitly destroyed by a Pascal program statement or the program finishes execution. Programs that use a lot of dynamic storage should make sure to destroy space once it is no longer needed (see Section 13.1.2). If this is not done, the program may eventually not be able to get new dynamic space.

Pointers can be moved from one dynamic variable to another. The pointer variable is defined in a TYPE statement of the form

```
TYPE
    <pointer name> = @<component name>
```

The component pointed to is usually a record. It is usually a record because the component usually contains at least two data elements: (a) some data and (b) a pointer reference to another component. An example of a simple list structure is shown in Figure 13.2.

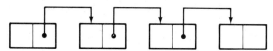

Figure 13.2   Simple list structure.

The TYPE for this list structure can be defined using the following declarations.

```
TYPE
   POINTER = @CELL;
   CELL = RECORD
              VALUE: INTEGER;
              NEXT: POINTER
          END;
VAR
   LAST: POINTER;
```

How a list structure is formed using these declarations is discussed in the following sections.

List structures violate Pascal's general principle that definition must precede use. Here CELL is used before its definition. There was no way around the problem. Either CELL or POINTER had to be used before definition. Pascal's designers chose the form shown.

13.1.2 Controlling Space

Objective
Introduce the Pascal statements used to create and destroy dynamic storage.

Suggested Background
The preceding sections in this chapter.

Dynamic variable storage space is controlled by the Pascal programmer using two standard procedures, NEW and DISPOSE. Dynamic variable space for a particular variable of a specific TYPE can be both created and destroyed. When storage is created, it is said to be *allocated* because new space is set aside for use within the computer. Storage is allocated using the NEW statement in the form

```
NEW(<pointer to new data component>)
```

The NEW statement allocates a new dynamic variable storage space. The dynamic storage space is referenced by the specified pointer variable. The TYPE of the data structure that is allocated is determined by the TYPE of the pointer used. For example, using the TYPE declaration of the previous section (13.1.1),

```
NEW(LAST)
```

would create a new dynamic variable space as defined by CELL in the TYPE declaration. The reference to be used to access this space will be the value of the pointer LAST.

Space that can be allocated dynamically is kept on an *available space list*. Pascal programmers do not have to be concerned with how to keep track of what space is currently available. This task is handled by the Pascal compiler. The Pascal programmer should be concerned with asking for new space and returning space once it is no longer used.

Space is returned to the available space list by the DISPOSE command. When space is returned, it is said to be *destroyed*, since it no longer is available for use in the Pascal program. The form of the command is

```
DISPOSE(<pointer to the space to be destroyed>)
```

The command destroys the space referenced by the pointer. All dynamic data of a particular TYPE is not destroyed by the execution of a DISPOSE statement, but only the specific space pointed to by the pointer. After the command is executed, the value of the pointer is undefined. For example,

```
DISPOSE(LAST)
```

would release space currently pointed to through LAST. If a program does not DISPOSE of space after it is no longer required, the program may eventually use up all of the available space and stop executing. (DISPOSE is not available in some implementations of Pascal.)

13.1.3 Pointer References

Objective
Discuss how dynamic data can be referenced by pointers.

Suggested Background
The preceding sections of this chapter.

Pointers either point to a dynamic component or they do not. If they do not point to a component, they are said to be *NIL pointers*. A pointer may be assigned a NIL value, for example,

```
LAST := NIL
```

The NIL pointer is shown graphically in this book as a box with a slash drawn through it. Pointers that are to point to a component need to be supplied with the reference to the component. This reference is first supplied when the NEW command is executed.

The values in a dynamic data structure are indirectly referenced through the pointer that references the data structure. The form of the reference is

```
<pointer>@.<variable>
```

The @ indicates that an indirect reference is being performed. (An indirect reference can also be called a *dereference*.) For example,

```
LAST@.VALUE := 5
```

stores the scalar value of 5 in the variable VALUE of the dynamic data structure pointed to by LAST.

Pointers can only be created by using NEW and destroyed only by DISPOSE. They can only be copied into another pointer pointing to the same TYPE. A pointer can only receive a copy of a pointer pointing to data of the same TYPE, or be set to NIL. Pointers can be compared to other pointers pointing to data of the same TYPE, but cannot themselves be operated upon by arithmetic.

13.2 LINKED LISTS

Objective
Discuss the formation of the linear linked list form of a dynamic data structure. This illustrates one use of dynamic storage.

Suggested Background
(a) The preceding sections of this chapter; (b) the chapter on user defined data, specifically the section on RECORDs; (c) the chapter on iterative control, specifically the section on WHILE.

The linked list is the simplest TYPE of dynamic data structure. It allows a Pascal programmer to maintain a list to which components may be added or deleted.

13.2.1 Creating a List

Objective
Demonstrate how a simple linear linked list can be created.

Suggested Background
The same as for Section 13.2.

Creating a linear linked list is a straightforward process. Every time a new component is to be added to the list, new space for that component is allocated and then the space is linked to the already existing list.

Example

Read in a list of integers and place them into a linked list. If the integers are

$$-3 \quad 27 \quad 12 \quad -17 \quad 4$$

the resulting linked list will be as shown in Figure 13.3.

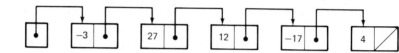

Figure 13.3   Resulting linked list.

build a linked list of numbers
1   define variables
    1.1   dynamic
    1.2   static
2   set pointer in last cell of list to NIL
3   while there may still be data, build the list
    3.1   try to read a new number
            3.1.1   if a new number was found, insert a new cell into the list
                    3.1.1.1   get a new dynamic data space
                    3.1.1.2   store the number in the dynamic variable
                    3.1.1.3   set dynamic variable's pointer to the base pointer
                    3.1.1.4   set the base pointer to the last pointer value used
4   problem finished

The steps in the development of a list using the program LINK are illustrated graphically in Figure 13.4.

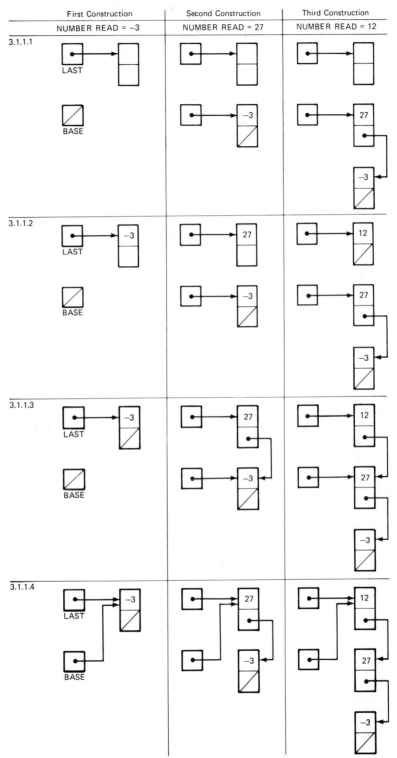

Figure 13.4

```
PROGRAM LINK(INPUT,OUTPUT);
   (* THIS READS IN NUMBERS AND PUTS THEM INTO A LINKED LIST *)
TYPE
   POINTER = @CELL;
   CELL = RECORD
              VALUE: INTEGER;
              NEXT: POINTER
          END;
VAR
   LAST: POINTER;
   BASE: POINTER;
   NUMBER: INTEGER;
BEGIN  (* BUILDING A LINKED LIST *)
   BASE := NIL;
   WHILE NOT EOF DO BEGIN  (* TRY TO BUILD A LINKED LIST *)
      READ(NUMBER);  (* TRY TO READ A NUMBER *)
      IF NOT EOF
         THEN BEGIN  (* INSERT A NEW CELL IF A NEW NUMBER IS READ *)
            NEW(LAST);
            LAST@.VALUE := NUMBER;
            LAST@.NEXT := BASE;
            BASE := LAST
         END  (* INSERT A NEW CELL *)
   END  (* TRYING TO BUILD A LINKED LIST *)
END.  (* LINK *)
```

The data stored in the list created by the program LINK is kept in inverse input order. That is, the first stored item is stored in the last available component of the list and the last stored item is stored in the first available component of the list. This is the simplest way to use a list structure. It is sometimes known as a *push down* stack.

More than one data value may be kept for each component in a list. Figure 13.5 illustrates how several different pieces of data might be kept in each component of a list. A component in a list is often called a *cell* or a *node*.

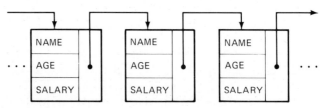

Figure 13.5   Example of a list where the components have several data values.

13.2.2 Writing a Simple List

Objective
Illustrate how the contents of a simple list can be printed.

Suggested Background
The same as for Section 13.2.

A simple PROCEDURE can be added to the program LINK in Section 13.2.1 to write the list out after it has been completed. Note that the data in the list is stored backward from the way that it was read in. When the list is printed, it will come out backward from the way it was read in. The invocation for the PROCEDURE named PRINTLIST should be placed directly before the program delimiter "END." The PROCEDURE is

```
PROCEDURE PRINTLIST;
BEGIN  (* ACTIVITIES IN THE PROCEDURE *)
   LAST := BASE;
   WHILE LAST <> NIL DO BEGIN  (* PRINTING LIST *)
      WRITE(LAST@.VALUE);
      LAST := LAST@.NEXT
   END  (* PRINTING THE LIST *)
END;  (* PROCEDURE PRINTLIST *)
```

If the list printed were constructed by the program LINK (Section 13.2.1), the list would have been constructued in an input inverse order. This results in PRINTLIST displaying the last item placed into the list first, the second to last item placed into the list second, and so forth, until the first item stored in the list is displayed last.

13.2.3 Deleting a Component

Objective
Illustrate the manipulation of a linked list by deleting a component.

Suggested Background
All of Section 13.2 along with the background suggested for Section 13.2.

Dynamic data structures are easy to modify. This is one of the reasons for using them. Modifying includes both adding components to and deleting components from the list. Deletion can be accomplished as a two step process: (a) move the pointer from the component to be deleted to the next component on the list [as shown in Figure 13.6(b)]; then (b) destroy the component being deleted [as shown in Figure 13.6(c)]. It is necessary to destroy the deleted component in a separate step after it is separated from the list, otherwise it will continue to exist.

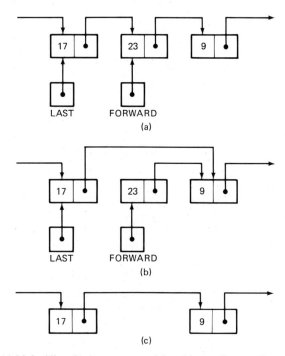

Figure 13.6 (a) Linked list. (b) A component deleted from a list. (c) The component deleted from the list destroyed by the DISPOSE statement.

If the data declarations include

```
TYPE
    POINTER = @CELL;
    CELL = RECORD
                VALUE: INTEGER;
                NEXT: POINTER
            END;
VAR
    LAST: POINTER;
    FORWARD: POINTER;
```

the statement

```
LAST@.NEXT := FORWARD@.NEXT
```

will move the NEXT pointer forward as in Figure 13.6(b). The statement

```
DISPOSE(NEXT)
```

would then destroy the unwanted component. The following PROCEDURE will delete the component pointed at by value of DELETE.

```
PROCEDURE TAKEOUT(KEEP:POINTER; DELETE:POINTER);
VAR
    FORWARD: POINTER;
BEGIN
    KEEP@.NEXT := DELETE@.NEXT;
    DISPOSE(DELETE)
END;
```

13.2.4 Inserting Components

Objective
Illustrate how to develop linear linked lists by inserting components into the list.

Suggested Background
The preceding sections of this chapter.

New components can easily be added to the middle of a list if a pointer is available to the component after which the new component is to be inserted. Insertion is a three step process: (a) create a new space to contain the data to be inserted, (b) set the new component's pointer to the cell it is to precede [as shown in Figure 13.7(b)], (c) set the pointer on the preceding cell to the new cell [as shown in Figure 13.7(c)]. If available, any other data values of the new list component can also be added.

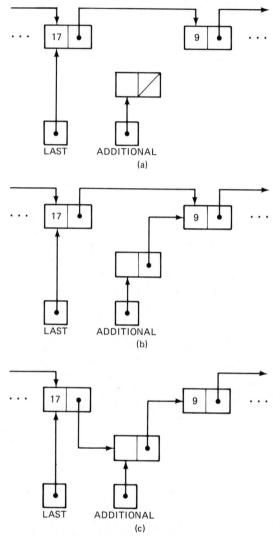

Figure 13.7   (a) A linked list with a new component to be added. (b) New component partially inserted in a linked list. (c) New component fully inserted into a list.

The following PROCEDURE will accomplish these steps.

```
PROCEDURE INSERT(VAR LAST; NEWDATA:INTEGER);
VAR
    ADDITION: POINTER;
BEGIN
    NEW(ADDITION);  (* CREATE NEW SPACE *)
    ADDITION@.VALUE := NEWDATA;  (* SET VALUE OF ELEMENT OF NEW SPACE *)
    ADDITION@.NEXT := LAST@.NEXT;  (* LINK SPACE TO BACK OF LIST *)
    LAST@.NEXT := ADDITION  (* LINK SPACE TO FRONT OF LIST *)
END;
```

13.2.5 Simultaneously Referring to Elements of Different Components

Objectives
Illustrate how to refer to two different list components in the same statement. Introduce the concept of multiple indirect references.

Suggested Background
The previous sections of this chapter. From previous chapters: (a) the section on IF-THEN-ELSE and (b) the section on recursive PROCE-DUREs.

Sometimes it is necessary to refer to two or more elements of different components of a dynamic data structure. For example, it may be necessary to compare particular values of two different components, such as employee age.

This need can occur in a wide range of data structures. When it does, a way must be found to provide pointer references to the components. One way of doing this is to have a separate pointer variable for each component that is to be used. It is also sometimes possible to make use of additional levels of indirect referencing. The two methods are illustrated in the PROCEDUREs named PAIRS and SCAN in the following example.

Example: PAIRS
This inserts a new component into an ordered linear list. An ordered linear list is one where the components are placed in a sequence that is dependent on one of the data values of the components that make up the list. This example is ordered on ascending or increasing values; that is, $-4, -3, -2, -1, 0, 1, 2, 3, 4$. For simplicity, this example does not consider how to handle the first and last components of the list. (However, one of the problems at the end of this chapter does.)

The PROCEDURE named PAIRS uses pointer values to adjacent components of the list. After finding the pair of components between which the new component is to be inserted, the PROCEDURE named INSERT is invoked to create a new component and to insert it.

```
PROCEDURE PAIRS(NUMBER:INTEGER; FIRST:POINTER; SECOND:POINTER);
BEGIN
    IF (FIRST@.VALUE < NUMBER) AND (SECOND@.VALUE >= NUMBER)
        THEN INSERT(FIRST,NUMBER)  (* INSERT NEW COMPONENT *)
        ELSE BEGIN  (* SHIFT DOWN LIST *)
            FIRST := FIRST@.NEXT;
            SECOND := FIRST@.NEXT;
            PAIRS(NUMBER,FIRST,SECOND)  (* EXAMINE NEXT PAIR *)
        END  (* SHIFTING DOWN LIST *)
    END;  (* PROCEDURE PAIRS *)
```

The way PAIRS works is illustrated in Figure 13.8. Figure 13.8(a) shows the case where a comparison can be made. Figure 13.8(b) illustrates the first part of the shift down the list; that is, after the execution of

```
FIRST := FIRST@.NEXT
```

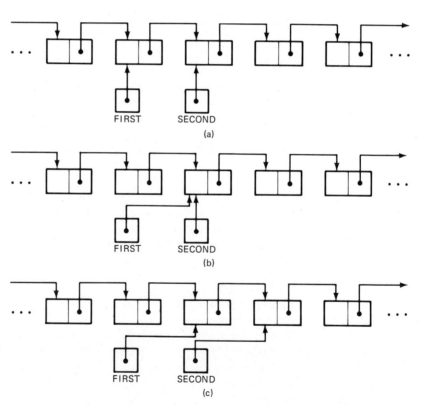

Figure 13.8 (a) FIRST and SECOND pointers identifying a pair of components of a list so they can be compared. (b) FIRST pointer shifted down list. (c) SECOND pointer shifted down list. SECOND pointer location was found in NEXT field of the component.

Figure 13.8(c) illustrates the state of things when the shift has been completed; that is, after the execution of

```
SECOND := FIRST@.NEXT
```

This returns to the situation first shown in Figure 13.8(a), only shifted down the list one position.

The PROCEDURE named SCAN accomplishes the same thing as PAIRS. However, it needs only a single pointer variable to refer to the adjacent components. The reference

```
CURRENT@.NEXT@.VALUE
```

provides the value for the next component following the one referred to by CURRENT. This is done indirectly through the NEXT pointer value of the component referred to by CURRENT.

```
PROCEDURE SCAN(CURRENT:POINTER;NEWDATA:INTEGER);
BEGIN
   IF (CURRENT@.VALUE < NEWDATA) AND (CURRENT@.NEXT@.VALUE >= NEWDATA)
      THEN INSERT(CURRENT,NEWDATA)
      ELSE BEGIN  (* MOVE FURTHER DOWN THE LIST *)
         CURRENT := CURRENT@.NEXT;  (* MOVE DOWN THE LIST *)
         SCAN(CURRENT,NEWDATA)  (* LOOK AT NEXT PAIR *)
   END  (* MOVING DOWN THE LIST *)
END;  (* PROCEDURE SCAN *)
```

13.3 SIMPLE RINGS

Objectives
Introduce the concept of a more complex use of a linked list, that is, rings. This provides a further insight into the complex structures that can be developed using Pascal.

Suggested Background
The preceding sections of this chapter.

A simple ring is a linked list that has the first and last components linked together. Figure 13.9 shows a ring.

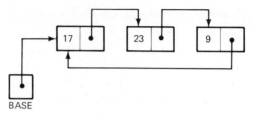

Figure 13.9   A simple ring.

A ring has the advantage over a simple list because the special cases of the first and last components of the list do not occur.

A ring is initially created by a two step process: (a) allocate new space and (b) assign the pointer to itself. The result of doing this is shown in Figure 13.10.

Figure 13.10   A single component ring.

For example, the following program RINGSTART will construct a ring of one component.

```
PROGRAM RINGSTART(INPUT,OUTPUT);
TYPE
   POINTER = @CELL;
   CELL = RECORD
              VALUE: INTEGER;
              NEXT: POINTER
          END;
VAR
   LAST: POINTER;
   NUMBER: INTEGER;
BEGIN  (* BUILDING A RING OF ONE ELEMENT *)
   NEW(LAST);
   LAST@.NEXT := LAST
END.
```

Note that VALUE of the component is not defined.

The following program RING is an extension of the previous program. It reads in data and constructs a ring. If the input data is

17   23   97

Figure 13.9 will be the result.

```
PROGRAM RING(INPUT,OUTPUT);
TYPE
   POINTER = @CELL;
   CELL = RECORD
              VALUE: INTEGER;
              NEXT: POINTER
          END;
VAR
   LAST: POINTER;
   NUMBER: INTEGER;
(* ================================================================ *)
PROCEDURE INSERT(VAR LAST:POINTER,NEWDATA:INTEGER);
   (* THIS INSERTS A COMPONENT INTO A LINKED LIST *)
VAR
   ADDITION: POINTER;
BEGIN  (* ACTIONS IN INSERT PROCEDURE *)
   NEW(ADDITION);
   ADDITION@.VALUE := NEWDATA;
   ADDITION@.NEXT := LAST@.NEXT;
   LAST@.NEXT := ADDITION;
   LAST := ADDITION
END;  (* PROCEDURE INSERT *)
(* ================================================================ *)
BEGIN  (* BUILDING A RING *)
   NEW(LAST);  (* INITIAL COMPONENT IN RING *)
   LAST@.NEXT := LAST;
   READ(NUMBER);  (* FIRST VALUE, INSERT INTO INITIAL COMPONENT *)
   IF EOF
      THEN WRITELN('NO DATA TO BE INSERTED INTO RING')
      ELSE LAST@.VALUE := NUMBER;
   WHILE NOT EOF DO BEGIN
      READ(NUMBER);  (* TRY TO READ A NUMBER TO PUT IN RING *)
      IF NOT EOF
         THEN INSERT(LAST,NUMBER)
   END  (* TRYING TO READ NUMBERS *)
END.  (* RING *)
```

Notice that the same PROCEDURE named INSERT was used to build a ring as well as the linear linked list.

Care should be taken when traversing a ring. Because there isn't any start or end (indicated by a NIL pointer), a program searching the list for a value that isn't there can continue going around and around the ring until it stops because it has used too much time. (Some Pascal compilers also stop when too many statements have been executed. How many is too many is set by each installation.)

The looping problem can be handled in several ways. Three among them are: (a) storing the pointer value for the place where the program starts a particular search and stopping when that value comes around again; (b) keeping a count of the components in the ring and only moving that many times around the ring; (c) having a pointer (such as BASE in Figure 13.9) where all searches start and terminating the search when that value again comes up. The technique of counting components is also useful for detecting when the ring has only one component left in it.

13.4 TREES

Objective
Discuss the formation of the tree form of dynamic data structures.

Suggested Background
(a) From this chapter, all parts of Section 13.1 are suggested. Sections 13.2 and 13.3 are not necessary. This section may precede Sections 13.2 and 13.3. (b) The chapter on user defined data, specifically the section of defining RECORDs. (c) The chapter on selection, specifically the section on IF-THEN-ELSE. (d) The chapter on iterative control, specifically the section on WHILE.

Trees are commonly used data structure. A tree is also known as a directed graph. It consists of nodes containing information with links between the nodes. A single, or root node, originates the tree. Rings, loops, or cycles are not formed. A tree is usually drawn upside down, that is, from its root node down. For example, a tree tracing a person's descendants might look like Figure 13.11.

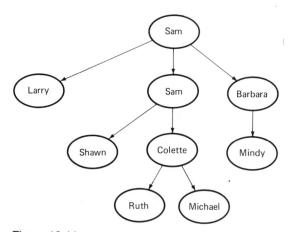

Figure 13.11

Tree structures are classified by the maximum number of branches that may exit from a node. The tree shown in Figure 13.11 is a *trinary* tree since three pointers exit the root node. Trees that allow any number of pointers to leave a node are known as a *n-ary*, or general, trees. There is a general theoretical result which states that any general tree may be represented as a binary tree (two exits per node). Consequently, some people prefer to represent most trees in computer programs as binary trees.

One use for trees is to store data in an ordered sequence, for example, alphabetically, or in increasing numeric order. For example, Figure 13.12 is a binary tree holding numeric data at its nodes. The data is sequence ordered from lowest value to highest value. The dotted line indicates how a program would read the tree to reflect this ordering.

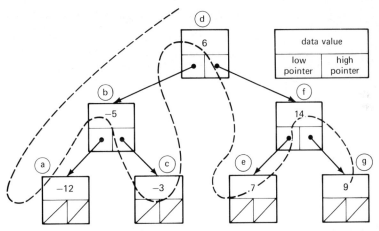

Figure 13.12   A binary tree holding data from lowest to highest. Each node of the tree has low and high pointers. The data in the tree was entered in the sequence 6, –5, 14, –12, 7, 19, –3. The letters in circles, ⓐ, ⓑ, . . ., ⓖ, indicate the sequential ordering of the nodes. The dotted line indicates the search path through the tree that a program would follow to display the data in an ordered list. (Consider that the contents of a node are displayed when the dotted line passes through the data value in the node.)

Example: TREE
Place a list of integers into a binary tree in a low to high sequence. After all the data has been placed in the tree, traverse the tree and print the integers out in low to high numeric order. The recursive PROCEDURE BUILD constructs the tree and the recursive PROCEDURE named SEQUENCE traverses and prints the tree.

The program plan for this example TREE is

build a tree
1   define variables
    1.1   dynamic
    1.2   static
2   initialize tree structure by setting pointers to NIL
3   while there may still be data, try to build a tree
    3.1   try to read a new data item
    3.2   if a new data item was found, process the data item
        3.2.1   echo print the data item
        3.2.2   insert the data into the tree by creating a node to hold it by finding a branch in the appropriate direction (high or low) which does not point to a node and then creating a node for this branch to hold the data
            3.2.2.1   if there is no next node pointed to along branch of tree where the new data should go, then create a node to hold the data
                3.2.2.1.1   create a new dynamic node for the tree
                3.2.2.1.2   set next low pointer in new node to NIL
                3.2.2.1.3   set next high pointer in new node to NIL
                3.2.2.1.4   store the new data into the new node
            3.2.2.2   else if there was a next node along the path followed, recursively search further down the tree
                3.2.2.2.1   if the new data is less than the data stored in the node in the tree where the tree search is
                    3.2.2.2.1.1   then follow low branch pointer by doing 3.2.2 again (recursively)
                    3.2.2.2.1.2   else follow high pointer and do 3.2.2 again (recursively)
4   display tree, lowest value to highest value
    4.1   start at top of tree (currently available from results of 3)
    4.2   recursive search repeated until NIL pointer in a tree's node found
        4.2.1   search along low pointer branch by again doing 4.2
        4.2.2   after NIL pointer has been found display data in node
        4.2.3   search along high pointer by again doing 4.2
5   end of problem

The program TREE follows this plan.

```
PROGRAM TREE(INPUT,OUTPUT);
   (* THIS STORES INTEGER DATA IN A TREE ORDERED LOW TO HIGH *)
TYPE
   BRANCH = @TREE;
   TREE = RECORD
               NUMBER: INTEGER;
               LOW: BRANCH;
               HIGH: BRANCH
            END;  (* TREE RECORD *)
VAR
   NODE: BRANCH;
   INPUTNUMBER: INTEGER;
(* ================================================================ *)
PROCEDURE BUILD(VAR NODE:BRANCH; NEWNUMBER:INTEGER);
   (* THIS INSERTS A NUMBER INTO THE TREE *)
BEGIN  (* INSERT A NUMBER INTO A NODE IN THE TREE *)
   IF NODE = NIL
      THEN BEGIN (* CREATE NEW NODE *)
         NEW(NODE);
         NODE@.LOW := NIL;
         NODE@.HIGH := NIL;
         NODE@.NUMBER := NEWNUMBER
      END  (* CREATE NEW NODE *)
      ELSE BEGIN  (* USE EXISTING NODE *)
         IF NEWNUMBER < NODE@.NUMBER
            THEN BUILD(NODE@.LOW,NEWNUMBER);
         IF NEWNUMBER >= NODE@.NUMBER
            THEN BUILD(NODE@.HIGH,NEWNUMBER)
      END  (* USING EXISTING NODE *)
END;  (* PROCEDURE BUILD *)
(* ================================================================ *)
PROCEDURE SEQUENCE(NODE:BRANCH);
BEGIN  (* PRINT DATA IN NODES OF TREE IN LOW TO HIGH SEQUENCE *)
   IF NODE <> NIL  (* TEST FOR STOPPING POINT *)
      THEN BEGIN  (* PRINTING NODE VALUES *)
         SEQUENCE(NODE@.LOW);
         WRITE(NODE@.NUMBER:4);
         SEQUENCE(NODE@.HIGH)
      END  (* PRINTING NODE VALUES *)
END;  (* PROCEDURE SEQUENCE *)
(* ================================================================ *)
BEGIN (* MAIN PART OF THE PROGRAM *)
   NODE := NIL;
   WRITELN('INITIAL DATA SEQUENCE:');
   WHILE NOT EOF DO BEGIN (* CONSTRUCTING TREE *)
      READ(INPUTNUMBER);  (* TRY TO READ DATA *)
      IF NOT EOF
         THEN BEGIN  (* INSERT NUMBER INTO THE TREE *)
            WRITE(INPUTNUMBER:4);  (* ECHO PRINT NUMBER *)
            BUILD(NODE,INPUTNUMBER)  (* INSERT NUMBER INTO TREE *)
         END  (* INSERTING NUMBER INTO TREE *)
   END;  (* READING NUMBERS TO PUT IN A TREE *)
   WRITELN;  (* NEEDED TO START NEXT TITLE LINE IN FIRST COLUMN *)
   WRITELN('SEQUENCE OF NUMBERS STORED IN THE TREE:');
   SEQUENCE(NODE)  (* PRINT OUT TREE *)
END.  (* TREE *)
```

if the initial data were

6 -5 14 6 7 -12 19 8 -6 15 21

the resulting tree is shown in Figure 13.13.

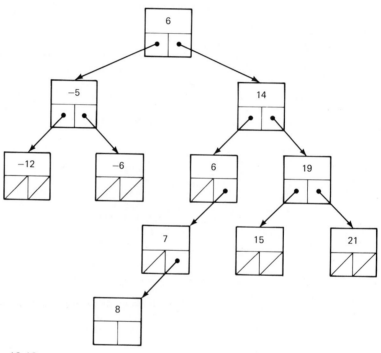

Figure 13.13

13.5 QUESTIONS

13.1 In what way does the storage space used for data declared as being dynamic differ from
      the storage space used for data declared as being static?
13.2 What does a pointer point to?
13.3 What is the difference between a direct and an indirect reference?
13.4 What two statements control the space allocated to dynamic variables.
13.5 In what ways are trees and lists the same? In what ways do they differ?
13.6 Describe a problem where dynamic storage is better for the problem's solution than
      static storage.
13.7 Why are records generally used for dynamically stored data?
13.8 Describe the relationship between a linked list and a tree.
13.9 Name five problems that can be solved using linked lists.

13.10   Name five problems that can be solved using trees.

13.11   After deleting a component from a linked list, why should it be destroyed?

13.6 PROBLEMS

13.1.   Input the following data and form a linear linked list. The data should be input in the sequence shown. The list should store the data as an ordered list, from low value to high value. The list should be initially formed as an ordered list. The data should not be input to a list and then reordered. This means that the program will have to insert new components at the ends and in the middle of the list as it is formed. Echo display each value as it is input. After all the data has been input, display the list. The program should work for any size list. The data is

$$-55 \quad 6 \quad -3 \quad 12 \quad 7 \quad -7 \quad 29 \quad -1 \quad 0 \quad 28$$

13.2.   Sort the following list of names by placing them into an ordered tree. Echo display each name as it is input to the program.

TOM   JANE   KATHERINE   SANDY   WILLIAM   HELENE   MOISE   KIM

13.3.   Ancient Greeks often felt honour bound to commit suicide if they survived a battle that was lost. One way of doing this was to sit in a circle and drink from a cup that was either poison or wine. The first person to drink sits in a special place and for the purposes of this problem can be identified as sitting on seat 1. Regardless of how many people were in the circle, every 17th cup was poison; the rest were wine. After a person drinks a cup of poison, a cup of wine is given to the next person and the count to seventeen begins again. Poisoned warriors are not given cups to drink after they drink their cup of poison. For this problem, assume that fourteen Greeks returned from a lost battle. Also assume that two friends, Hero and Hector, decide that they want to avoid drinking a cup of poison. In order to survive, they must be the last two in the circle. Also assume that you and your computer have been trapped in ancient Greece by a time warp. Hero and Hector have appealed to you to help them—quickly. They need to know the seat numbers of where they should sit. You are to do this by forming a linked list of 14 components into a ring. Each component is to contain a data value numbering the component (1,2,3,..,14). Start counting the component 1. As a person is given poison at a seat associated with a component, eliminate that component from the ring. Start the count again at the next component in the ring. Display the number of each seat as its occupant is poisoned. When only two components are left in the ring, display these numbers, indicating that Hector and Hero should sit on them.

13.4.   Input a list of names into an ordered dynamic data structure (either a list or a tree). Input the names in the sequence shown. If a name is found more than once, do not create an additional node, but add to the count of occurrences of that name. A count of the occurrences of each name should be kept in the same dynamic structure node that stores the name. Test your program with the following data.

BILL   FRAN   KAREN   FRAN   SALLY   TIM   ANNE   BILL
ANN   KAREN   SUSAN   JUDITH   VELMA   MAUREEN   ANNE
MARVIN   SALLY   JAY   BILLY   KURT   TIM   ZACK

Echo display each name as it is input.

13.5. Ruth has a personal library of several different computer books. She wants to have several lists of her books ordered on different things identifying them. She wants the titles listed in the following ways

Alphabetically by author
Alphabetically by title
Alphabetically by publisher
By publication date

Each one of these lists is to contain all of the information and is to be displayed in the following form.

```
AUTHOR              TITLE                   PUBLISHER                YEAR
----------------    --------------------    ------------------------ ---
```

You are to construct these different lists by placing each input record into four different ordered data structures as they are input. Also echo display the data as it comes in. Test your program by combining the following data with information about at least five more books.

```
TUCKER              PROGRAMMING LANGUAGES   MCGRAW-HILL              1977
KNUTH               FUNDAMENTAL ALGORITHMS  ADDISON-WESLEY          1973
MAZLACK             PLC ESSENTIALS          MCGRAW-HILL              1978
POLLACK,STERLING    ESSENTIALS OF PL/I      HOLT,RINEHART,WINSTON   1974
AHO,ULLMAN          COMPILER DESIGN         ADDISON-WESLEY          1978
```

13.6. Write a program using dynamic data storage to do the following.

(a) An ordered tree data structure is to be created to accomplish the problem solution.

(b) Each major node of the tree is to be an account balance record. Attached to each major node is to be the supporting detail.

(c) The major nodes are to be ordered by account number.

(d) The detail data for each major node is to be attached to it and ordered by date. (The dates in the test data are Julian dates.)

(e) No sorting of the data is permitted.

(f) Each record is to be echo printed as it is input.

(g) After all the data has been input to the tree, the results are to be displayed in the following form.

```
                              ---DETAIL----
        ACCOUNT    BALANCE    DATE   AMOUNT
        -------    -------    -----  ------
          xxx      xxxx.xx
                              xxxxx  xxx.xx
                              xxxxx  xxx.xx
                                .       .
                                .       .
                              xxxxx  xxx.xx
          xxx      xxxx.xx
                              xxxxx  xxx.xx
                              xxxxx  xxx.xx
                                .       .
                                .       .
```

The first detail date and amount should be the date upon which the account is initiated and the initial balance.

(h) The form of the incoming records is

account master
columns   1–3: account number
          5–10: initial balance
          12–16: initiating date
          18: an integer "1"

detail record
columns   1–3: account number
          5–10: transaction amount
          12–16: transaction date
          18: an integer "2"

(i) Use the following data to test your program.

```
321   32.01 81231 1
486    0.00 81146 1
321 -15.12 81235 2
321 871.49 81234 2
321   71.98 81236 2
281 -26.91 81023 1
486  16.96 81295 2
321  78.41 81301 2
281 107.42 81284 2
486 -69.71 81329 2
105 294.59 81121 1
105 -79.81 81211 2
312    4.04 81002 1
105  78.21 81351 2
301 984.01 81014 1
486 -22.95 81147 2
311    0.00 81095 1
395  42.68 81111 1
395 -21.98 81201 2
395  68.41 81201 2
395 768.21 81200 2
561  21.24 81365 1
321   -0.21 81365 2
311  16.48 81281 2
```

The detail data found in a type 2 record should be attached to a node in the tree representing the data that is found in a type 1 record. This means that separate trees of detail data should be formed to represent the detail data for each account and that these detail trees should be attached to the major account nodes.

13.7. Mr. Bill has an auto parts store with many transactions each year. He wants you to store these invoices in his computer in a tree structure keyed on invoice number so that they can be retrieved easily by invoice number. After all the data has been displayed, display the invoices that involve part B as well as the invoices that involve company D.

Test your program with the following data.

INVOICE NUMBER	DATE	PART	COMPANY
1	2	F	D
2	2	B	A
3	2	Y	C
4	3	B	D
5	3	W	E
6	4	A	C
7	5	T	D
8	6	B	D
9	6	G	M
10	6	F	C
11	6	S	D
12	7	U	P

Chapter 14

FILES

Objectives
Discuss and define how Pascal provides auxiliary data storage through the use of files.

Suggested Background
Beyond the basic material in the first four chapters, this chapter makes use of the material on WHILE, IF-THEN-ELSE, and RECORD.

Some problems use data only one time to produce a single set of results. For example, when a clerk in a grocery store adds up the total bill, the prices are used only one time to come up with the bill. After the bill has been paid, the store usually discards the list of prices. Similarly, the problems that we have been interested in solving with the aid of Pascal have been concerned with processing some data once to produce a final result. The data and results have not been saved in the computer for use at another time.

Some problems require that data and/or results be stored for use at another time. For example, an employee's payroll record is used several different times. Every pay period, the data stored in the payroll record is used to determine how much the person is to be paid per hour. Then, to calculate the amount to be paid this time, the hourly pay rate is multiplied by the number of hours worked. Once this is done, the payroll record itself is changed to reflect the total money that was earned in the year and the total amount of taxes that have been paid. Often the payroll record may be used in several different programs. For example, one program may calculate how much the person is to be paid while another program may report to the government how much money the person made in the year. Although different, both programs could use the same record as the source of their input data.

Data that are to be used by several programs or used at different times by the same program can be kept in a *file*. Files are usually stored on an auxiliary storage medium such as a disk or a tape. When a program finishes execution, the data that were stored in the computer disappear. Only data that is stored on an auxiliary storage device are available for reuse by another program.

This chapter discusses the use of Pascal to solve problems that need files. The Pascal programmer does not have to be concerned with how the computer physically gains access to the files. This changes from computer to computer and is not part of Pascal. Likewise, the physical description of the files is not of direct concern. Pascal

FILEs are an abstraction of the actual physical files. It is a function of the operating system and the Pascal compiler to assign physical files to a program.

14.1 FILE DEFINITION

Objectives
Discuss the differences between a FILE and an ARRAY and describe how a sequential Pascal FILE is defined.

Suggested Background
The previous material in this chapter and the section on defining RECORDs.

In Pascal a FILE contains a sequence of components of the same structured data TYPE. Section 11.3 discussed how an ARRAY of RECORDS could serve for temporary storage in a way that could be thought of as being a file. (A collection of like records is a file.) There are significant differences between using an ARRAY and using a FILE. In an ARRAY, the desired element can be made immediately available by specifying the desired element. For example,

```
<structured variable name>(.5.)
```

would make element 5 of the ARRAY available. This is possible because the entire ARRAY is available at the same time so that any element desired can be chosen. In a FILE, only a single component is available at one time.

Another significant difference is that the number of elements in an ARRAY must be defined when it is declared. A FILE can have any number of components. The number of components in a FILE does not have to be known by the program.

A FILE TYPE is declared in the form

```
TYPE
    <type identifier> = FILE of <basetype>
```

For example,

```
TYPE
    AGE = FILE OF INTEGER;
VAR
    PEOPLE: AGE;
```

would create a FILE of INTEGERs representing AGEs. For most problems, a variety of different TYPEs of information is kept for each FILE component. Each component may then have elements of different TYPEs. These elements can be kept together in RECORDs. FILEs are usually collections of RECORDs. For example,

```
TYPE
   DELIVERED =
      RECORD
         COLOUR: CHAR;
         AMOUNT: INTEGER;
         PRICE: REAL
      END;  (* DELIVERY RECORD *)
VAR
   CORN: FILE OF DELIVERED;
```

A component of a FILE often is known as a record of the FILE.

The name of any FILEs that are placed on auxiliary storage must be included in the program heading. For example,

```
PROGRAM EXAMPLE(INPUT,OUTPUT,AGE,CORN)
```

The standard files INPUT and OUTPUT are not declared in the VAR section. However, INPUT must appear in the program if READ, EOF, or EOLN are used in the program without a file name. OUTPUT must appear in the program heading if WRITE is used in the program without a file name. The order in which file names appear in the program heading does not matter.

14.2 SEQUENTIAL ACCESS OF FILES

Objectives
Discuss the concept of sequential files. Discuss and identify how Pascal makes sequential files available.

Suggested Background
The previous material in this chapter.

Standard Pascal allows only one means of accessing data stored in files. This is *sequential* access. Some implementations of Pascal allow *index sequential* access. This chapter is restricted to sequential files.

A Pascal FILE is constructed as a sequence of components. A sequence can be thought of as a column of spaces that can be used to hold data, as in Figure 14.1(a).

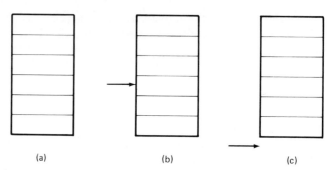

(a)   (b)   (c)

Figure 14.1   (a) A sequence of spaces. (b) Marker indicating the next space to be used. (c) Marker past the last space in the FILE.

A marker is used to indicate the next component that is to be used, as in Figure 14.1(b).

After a component is used by either writing into it, or reading from it, the marker is moved to the next component. The marker always moves forward to the next component after a component is used. It cannot stay in the same place or move backward. The marker may move past the last component that is already in the file, as in Figure 14.1(c).

If the program writes when the marker is past the end of the FILE, a new component will be added to the FILE. If the program attempts to read when the marker is past the end of the FILE, the EOF value associated with the FILE being read will be changed from FALSE to TRUE.

At any one time, exactly one component of the FILE is accessible to the program. The component that is currently accessible is known as the *buffer variable*. The buffer variable is written as

```
<file name>@
```

For example,

```
AGE@
CORN@
```

When a FILE component is accessed through the buffer variable, the buffer variable should be part of any reference. For example, assignment statements might be

```
AGE@ := 25;
CORN@.PRICE := 1.25;
NETCOST := CORN@.PRICE * ( 1.0 - DISCOUNT );
```

There are five predefined subprograms that are used to control and test FILEs and buffer variables. They are: EOF, REWRITE, PUT, WRITE, RESET, and GET. These are discussed in the next sections.

14.2.1 EOF

Objective
Discuss how the end of a FILE is recognized.

Suggested Background
The previous material in this chapter.

EOF is used to indicate whether or not the file position marker points to a component in a FILE. The marker does not point to a record either (a) when the FILE is first initialized by the REWRITE statement (Section 14.2.2) and there are no records in the file, or (b) when a READ or GET (section 14.2.3) has moved the file position marker past the end of the file, as in Figure 14.1(c). There is an EOF indicator available for each FILE that is used for input. The form of the EOF for a specific file is

```
EOF(<file name>)
```

If the file name is not specified, the standard FILE named INPUT will be used.

14.2.2 REWRITE

Objective
Discuss how a Pascal FILE is initialized for use.

Suggested Background
The previous material in this chapter.

REWRITE clears a FILE and initializes it for use. The form of the statement is

```
REWRITE(<file name>)
```

The REWRITE statement clears the file and sets EOF (<file name>) to TRUE. All output FILEs, except for the standard FILE named OUTPUT, must be cleared before initial use. REWRITE should not be used with the standard file OUTPUT.

14.2.3 PUT and WRITE

Objective
Discuss how to place information on a FILE.

Suggested Background
The previous material in this chapter.

PUT writes the contents of a buffer variable onto the end of a FILE. The form of the statement is

```
PUT(<file name>)
```

Before the contents of the buffer variable are written to the FILE, data should be put into the buffer variable. This can be done by an assignment statement such as

```
<file name>@ := <value>
```

For example,

```
AGE@ := 23;
PUT(AGE);
```

would append 23 to the end of the FILE named AGE. After writing, the file position marker is advanced.

The writing process can be compressed into one statement by using the WRITE statement. The form is

```
WRITE(<file name>,<expression>)
```

where the TYPE of the expression is the same as the component TYPE of the FILE. For example,

```
WRITE(AGE,23)
```

will append 23 to the end of the FILE named AGE. When writing to the standard output FILE named OUTPUT, the file name does not have to be specified. After executing either PUT or WRITE, the value of EOF (<file name>) remains TRUE.

14.2.4 RESET

> **Objective**
> Discuss how to prepare an existing file for reading by moving the file marker to the beginning of the file.
>
> **Suggested Background**
> The previous material in this chapter.

RESET prepares a FILE for initial reading by moving the file position marker to the beginning of the FILE. It also transfers the contents of the first component of the file to the buffer variable, <file name>@. For example,

```
RESET(AGE)
```

places the contents of the first component of the FILE named AGE into

```
AGE@
```

If the FILE is empty, the value of EOF (<file name>) will be TRUE. If there is at least one component in the FILE, it will be set to FALSE.

14.2.5 GET

> **Objective**
> Discuss how to read a component from a Pascal file.
>
> **Suggested Background**
> The previous material in this chapter.

GET is used to read a component from a FILE. It reads the value of the component indicated by the file position marker into the buffer variable. The file position marker is then advanced. If there is nothing to be read, the value of EOF(<file name>) is TRUE. If a component was read, the value remains FALSE. For example,

```
GET(AGE)
```

reads a component of the FILE named AGE into the buffer. If the component was then to be printed, it could be done by

```
WRITELN(AGE@)
```

14.3 CREATING A FILE

Objectives
Discuss how a Pascal FILE may be created and provide an example of the creation process.

Suggested Background
The previous material in this chapter. The sections on WHILE and IF-THEN-ELSE.

FILEs are created at two different times. When a FILE is first developed, data is inserted into the empty FILE. Later, when an existing FILE is changed, it is said to be *updated*. FILEs are updated when either (a) new components are added to the FILE, or (b) values in existing components are changed. The result is that a new FILE, is created by combining the old and new data.

14.3.1 Creating a New File

Objective
Illustrate how a new FILE can be created.

Suggested Background
The previous material in this chapter.

The components in a sequential FILE often are kept in an order determined by some element of the component. This element usually is a data item that also is used for something else. It is called a *key*. For example, if the FILE components were RECORDs containing data about automobile parts, the FILE might be sequenced on the part number. For example,

part number	weight	price	quantity on hand
15	2.3	0.18	15
17	24.6	2.09	175
342	1.4	0.05	6743
791	14.7	10.12	32

The following example illustrates how a FILE could be built to hold this data.

Example: Build
Store an unknown amount of data about parts in a FILE. The data about each part includes part number, weight, price, and quantity on hand.

```
PROGRAM BUILD(INPUT,OUTPUT,STOCKFILE);
   (* THIS BUILDS A FILE DESCRIBING A PARTS INVENTORY *)
TYPE
   PART =   (* DEFINES A RECORD OF THE PARTS FILE *)
      RECORD
         NUMBER: INTEGER;  (* PART IDENTIFICATION NUMBER *)
         WEIGHT: REAL;  (* WEIGHT OF THE PART *)
         PRICE: REAL;  (* PRICE OF THE PART *)
         QUANTITY: INTEGER  (* COUNT OF THE PART THAT IS AVAILABLE *)
      END;  (* PART RECORD *)
   PARTSFILE = FILE OF PART;
VAR
   STOCKFILE: PARTSFILE;
   NEWDATA: PART;
(* ================================================================ *)
PROCEDURE TITLES;
BEGIN  (* ACTIONS IN TITLES PROCEDURE *)
   WRITELN('IDENTIFICATION                    QUANTITY');
   WRITELN('   NUMBER       WEIGHT    PRICE   ON HAND');
   WRITELN('--------------   ------   -----   --------')
END;  (* PROCEDURE TITLES *)
(* ================================================================ *)
BEGIN  (* MAIN PART OF PROGRAM *)
   TITLES;
   REWRITE(STOCKFILE);  (* INITIALIZE PARTS FILE *)
   WHILE NOT EOF DO BEGIN  (* READ DATA FOR FILE AND INSERT INTO FILE *
      READ(NEWDATA.NUMBER);  (* TRY TO READ THE ID NUMBER OF INPUT DATA
      IF NOT EOF  (* IF AN ID NUMBER FOR A PART WAS READ, PROCESS DATA
         THEN BEGIN  (* READ THE REST OF THE DATA *)
            READ(NEWDATA.WEIGHT,NEWDATA.PRICE,NEWDATA.QUANTITY);
            WRITELN(NEWDATA.NUMBER:7,NEWDATA.WEIGHT:10:1,
                    NEWDATA.PRICE:8:2,NEWDATA.QUANTITY:7);  (* ECHO PRI
            WRITE(STOCKFILE,NEWDATA);
         END  (* BUILDING A RECORD *)
      END  (* READING DATA *)
END.  (* BUILD *)
```

If the input values are the same as the table shown before in this section, the resulting FILE is illustrated in Figure 14.2.

15	2.3	0.18	715

17	24.6	2.09	175

342	1.4	0.05	6734

791	14.7	10.12	32

Figure 14.2   Abstracted illustration of the file resulting from Example 11.3.1.

Note that data that is written to the OUTPUT File is formatted; that is, includes any spaces specified as part of the output display. In comparison the data written to STOCKFILE is compressed; that is, contains only the spaces needed to separate data values.

14.3.2 Merging Files

Objective
Illustrate how an updated FILE can be created by merging new data into an existing FILE to create a new, updated FILE.

Suggested Background
The previous material in this chapter. The sections on WHILE, IF-THEN-ELSE, and RECORD.

One way that FILEs can be updated is by adding new components to an existing FILE. If the FILE is not ordered on a key, this is easy to do. The new component simply can be appended to the end of a FILE by using either PUT or WRITE. However, if new components are to be added to an existing FILE that is sequenced, the new components must be "merged" with the old. This can be done if the new components are ordered in the same way as the old FILE. A new merged FILE can then be created. The process is illustrated in Figure 14.3. It is not possible to insert new components into an existing ordered, sequential FILE without creating a new FILE.

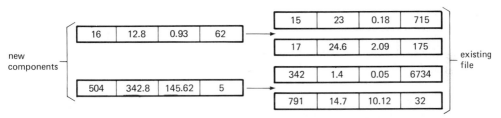

Figure 14.3   New components merged into an existing file.

Example: Update
The program MERGE illustrates how a new, merged FILE can be created.

```
PROGRAM MERGE(INPUT,OUTPUT,STOCKFILE,MERGEFILE);
   (* THIS BUILDS A MERGED FILE DESCRIBING A PARTS INVENTORY *)
TYPE
   PART =  (* DEFINES A RECORD OF THE PARTS FILE *)
      RECORD
         NUMBER: INTEGER;  (* PART IDENTIFICATION NUMBER *)
         WEIGHT: REAL;  (* WEIGHT OF THE PART *)
         PRICE: REAL;  (* PRICE OF THE PART *)
         QUANTITY: INTEGER  (* COUNT OF THE PART THAT IS AVAILABLE *)
      END;  (* PART RECORD *)
   PARTSFILE = FILE OF PART;
VAR
   STOCKFILE: PARTSFILE;  (* INITIAL FILE *)
   MERGEFILE: PARTSFILE;  (* UPDATED FILE *)
   NEWDATA: PART;
(* ================================================================ *)
PROCEDURE TITLES;
BEGIN  (* ACTIONS IN TITLES PROCEDURE *)
   WRITELN('IDENTIFICATION                   QUANTITY');
   WRITELN('    NUMBER       WEIGHT    PRICE   ON HAND');
   WRITELN('--------------   ------    -----   --------')
END;  (* PROCEDURE TITLES *)
(* ================================================================ *)
PROCEDURE LOWMASTER;
BEGIN  (* READ THE MASTER FILE STOCKFILE UNTIL INSERT PLACE FOUND *)
   WRITE(MERGEFILE,STOCKFILE@);  (* WRITE NEW, MERGED FILE *)
   GET(STOCKFILE);
   IF NOT EOF(STOCKFILE)
      THEN IF STOCKFILE@.NUMBER < NEWDATA.NUMBER
         THEN LOWMASTER  (* MOVE FURTHER DOWN ORIGINAL FILE *)
END;  (* PROCEDURE LOWMASTER *)
(* ================================================================ *)
BEGIN  (* MAIN PART OF PROGRAM *)
   TITLES;
   REWRITE(MERGEFILE);  (* INITIALIZE NEW FILE TO HOLD UPDATED FILE *)
   RESET(STOCKFILE);  (* START AT TOP OF EXISTING PARTS FILE  *)
   WHILE NOT EOF DO BEGIN  (* READ DATA TO BE INSERTED INTO FILE *)
      READ(NEWDATA.NUMBER);  (* TRY TO READ ID NUMBER OF INPUT DATA *)
      IF NOT EOF  (* IF AN ID NUMBER FOR A PART WAS READ, PROCESS DATA
         THEN BEGIN  (* READ THE REST OF THE DATA *)
            READ(NEWDATA.WEIGHT,NEWDATA.PRICE,NEWDATA.QUANTITY);
            WRITELN(NEWDATA.NUMBER:7,NEWDATA.WEIGHT:10:1,
                  NEWDATA.PRICE:8:2,NEWDATA.QUANTITY:7);  (* ECHO *)
            IF (STOCKFILE@.NUMBER < NEWDATA.PRICE )
               AND (NOT(EOF(STOCKFILE)))
               THEN LOWMASTER  (* MOVE DOWN STOCKFILE TO FIND INSERT *)
               ELSE WRITE(MERGEFILE,NEWDATA);
         END  (* BUILDING A RECORD *)
      END;  (* READING NEW DATA TO BE MERGED INTO OLD MASTER FILE *)
   (* MOVE THE REST OF THE OLD MASTER FILE TO THE NEW, MERGED FILE *)
   WHILE NOT EOF(STOCKFILE) DO BEGIN  (* READ AND WRITE UNTIL ALL IN *)
      GET(STOCKFILE);
      IF NOT(EOF(STOCKFILE))
         THEN WRITE(MERGEFILE,STOCKFILE@)
   END  (* MOVING THE REMAINDER OF THE ORIGINAL FILE OVER *)
END.  (* MERGE *)
```

In order to make it easy to keep track of where the data is stored, updated FILEs are kept in the same place and are known by the same name before and after a program is executed. After the merged FILE is created, it is usually copied back over the original FILE so that the updated FILE will be in the same place and have the same name. The original FILE if often called the *master* FILE and the FILE with the new components the *update* FILE.

14.4 TEXT FILES

Objective
Discuss a special type of FILE known as text FILEs. A text FILE is the TYPE of FILE used for INPUT and OUTPUT.

Suggested Background
The previous material in this chapter.

Pascal defines a special file TYPE called TEXT. A TEXT FILE can be declared as

```
TYPE
    TEXT = FILE OF CHAR;
```

The standard system FILEs INPUT and OUTPUT are examples of this special file TYPE. INPUT and OUTPUT are predefined as TEXT FILES. The programmer does not have to so define them.

14.4.1 Line Control

Objective
Discuss how to manipulate the components of a text file known as lines.

Suggested Background
The previous material in this chapter.

A text FILE can be thought of as a FILE of variable length units called lines. Each line is separated from the next line by a special line separator character that normally cannot be printed. Different computer systems use different characters to separate one line from another. Pascal provides a special function to recognize that the last character of a line has been reached. The FUNCTION

```
EOLN(<file name>)
```

returns a TRUE value when at the end of the line. It is FALSE everywhere else. Pascal also provides a predefined PROCEDURE to read and skip characters in a line until the last character of the line is found.

```
READLN(<file name>)
```

skips over the characters in the current input line until the last character in the line is found. In both EOLN and READLN, if a file name is not specified, INPUT is assumed.

A peculiarity of Pascal should be noted. When reading BOOLEAN or numeric data, the last character of the line may not be the last character of the last value on the line. For example, if punched card input is used and the integer value 123 is punched into the first three columns of the card, the last character of the input line still will be in column 80, not in column 3 where the last digit is punched. Consequently the careful programmer should restrict usage of EOLN to reading CHAR data from text FILEs.

14.4.2 Text File Input/Output

Objective
Discuss how data requiring more than one character to represent the data is stored on text files.

Suggested Background
The previous sections of this chapter.

FILEs usually allow only one component at a time to be read or written. In a text FILE, a component is a single character since all data in a text FILE is stored in character form. When a data item requiring several characters to represent it is read from a text FILE using READ or written to a text FILE using WRITE, enough components are handled to complete the value being processed. On input the compiler converts the string of input characters to the requested input value TYPE. On output the compiler converts the values in the output list to CHAR components. For example, if the INTEGER value "–3645" is written to a text FILE (such as OUT-PUT), the value will be converted into a character representation and then written to the file. It will take five characters on the text FILE to represent this value.

14.5 QUESTIONS

14.1   Identify two reasons why FILES are used.

14.2   Identify the ways in which FILEs and ARRAYs of RECORDs differ.

14.3   What does "sequential access" imply? Provide an example of sequential data access.

14.4   What is the "buffer" variable used for?

14.5   What information is EOF intended to communicate?

14.6   How do the commands REWRITE and RESET differ in their results?

14.6 PROBLEM

14.1.   Input the following list of words onto a file. As the words are input, count and echo report them. Next input the file and count and display all the words beginning with the letter "A". Then input the file again and count and display all the words beginning with the letter "B". Repeat the process for the remaining letters of the alphabet, in sequence from "C" to "Z". The words your program is to process are

He calls us to open our eyes. He asks us why we are here, what we wish for, what forces we obey. He asks us, above all, if we understand what we are. He wants us to bring everything back into question.

You do not have to include punctuation in your input. You do not have to place more than one word on an input line.

Chapter 15

STRUCTURED WALKTHROUGHS

Objectives
Complement the discussion of how to solve problems using a programming language with a method that helps people help each other to solve a problem with the help of a computer.

Suggested Background
Chapters 1 and 2. The same background is suggested for all of the sections of this chapter. The sections of this chapter should be read in sequence.

Solving problems outside of the classroom with the aid of a computer usually involves more than one person. This is because the problems being solved usually are too large for one person to complete in the time available. Also, the resulting program is usually used by someone other than the author. In Chapter 1, the different roles that people may come to play in the development of a problem's solution were discussed. This chapter discusses how people who are working for the same organization can use a particular technique to help each other with their separate problems. This technique is called a *structured walkthrough*. Structured walkthroughs review documents that describe the stages of a computer software product's development.

15.1 ADVANTAGES

In a structured walkthrough, people at the same level of authority in the organization form a group to review a particular product. (Computer programs are products since they are produced to satisfy the needs of a customer.) It is called *peer review* when people at the same level of authority in an organization review each other's work. The members of a structured walkthrough review group may change from time to time and from product to product.

The product reviewed is usually one of three things:

(a) a program planning document,
(b) a program, or
(c) the description of the functions that eventually are to be performed by a program or by people in support of the actions of a program.

Walkthroughs are one of the most effective ways known to improve the quality of a program. (The most important measure of program quality is: Does it do the job that it was supposed to do?) Structured walkthroughs result in programs with few invalidly performing statements. Walkthroughs also produce programs with fewer design and analytical errors. One of the reasons that these improvements come about is that many errors are caused by individual oversights and misconceptions that can be seen by others. Simple errors include program construction mistakes where misconceptions include misunderstanding of what needs to be done and faulty knowledge of the interfaces between separate modules.

Besides valid solutions, structured walkthroughs offer other benefits to an organization. For one thing, readability is increased. This happens because the producer has to explain what is being done at an early point in the program's development. This is useful because it helps the original person to develop a better product. More importantly, other people can understand what is being done.

Walkthroughs increase programmer adherence to whatever documentation and programming standards are required. Additionally, a walkthrough helps to train people with less experience by putting them in a good position to examine the program development process. They can see how more experienced workers approach the development of a solution to a problem. Moreover, their own work is guided in a positive atmosphere.

Lastly, walkthroughs provide some insurance against projects being disrupted by people leaving. It is a fact of life that people may depart from a computer project before it is completed. Walkthroughs lessen the problems created by a need to restart the work of an employee who has departed and left behind poor notes, documentation, etc.

15.2 WHEN A WALKTHROUGH SHOULD BE DONE

Walkthroughs should be done at the major checkpoints of a program product's development. Major checkpoints are sometimes called *milestones*. They occur:

(a) after the specifications have been written,
(b) after the design has been completed,
(c) after the test data has been defined, and
(d) after the program has been written—after a reasonably error-free compilation has been made, but before any significant testing has taken place.

15.2.1 Specification Walkthrough

A specification walkthrough is the review of the product's functional requirements or specifications. The purpose is to spot any problems, inaccuracies, and omissions. It should involve the customer, the systems analyst, and one or more programmers. The reviewed document is a high level program planning document that describes what is to be done by the entire product.

15.2.2 Design Walkthrough

A design walkthrough reviews the proposed solution to the specified functional needs. The program planning documents are reviewed. The logical program planning documents may include pseudo-code.

The physical design documents may include descriptions of such subsystems as teleprocessing and database. What to do when the computer stops unexpectedly because of a software failure, hardware failure, or a disaster is called backup and recovery. A backup and recovery plan may also be discussed as part of the physical design document.

The procedural documents specify low level module design. This may be done using pseudo-code.

15.2.3 Program Walkthrough

The document used in the program walkthrough is the actual program statement listing. It sometimes uncovers design or analysis problems. The purpose is to clarify and validate the program statements.

15.2.4 Test Walkthroughs

A test walkthrough helps ensure the adequacy of the test data. Good test data should test every condition that the program has been designed to meet. A test walkthrough does not examine output from the program. The attendees include the program author and the person developing the test data. These should be different people. Other programmers and the customer's representative should also be present.

15.3 ROLES IN A WALKTHROUGH

The people involved in a walkthrough review group should be peers. (Peers are people with the same level of management authority in the organization.) Higher management authority figures should not be present because this discourages free and open discussion. The roles are not permanent; different people may take on different roles in different walkthroughs and the same person may play more than one role in a single walkthrough.

15.3.1 Presenter

The presenter presents the product that is under review. Usually the presenter is the producer or author of the product. The presenter is the person who want/needs to know the flaws in the document.

15.3.2 Coordinator

The coordinator ensures that activities are properly planned. During the walkthrough, the coordinator ensures that the discussion does not stray from the product being reviewed.

15.3.3 Scribe

The scribe develops a permanent record of the results. The record is used in ongoing quality assurance. The scribe does not produce a complete transcript of what happened, but does produce an intelligent summary.

15.3.4 Maintenance Representative

The maintenance representative is concerned with maintenance of the program after it has been developed, tested, and accepted by the customer. Often the maintenance representative is not part of the production group. At a walkthrough, he should be concerned with the future ease of modification of the program.

15.3.5 Standards Leader

Most modern programming organizations have their own standards as to what is acceptable documentation and how programs should be laid out. (This text has a program layout convention that is described in Appendix F.) The standards leader encourages people to conform to the organization's specified standards.

15.3.6 Customer Representative

The ultimate user of the product under construction is the customer for whom the product is being developed. If the product does not meet the customer's needs, it is useless.

The customer's representative assures that the product meets the customer's needs. The representative keeps the functional needs in mind so that the right problem is solved.

15.3.7 Others

Other reviewers give general opinions on correctness and quality. They usually are working on different parts of the same project. Outsiders may be brought in to supply a fresh, objective viewpoint.

15.4 ACTIVITIES BEFORE A WALKTHROUGH

After choosing a product that can be reviewed in 30 to 60 minutes, the producer announces an intention to hold a walkthrough, usually about two days in advance. The producer also provides the documents to the coordinator.

The coordinator selects an acceptable time and place. The coordinator also ensures attendance by the other members, sometimes by nagging. In addition, the coordinator distributes the documentation.

The participants are to review the documents carefully. They each should come prepared with at least one positive and one negative comment.

15.5 ACTIVITIES DURING THE WALKTHROUGH

Everyone should agree to follow the same rules. The discussion should be organized and methodical. It should not drift off into aimless argument between two people. The discussion should be focused on the document, not the producer. It should be well understood that it is the product being reviewed, not the producer.

The proceedings begin when the coordinator calls the group to order.

Then the producer takes the floor. The producer begins with a general overview and then presents the product piece by piece. If the reviewers have had enough opportunity to study the document, the presentation can be kept brief. Alternately the reviewers may prefer to restrict their initial review to the document itself, without a verbal presentation, thereby reducing the possibility of brainwashing.

If this is a second walkthrough on the same product, the discussion can begin with a point by point review of the last discussion.

The reviewers should make constructive comments, criticisms, and suggestions. To save time, both the producer and the scribe are to be given a list of errors that require no explanation: program syntax, spelling, etc. They are to direct their comments to the product and not to the producer.

The producer should not argue about the comments or defend the product. This consumes time and causes ego confrontations. The purpose is to detect possible errors, not to correct them immediately. After the walkthrough is over, the producer can review the comments calmly. If it is necessary to argue, it can be done in private.

The scribe takes notes and collects any written comments.

The group then recommends one of three actions:

(a) accept the product as is,
(b) accept with revisions, or
(c) require another walkthrough with a revised product.

15.6 ACTIVITIES AFTER A WALKTHROUGH

The coordinator carries out the clean-up activities. The coordinator provides management with a summary that fits on a single page. The summary includes:

(a) what is reviewed,
(b) when it happened, and
(c) who was there.

Detailed comments are not included as (a) management might not understand, (b) management is really not interested, and (c) the internal objectivity of the review process would be threatened since the participants might be more interested in impressing the manager than in producing a product.

The coordinator also is responsible for placing a file copy with the project's librarian. The file copy should include:

(a) the management summary,
(b) detailed comments, and
(c) the reviewed documentation.

The coordinator also delivers detailed comments to the participants quickly, preferably within the hour, so they can be reviewed while everything is still fresh.

The participants review the comments for errors. They also should make themselves available for discussion with the producer.

The producer is to come to understand the comments. Either the suggestions should be accommodated or rational arguments should be developed as to why the suggestions should not be adopted. The producer then starts the cycle over again.

15.7 GENERAL GUIDELINES

Keep it short. Less than 30 minutes is best. A walkthrough should never run more than two hours. Short walkthroughs are much more likely to have willing participants who can concentrate during the entire session.

Don't schedule more than two in a row. This prevents mental exhaustion. The first walkthrough usually is very productive. The second produces acceptable results, while the results from a third are usually less than successful.

Use standards to avoid style disagreements.

Let the coordinator maintain decorum. Agree beforehand to respect the coordinator's role. Computer people love to argue; however, argument is not very productive in a walkthrough.

15.8 QUESTIONS

15.1 Why is a structured walkthrough performed?

15.2 In one sentence, describe what a structured walkthrough is to do.

15.3 What are the three types of products often reviewed in a structured walkthrough?

15.4 What is the difference between a specification and a design walkthrough?

15.5 Why is management usually excluded from a walkthrough?

15.6 Why should a test walkthrough be held?

15.7 When should a walkthrough be held?

15.8 How much time should a walkthrough take?

Appendix A

SYNTAX DIAGRAMS

The following syntax diagrams provide a complete description of Pascal's syntax. These diagrams should be referred to in case of doubt as to the proper construction of a Pascal statement.

This appendix is taken from Appendix D, pages 116–118, of Jensen and Wirth, *Pascal Users Manual and Report,* Springer-Verlag, 1974, with their permission.

Syntax diagrams for the Pascal language.

Used to represent Pascal reserved words or syntactic entities that are not defined further (for example, a letter or a digit)

Used to represent a Pascal operator

Used to represent a syntactic entity that is defined by another diagram

identifier

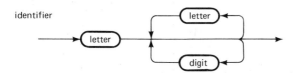

unsigned integer

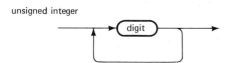

unsigned number

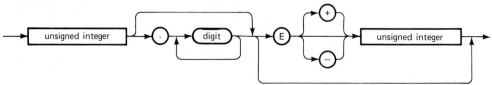

unsigned constant

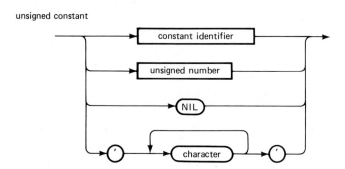

constant

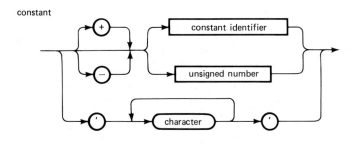

simple type

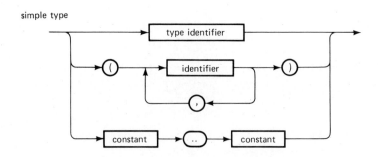

type

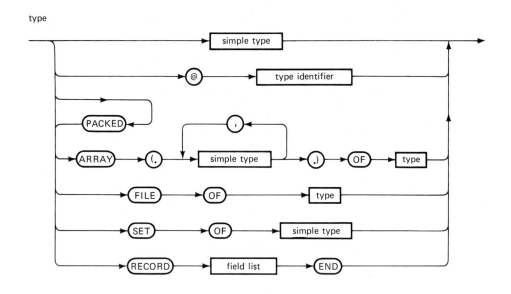

field list

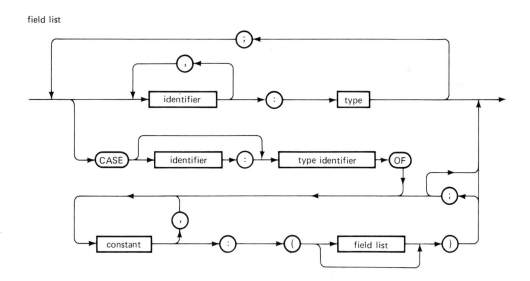

variable

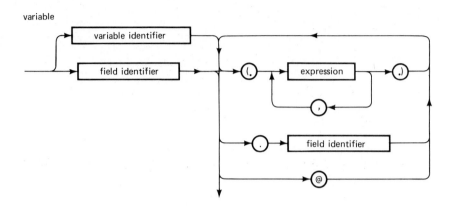

factor

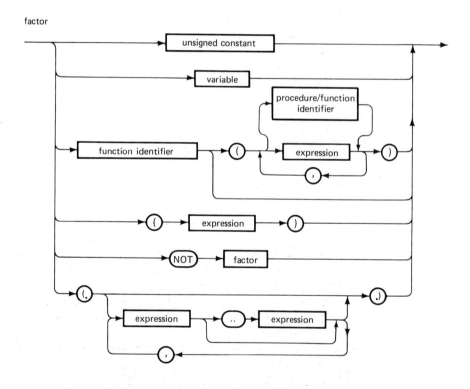

term

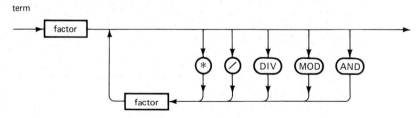

simple expression

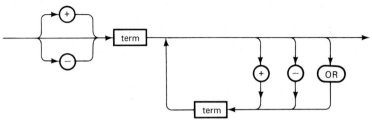

expression

parameter list

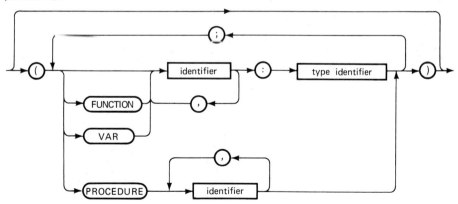

statement

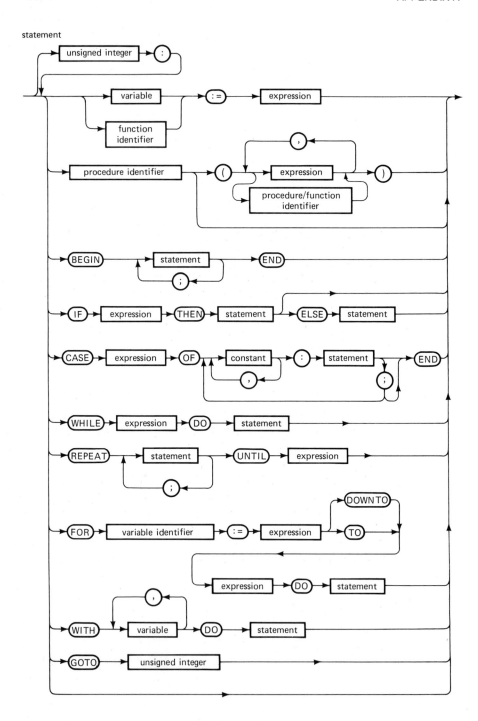

block

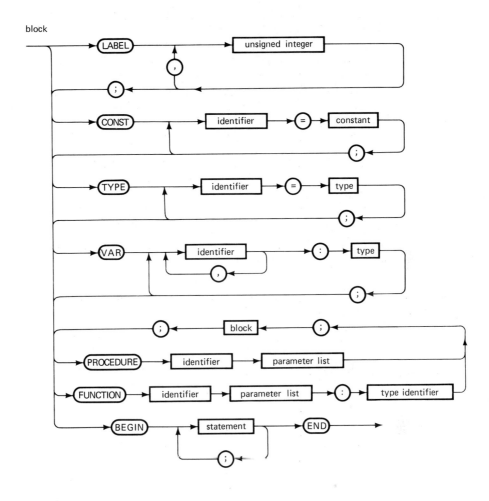

program

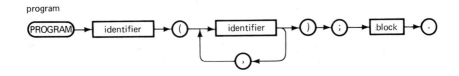

Appendix B

STANDARD PASCAL TERMS

B.1 RESERVED WORDS

AND	ARRAY	BEGIN	CASE	CONST	DIV
DO	DOWNTO	ELSE	END	FILE	FOR
FUNCTION	GOTO	IF	IN	LABEL	MOD
NIL	NOT	OF	OR	PACKED	PROCEDURE
TO	PROGRAM	RECORD	REPEAT	SET	THEN
TYPE	UNTIL	VAR	WHILE	WITH	

B.2 STANDARD INDENTIFIERS

B.2.1 Constants

FALSE   TRUE   MAXINT

B.2.2 Types

BOOLEAN   CHAR   INTEGER   REAL   TEXT

B.2.3 Files

INPUT   OUTPUT

B.2.4 Functions

name	TYPE of		description
	parameters	result	
ABS(X)	INTEGER or REAL	same as parameter	absolute value
ARCTAN(X)	INTEGER or REAL	REAL	inverse tangent
CHR(X)	INTEGER	CHAR	character whose ordinal number is X
COS(X)	INTEGER or REAL	REAL	cosine of X
EOF(F)	FILE	BOOLEAN	end-of-file indicator INPUT if F not given
EOLN(F)	FILE	BOOLEAN	end-of-line indicator INPUT if F not given
EXP(X)	REAL or INTEGER	REAL	e raised to the power X
LN(X)	REAL or INTEGER	REAL	natural logarithm
ODD(X)	INTEGER	BOOLEAN	TRUE if X is odd
ORD(X)	BOOLEAN, CHAR, or user defined scalar	INTEGER	ordinal number of X in the scalar data type of which X is a member
PRED(X)	scalar, not REAL	same as parameter	predecessor of X
ROUND(X)	REAL	INTEGER	X rounded
SIN(X)	REAL or INTEGER	REAL	sine of X
SQR(X)	REAL or INTEGER	same as parameter	square of X
SUCC(X)	scalar, not REAL	same as parameter	successor of X
TRUNC(X)	REAL	INTEGER	X truncated

B.2.5 Standard Procedures

name	description
DISPOSE(P)	returns the dynamic variable referenced by the pointer P to the available space list
GET(F)	advances file F to the next component and places the value of the component in F@
NEW(P)	allocates a new variable that is accessed through the pointer P
PACK(A,I,Z)	takes the elements beginning at subscript position I of array A and copies them into packed array Z beginning at the first subscript position
PAGE(F)	tells the printer to skip to the top of a new page before printing the next line of text file F
PUT(F)	appends the value of the buffer variable F@ to the file F
READ(. . .)	reads data from text files
READLN(. . .)	reads data from text files, tries to advance input pointer to a new input line
RESET(F)	positions file F at its beginning for reading
REWRITE(F)	empties file F and allows it to be written into
UNPACK(Z,A,I)	takes the elements starting at the first subscript position of packed array Z and copies them into array A starting at subscript position I
WRITE(. . .)	writes data to text files
WRITELN(. . .)	writes data to text files, moves output pointer to next output line

B.3 SUMMARY OF OPERATORS

operator	description	type of	
		operand(s)	result
:=	assignment	any, except FILE	same as left most operand
+	addition	INTEGER or REAL	INTEGER or REAL
	set union	any SET type	same as operand
−	subtraction	INTEGER or REAL	INTEGER or REAL
	set difference	any SET type	same as operand
*	multiplication	INTEGER or REAL	INTEGER or REAL
	set intersection	any SET type	same as operand
DIV	integer division	INTEGER	INTEGER
/	real division	REAL	REAL
MOD	modulus	INTEGER	INTEGER
NOT	logical negation	BOOLEAN	BOOLEAN
OR	disjunction	BOOLEAN	BOOLEAN
AND	conjunction	BOOLEAN	BOOLEAN
<=	less than or equal	any scalar type	BOOLEAN
	set inclusion	any set type	BOOLEAN
	implication	BOOLEAN	BOOLEAN
=	equality	scalar, SET, or POINTER	BOOLEAN
	equivalence	BOOLEAN	BOOLEAN
<>	inequality	scalar, SET, or POINTER	BOOLEAN
	exclusive OR	BOOLEAN	BOOLEAN
>=	greater than or equal set	any scalar type	BOOLEAN
	inclusion	any SET type	BOOLEAN
<	less than	any scalar type	BOOLEAN
>	greater than	any scalar type	BOOLEAN
IN	set membership	left operator: scalar right operand: SET with the base type the type of the left operand	BOOLEAN

Appendix C

CHARACTER SETS

Different computers are capable of using different characters. Pascal has specified a set of punctuation marks along with alternative symbols for them. Not all computers can supply a complete set of the specified characters. However, most can provide a reasonable approximation.

C.1 ALTERNATE PASCAL SYMBOLS

Figure C.1   Alternate Pascal Symbols.

Standard	Alternate
^	@ or
{	(*
}	*)
[	(.
]	.)

C.2 EBCDIC

Figure C.2   EBCDIC (Extended Binary Coded Decimal Interchange Code).

Left Digit(s) \ Right Digit	0	1	2	3	4	5	6	7	8	9
6										
7					¢	.	<	(	+	|
8	&									
9	!	$	*	)	;	¬	_	/		
10							^	,	%	—
11	>	?								
12			:	#	@	'	=	"		a
13	b	c	d	e	f	g	h	i		
14						j	k	l	m	n
15	o	p	q	r						
16			s	t	u	v	w	x	y	z
17								/	{	}
18	[	]								
19				A	B	C	D	E	F	G
20	H	I								J
21	K	L	M	N	O	P	Q	R		
22							S	T	U	V
23	W	X	Y	Z						
24	0	1	2	3	4	5	6	7	8	9

Codes 00 to 63 and 250 to 255 represent nonprintable control characters.

C.3 ASCII

Figure C.3 ASCII (American Standard Code for Information Interchange).

Left Digit(s) \ Right Digit	0	1	2	3	4	5	6	7	8	9
3				!	"	#	$	%	&	'
4	(	)	*	+	,	−	.	/	0	1
5	2	3	4	5	6	7	8	9	:	;
6	<	=	>	?	@	A	B	C	D	E
7	F	G	H	I	J	K	L	M	N	O
8	P	Q	R	S	T	U	V	W	X	Y
9	Z	[	1/8	]	$\wedge$	—	`	a	b	c
10	d	e	f	j	h	i	j	k	l	m
11	n	o	p	q	r	s	t	u	v	w
12	x	y	z	{	|	}	—			

Codes 00 to 31 and 127 (decimal) represent special control characters that are not printable.

C.4 CDC SCIENTIFIC

Figure C.4 CDC Scientific, with 64 Characters.

Left Digit(s) \ Right Digit	0	1	2	3	4	5	6	7	8	9
0	:	A	B	C	D	E	F	G	H	I
1	J	K	L	M	N	O	P	Q	R	S
2	T	U	V	W	X	Y	Z	0	1	2
3	3	4	5	6	7	8	9	+	−	*
4	/	(	)	$	=		,	.	$\equiv$	[
5	]	%	$\neq$	↱	$\vee$	$\wedge$	↑	↓	<	>
6	$\leq$	$\geq$	¬	;						

Appendix D

LEXICAL STRUCTURE

Objective
Provide a fairly formal description of Pascal's lexical structure. This material will probably not be of interest to all readers. It should only be referenced if there is a need for a precise description of Pascal's lexical structure.

Suggested Background
This section is a formal description of the basic elements of the Pascal language. This is simplified from the appropriate sections of the Pascal standard. However, it probably requires a greater understanding of programming language construction than most beginning students have.

The lexical structure of a programming language defines the basic building blocks of the language. The lexical structure is described by *lexical tokens*. Lexical tokens are the basic elements or building blocks of a programming language. The Pascal syntax diagrams in Appendix A show how the elements of the lexical structure can be used to form Pascal statements.

This appendix is a simplified version of Section 6.1 of the Pascal standard. In case of a need for additional clarification, that source should be consulted.

The lexical tokens used to construct Pascal programs are classified into

special symbols
identifiers
directives
unsigned numbers
labels
character strings

D.1 LETTERS AND DIGITS

The representation of any letters (uppercase, lowercase, etc.) that occur anywhere outside of a character string (see D.7) is insignificant in that it does not cause a change in meaning.

the letters are

"A" "B" "C" "D" "E" "F" "G" "H" "I" "J" "K" "L" "M"
"N" "O" "P" "Q" "R" "S" "T" "U" "V" "W" "X" "Y" "Z"

the digits are

"0" "1" "2" "3" "4" "5" "6" "7" "8" "9"

D.2 SPECIAL SYMBOLS

The special symbols are tokens having special meanings and are used to delimit the syntactic units of the language.
special symbols

"+" "−" "*" "/" "=" "<" ">" "[" "]" "." "," ":" ";" "^" "("
")" "<>" "<=" ">=" ":=" ".."

and include the word-symbols

AND	ARRAY	BEGIN	CASE	CONST	DIV
DO	DOWNTO	ELSE	END	FILE	FOR
FUNCTION	GOTO	IF	IN	LABEL	MOD
NIL	NOT	OF	OR	PACKED	PROCEDURE
TO	PROGRAM	RECORD	REPEAT	SET	THEN
TYPE	UNTIL	VAR	WHILE	WITH	

D.3 IDENTIFIERS

Identifiers may be of any length. All characters of an identifier are significant. No identifiers can have the same spelling as any word-symbol. The first character of an identifier is a letter; subsequent characters may be letters and/or digits.

D.4 DIRECTIVES

A directive can only occur in a procedure-declaration or a function-declaration. The directive FORWARD is the only required directive. Specific Pascal implementations may have other directives.

D.5 NUMBERS

A fuller discussion may be found in Sections 3.1.2.1 and 3.1.2.2. The letter E preceding a scale factor means "times 10 to the power of." The value of an unsigned integer is in the closed interval 0 to MAXINT.

digit-sequence
    one or more digits grouped together
unsigned-integer
    a digit-sequence
unsigned-real
    unsigned-integer "." digit-sequence
    unsigned-integer "." digit-sequence "e" scale-factor
    unsigned-integer "e" scale-factor
unsigned-number
    a unsigned-integer or a unsigned-real
scale-factor
    signed integer
sign
    "+" or "−"
signed-integer
    sign unsigned-integer
    unsigned-integer
signed-real
    sign unsigned-real
    unsigned-real
signed-number
    signed-integer
    signed-real

D.6 LABELS

Labels are digit sequences. One label is distinguished from another label by its apparent integral value. Labels must be in the closed interval 0 to 9999.

D.7 CHARACTER STRINGS

Any of the characters that have been defined as legal for a particular implementation of Pascal can be a string element. A character string is made up of one or more string elements. In a Pascal program, a character string can be defined by placing the character string between a pair of apostrophes. For example,

'ABCDEFG'

is a character string definition. A character string containing a single string element denotes the value of a CHAR TYPE. A character string containing more than one string element denotes the value of a STRING TYPE. If a string includes an apostrophe, the apostrophe is denoted by two adjacent apostrophe marks ('').

D.8 TOKEN SEPARATORS

Everything between the pair of comment delimiters "(*" and "*)" is considered to be a comment if the "(*" does not occur within a character string or a comment.

Comments, spaces (except in character strings), and the separation of consecutive lines are considered to be token separators. Zero or more token separators may occur between any two consecutive tokens, or before the first token of a program text. There must be at least one separator between any pair of consecutive tokens made up of identifiers, word-symbols, labels, or unsigned-numbers. Separators may not occur within tokens.

Appendix E

WATERLOO PASCAL

Suggested Background

This appendix presumes some knowledge of the details of implementing computer systems. Although a person relatively new to computers may find much that is useful, some terminology will be new. A knowledge of this appendix is not necessary to learn Pascal. This section should be used when it is necessary to answer questions about how the Waterloo Pascal compiler was implemented or the limits of the Waterloo Pascal compiler.

This book uses the Waterloo implementation of Pascal to provide its examples. As with most implementations of Pascal, it varies in some ways from the Pascal standard. This appendix is largely drawn from *Waterloo Pascal, User's Guide and Language Description, 1981, University of Waterloo*. The *User's Guide* is designed to provide information about implementation details and not to serve instructional purposes. A copy of the *User's Guide* may be obtained from

The Computer Systems Group
University of Waterloo
Waterloo, Ontario N2L 3G1
Canada

This group has given its permission to use its material. This help is gratefully acknowledged.

E.1 OVERVIEW

The Waterloo Pascal is a "debugging" compiler. The compiler has a special set of objectives, which include:

(1) A fast compilation rate.
(2) A comprehensive set of readily understandable compile-time diagnostics, in full English text (as opposed to error codes or numbers).

(3)   An environment that ensures that all errors that occur when the program is executing will be detected and diagnosed.

These are the goals of a compiler designed for instructional use. Such a compiler may tend to sacrifice execution speed in order to meet these objectives, as compared with production compilers. This, however, is an acceptable trade-off, since most student programs are not usually executed more than a few times (it has been observed that once a student obtains a working program, it is rarely run again).

E.2 FEATURES

In order to achieve a reasonable compilation rate, it was decided to implement a one-pass, compile and execute processor, eliminating the overhead associated with such things as temporary work files and the linkage edit step.

The compiler produces two output files: a listing file and a diagnostics file. Particular attention is paid to the problem of *cascading error messages* (that is, a situation in which one error message may cause many other error messages).

The classes of errors that Waterloo Pascal detects during program execution are

(a)   Attempts to use a variable that has not been assigned a value.
(b)   Attempts to assign a value that is outside the declared range of a variable.
(c)   Array subscripting errors.
(d)   Attempts to use a NIL pointer, or to use previously disposed memory.
(e)   Dynamic storage resources exhausted.
(f)   Run-stack overflow (for example, infinite recursion detection).
(g)   Attempts to violate variant record rules.
(h)   Control statement semantics: branching into an inactive FOR or WITH statement; no case match in a CASE statement.

In the case of any error during program execution, Waterloo Pascal displays:

(a)   The name of the variable involved (if any).
(b)   The source-file line number where execution was taking place when the error occurred.
(c)   A traceback of all functions and procedures and their points of activation.

E.3 IMPLEMENTATION PARTICULARS

E.3.1 Implementation Defined Attributes

The Pascal standard allows an implementor to define various attributes of an implementation. Those that are noted here pertain to the IBM 360/370 version of Waterloo Pascal.

(a) MAXINT is defined to be 2,147,483,647 (that is, 1 less than 2 to the 31st power).
(b) The largest REAL value is approximately 7.2E+75.
(c) The smallest positive REAL value is approximately 5.4E-79.
(d) The data type CHAR is defined to be all 256 EBCDIC character codes. (This includes all upper and lower case letters, and all special characters. Note that the alphabetic characters are not contiguous in the collating sequence.)
(e) Sets may have a maximum of 50,000 elements.
(f) The default widths used by the procedures WRITE and WRITELN are 12, 5, and 16 for INTEGERs, BOOLEANs, and REALs (respectively).
(g) The default number of decimal places displayed by WRITE or WRITELN for a floating-point number (exponential notation) is 16.

E.3.2 Implementation Dependent Attributes

The Pascal standard allows an implementer to specify various other attributes about an implementation.

(a) The only procedure directive in Waterloo Pascal is the FORWARD directive.
(b) There are some additional standard functions/procedures (see E.3.4).
(c) Attempting to write onto a file that was opened for reading will result in an error when the program is executed.
(d) The operands of a binary operator are evaluated left to right so that in the following expression, the left-hand expression is evaluated first.

<left-hand expression> <operator> <right-hand expression>

(e) Boolean expressions are always evaluated completely.
(f) The order of evaluation and binding of function and procedure actual parameters is strictly left to right.
(g) The effect of resetting or rewriting a standard file is the same as for any other file.

(h) The default size of the run stack is 10,000 bytes (all variables, both global and local, are allocated from this area).

(i) Data items of the type CHAR are stored in one byte.

(j) INTEGERs, enumerated types, and subrange types are stored in 4 bytes.

(k) Data items of the type REAL are stored in eight bytes.

(l) Declaring a structured type to be PACKED has no effect on the internal representation.

E.3.3 Options

Options in Waterloo Pascal are specified by the same syntax as described by Jensen and Wirth (*Pascal User Manual and Report,* 2nd edition, Springer-Verlag, New York, 1974) for the options in CDC 6000 Pascal. The options are enclosed between two comment brackets. The option itself is preceded by a "$." There are no blanks in the specification. For example, the stack control option can be specified as (*$S6000*). The options currently implemented are

(a) 1+,1− (these are lower case "L"s)
Source listing control. The default is "1+" (list the source).

(b) c+,c−
Compiler output case control. Since some I/O devices may not support lower-case alphabetic characters, Waterloo Pascal will translate all compiler output (the diagnostic file, the source listing portion of the listing file, and terminal messages) into upper case. The default is "c−" (do not translate).

(c) s n
Run stack size control. The default is n = 10000 bytes, and the minimum allowed is n = 1000 bytes.

(d) x n
Statement execution control. Waterloo Pascal limits the number of statements that a program may execute. The default is n = 25000. Each installation sets an absolute limit for this option; it may be specified as n = 0.

(e) p n
Standard output control. The "p" option controls the number of physical lines that may be written (by a program) on the listing file. The default is n = 1000. Like the "x" option, there is an installation maximum for the "p" option that may be specified as p = 0.

(f) w+,w−
Warning message control. There are a few situations where Waterloo Pascal will issue a warning, rather than an error (for example, a semicolon detected inside a comment). These messages may be controlled with the "w" option: "w+" for notification, "w−" for no notification. The default is "w+."

The "s", "x", and "p" options have no effect until the program begins execution; thus, if they are specified more than once, the last textual occurrence in the source program is the one used. The "c" and "w" options have effect during both the compilation and execution of a program. During compilation they may be changed as desired, but it is the last textual occurrence of the option that is used throughout the execution of the program.

E.3.4 Standard Functions and Procedures

Waterloo Pascal provides three additional built-in routines beyond those specified for standard Pascal. They are RTOS, STOR, and ARCTAN2.

E.3.4.1 RTOS

RTOS ("real to string") converts a REAL or INTEGER value to a sequence of characters. There are two or three parameters, as follows:

Parameter 1: The value to be converted. It may be INTEGER or REAL.
Parameter 2: The "array of CHAR" variable into which the result is to be placed. The result is right justified in the string, and padded with blanks on the left.
Parameter 3: Optional. If specified, it must be an INTEGER value giving the number of decimal places to the right of the decimal point in the result.

For example,

```
   .
   .
VAR
    STRING: ARRAY(. 1..10 .) OF CHAR;
   .
   .
RTOS(2+3+4+,STRING,3);
```

would result in the variable STRING containing

```
"    9.000"
```

If the parameters were instead

```
RTOS(2+3+4,STRING)
```

the resulting value of STRING would be

```
"        9"
```

If the decimal point width is specified as zero, only the decimal point will appear. If it is negative, the result is as if the parameter had not been specified at all.

E.3.4.2 Function STOR

STOR ("string to real") converts an array of CHAR representing a REAL or INTEGER value into a REAL number (which may be then converted into an INTEGER by use of the ROUND or TRUNC standard functions). It takes one parameter—namely, the array of CHAR—to be converted. For example,

```
VAR
    X: REAL;
    .
    .
    X := STOR('12.34E+5');
```

would cause the variable X to have the correct internal representation of the given REAL number. The format of the numbers that may be converted is the standard Pascal REAL number format.

E.3.4.3 Function ARCTAN2

ARCTAN2(y,x) computes the inverse tangent of (y/x), where x and y may be either INTEGER or REAL. The only values for which ARCTAN2 is not defined are $y=x=0$.

The motivation for ARCTAN2(y,x) [as opposed to ARCTAN (x/y)] is that, given y and x separately, it is possible to compute the mathematical principal value.

E.3.4.4 Character Set Extensions

The Waterloo Pascal compiler uses the specified alternate character set for certain symbols. They are

(* left brace bracket
*) right brace bracket
(. left square bracket
.) right square bracket
@ upward pointing arrow

In addition the cent sign and not sign (or tilde) may be used instead of the upward pointing arrow.

E.3.4.5 Miscellaneous

(a) Identifiers and keywords are case insensitive. This means that it doesn't matter whether the program is written in upper or lower case alphabetic characters.
(b) The underscore character "_" is permitted in identifiers.
(c) Instead of the $ENTRY used for separating the program source and the standard input file, a %EOF may be used.
(d) The $PAGE directive is available to force the compiler to begin the next line of the listing file at the top of a new page.
(e) The compiler should not be used with source files that have a record length greater than 100.
(f) Sequence numbers are not part of the Pascal language; thus the compiler will not accept programs that have them.

E.3.4.6 Permanent Restrictions

To ensure the security of the execution environment of Waterloo Pascal (that is, to allow complete semantic checking while the program is executing), the restriction that file types may contain neither file nor pointer types is enforced.

Appendix F

STATEMENT LAYOUT CONVENTIONS

Suggested Background
This section describes a convention for laying out or formatting Pascal program statements. As readers progress in their knowledge of Pascal, greater use can be made of this section.

This section serves as a guide to laying out or indenting a Pascal program to enhance its readability. It describes the layout convention used for the example programs in this book. Pascal does not require that program statements be written as they are shown here. Pascal does not have a required layout convention. Most programmers will find it best to adopt a convention that uses some form of indentation to indicate groups or sub-clauses.

In general this book has indented three columns to indicate a subgroup. (In some installations, programs called something like "pretty print" are available to place programs in a consistent layout.)

F.1 PROGRAM SHELL

Major sections are to start on the first column used. On most systems, the starting column will be either column 1 or 2. (Pascal allows statements to start on any column.) The major sections that are to start this way are

PROGRAM
LABEL
CONST
TYPE
VAR
PROCEDURE
FUNCTION

The BEGIN delimiting the beginning of the main part of a program or a subprogram is to start on the same column. The END paired with such a BEGIN is to be aligned with the BEGIN.

F.2 IF-THEN-ELSE STRUCTURES

The resulting subclauses are indented three columns in from the initiation of the IF.

```
IF <boolean expression>
   THEN <statement1>
   ELSE <statement2>;
```

Additional IF-THEN-ELSE structures are in turn indented three columns.

```
IF <boolean expression>
   THEN IF <boolean expression>
      THEN <statement>
      ELSE <statement>
   ELSE <statement>

IF <boolean expression>
   THEN IF <boolean expression>
      THEN <statement>
      ELSE <statement>
   ELSE IF <boolean expression>
      THEN IF <boolean expression>
         THEN <statement>
         ELSE <statement>
      ELSE IF <boolean expression>
         THEN <statement>
         ELSE IF <boolean expression>
            THEN <statement>
            ELSE <statement>;
```

F.3 IF CONTROLLED COMPOUND GROUPS

The BEGIN for the compound statement containing a group of statements follows the THEN or ELSE. The statements in the group are indented three columns from the THEN or ELSE. The END for the group is aligned with the THEN or ELSE.

```
IF <boolean expression>
   THEN BEGIN
      <statement>;
      <statement>;
         .
         .
      <statement>
   END
   ELSE <statement>;
```

Some other references place the BEGIN on another line, indented three columns from the THEN. Statements are indented three columns from the BEGIN and the END is aligned with the BEGIN. This practice does have some aesthetic advantages; however, this practice consumes excessive space when there is a significant amount of nesting.

F.4 WHILES

The statement controlled by the WHILE is indented three columns from the initiation of the WHILE.

If the WHILE controls a compound statement, the BEGIN for the compound statement is on the same line as the WHILE. The matching END is aligned with the start of the WHILE. The compounded statements are indented three columns.

```
WHILE <boolean expression> DO
   <statement>;

WHILE <boolean expression> DO BEGIN
   <statement>;
   <statement>;
      .
      .
   <statement>
END;
```

Some other references place the BEGIN for the compound statement on the next line following the WHILE-DO, three columns from the THEN. Compounded statements are indented three columns from the BEGIN and the END is aligned with the BEGIN. This practice does have some aesthetic advantages; however it consumes excessive space when there is a significant amount of nesting.

F.5 REPEAT-UNTIL

The controlled statements are indented three columns from the first column of REPEAT. The REPEAT and UNTIL are aligned.

```
REPEAT
   <statement>;
   <statement>;

      .
      .
   <statement>
UNTIL <boolean expression>;
```

F.6 FOR

The controlled statement is indented three columns from the first column of the FOR.

When the controlled statement is a compound statement, the BEGIN delimiting the start of the compound statement is on the same line as the DO. The END delimiting the termination of the compound statement is aligned with the FOR.

```
FOR <control variable> := <initial value> TO <final value> DO
   <statement>;

FOR <control variable> := <initial value> TO <final value> DO BEGIN
   <statement>;
   <statement>;

      .
      .
   <statement>
END;
```

Some other references place the BEGIN for the compounded statements on the next line following the FOR-DO, indented three columns from the THEN. Compounded statements are indented three columns from the BEGIN, and END is aligned with the BEGIN. This practice does have some aesthetic advantages; however, it consumes excessive space when there is a significant amount of nesting.

F.7 CASE

The CASE labels are indented three columns from the start of the CASE statement. Statements compounded into a group are indented three columns from the start of the BEGIN delimiting the group.

```
CASE <selector expression statement> OF
   <case label>: <statement>;
   <case label>: <statement>;
   <case label>: BEGIN
                    <statement>;
                    <statement>;
                       .
                       .
                    <statement>
                 END;
   <case label>: <statement>;
   <case label>: BEGIN
                    <statement>;
                    <statement>;
                       .
                       .
                    <statement>
                 END;
   <case label>: <statement>;
      .
      .
   <case label>: <statement>
END;
```

F.8 GOTO

The target label for the GOTO is aligned with the preceding statement at the same nesting level. A GOTO in an IF-THEN-ELSE structure follows either the THEN or the ELSE on the same line.

```
<statement>;
IF <boolean expression>
   THEN <statement>
   ELSE GOTO <label>;
<statement>;
<label>: <statement>;
<statement>;
GOTO <label>;
<label>: <statement>;
<statement>;
```

F.9 PROGRAM AND SUBPROGRAM NAMES IN MATCHING ENDS

Pascal requires that user defined identifiers including program and subprogram names be a character string. No mechanism is provided to force an association between the terminating END and the name of the program or subprogram. The convention adopted is that a program or subprogram name be informally associated with the END terminating the program or subprogram by using a comment after the END.

```
PROGRAM EXAMPLE(INPUT,OUTPUT);
 .
 .
END.  (* EXAMPLE *)

FUNCTION EXAMPLE:TYPE;
 .
 .
END;  (* EXAMPLE *)

PROCEDURE EXAMPLE;
 .
 .
END;  (* EXAMPLE *)
```

Appendix G

DIFFERENCES BETWEEN STANDARD PASCAL AND UCSD PASCAL

Objective

Summarize the differences between Standard Pascal and UCSD Pascal. For the most part, a programmer can use this text with the UCSD Pascal compiler. Once a programmer who is using a microcomputer with UCSD Pascal on it has mastered access to the compiler, this appendix can serve as a guide to most of the differences between Standard Pascal and UCSD Pascal that the programmer will find important.

A version of Pascal has been implemented at the University of California, San Diego (UCSD). This version was originally developed for the Apple microcomputer. It is known as UCSD Pascal. It is available on a variety of computers. This appendix provides a brief summary of the differences between UCSD and standard Pascal.

The differences between UCSD and standard Pascal are not great. Many of the differences derive from the interactive entry of programs and data under UCSD Pascal.

G.1 CASE

In standard Pascal, if there is no label equal to the value of the CASE statement selector, then the result of the CASE statement is undefined. In UCSD Pascal, the CASE statement is exited normally with no action taken.

G.2 COMMENTS

In UCSD Pascal, comments appear between the delimiters "(*" and "*)". If the comment begins with "(*$", then the rest of the comment is considered to be a directive to the compiler. The UCSD directive "(*$G+*)" tells the compiler to allow the use of the GOTO statement (see Section G.5).

G.3 EOF

In UCSD Pascal, EOF (<file name>) is set to TRUE for a text file (including the standard INPUT file) by the "ETX" or "ENTER" keys ("CONTROL" "C" will also do).

If the file is closed, EOF will return TRUE. For a text file, if EOF is TRUE, then EOLN is also TRUE. After RESET(<file name>), EOF(<file name>) returns FALSE if the file is present.

When a program is initialized, RESET is automatically performed on the files INPUT, OUTPUT, and KEYBOARD.

G.4 EOLN

In UCSD Pascal, EOLN(<file name>) is only defined for text files. EOLN becomes TRUE following a READ during which the end-of-line character is received. The end-of-line chracter is established by the "RET" or "RETURN" key or button.

G.5 GOTO AND EXIT

UCSD Pascal allows GOTO statements to be used only in the same block as the declaration of the target label. Unless instructed otherwise, UCSD Pascal will not allow the use of GOTO anywhere in the program. The GOTO statement can be enabled by the compiler directive "(*$G+*)".

In UCSD Pascal, EXIT provides a limited equivalent GOTO capability. A single parameter is specified in the form:

```
EXIT(<procedure identifier>)
```

When executed the last invocation of the PROCEDURE specified in the EXIT statement will be terminated normally. This was designed to provide a way to exit a nest of procedure calls.

G.6 PACKING

UCSD Pascal does not support PACK and UNPACK as predefined PROCE-DUREs. It does support packed arrays of characters and packed RECORD TYPEs. Characters are packed two to a 16-bit word. Packing and unpacking are done automatically as needed.

G.7 PROCEDURES AND FUNCTIONS AS FORMAL PARAMETERS

Except for EXIT, the use of PROCEDURE and FUNCTION identifiers as formal parameters is not supported in UCSD Pascal; they are in Standard and Waterloo Pascal.

G.8 READING TEXT FILES

Standard Pascal defines READ(<file name>,<character variable>) to be equivalent to the sequence:

```
<character variable> := <file name>@;
GET(<file name>);
```

In UCSD Pascal, this sequence is reversed when the file is either one of the UCSD standard input files INPUT or KEYBOARD. This makes it easier to write interactive programs.

G.9 RESET

In standard Pascal, RESET(<file name>) moves the file marker to the first component of the file and sets the associated variable value to <file name>@. UCSD Pascal does not set the associated variable value with the RESET statement. To achieve the equivalent effect of the Standard Pascal RESET in UCSD Pascal, the following must be used in UCSD Pascal.

```
RESET(<file name>);
GET(<file name>);
```

G.10 SETS

A UCSD Pascal set is limited to 255 elements.

G.11 STRING

UCSD has a predeclared data TYPE known as STRING. To get the equivalent TYPE in Standard Pascal, the programmer would have to specify

```
TYPE
    STRING = PACKED ARRAY(. 1..80 .) OF CHAR;
```

There is an associated length attribute of an INTEGER data TYPE. The default length of 80 characters may be overridden by a declaration specifying the maximum length; for example,

```
NAME: STRING(. 30 .)
```

The maximum length that can be specified in UCSD Pascal is 255 characters.

G.12 WRITING BOOLEAN VALUES

In UCSD Pascal, values of the TYPE BOOLEAN may not be written by the use of the WRITE statement where as they can be in Standard Pascal.

G.13 GRAPHICS

UCSD Pascal has a graphics package called *Turtle Graphics*. It is not defined in standard Pascal. Turtle Graphics was originally designed to aid in the computer instruction of children.

G.14 FILE STRUCTURE

Standard Pascal supports only sequential files. UCSD Pascal supports the use of both sequential and indexed sequential files. Indexed sequential files are particularly useful when only a few out of many records of a file need to be accessed. The use of indexed sequential files is not usually presented in a first course in programming.

GLOSSARY

The number in the parenthesis indicates where the term is first discussed.

Ada (8)   A structured general purpose programming language which can be considered to be an extension of Pascal. Ada has recently been selected for use by the United States Air Force.

ALGOL (8)   A structured general purpose language. Pascal can be considered an improvement of ALGOL.

algorithm (4)   A complete, unambiguous plan for solving a specified procedure in a finite number of steps.

auxiliary storage (3)   A place to store data in a computer system other than in the computer's memory. The devices used most often to provide auxiliary storage include magnetic tape and magnetic disk drives.

card, punched (3)   A medium for storing data. A punched card is rectangular and the data is encoded by punching holes in the card.

character data (35)   Symbols that can be internally represented in a computer.

character string (233)   Several items of character data that are linearly grouped together; for example, ABC, C2389G.

COBOL (7)   A programming language often used to solve problems in business.

compiler (8)   A program which translates statements written in a particular programming language (such as Pascal) into instructions that the computer is to follow.

computer (2)   A machine which can perform the following five functions: (a) input data, (b) output data, (c) store data, (d) manipulate data, and (e) make decisions based on previously supplied instructions.

computer system (3)   A collection of connected and integrated hardware and software.

control structure (118)   A decision framework which controls the conditional execution of a portion of a program.

database (14)   An organized collection of machine stored data.

database management system (DBMS) (14)   Software which provides an environment for a database. A DBMS provides facilities which help in the access and maintenance of a database.

debugging (49)   The process of detecting and correcting errors in a program.

diagnostic message (8)   A message indicating either that the syntax of a statement is improper or that the program has stopped execution because of a semantic error in the program's design.

digital computer (2)   A computer which manipulates discrete symbols.

disk, magnetic (3)   An auxiliary storage medium which is used to store data. Disks are sometimes said to resemble phonograph records.

dynamic data storage (191)   The amount of storage space allocated to data of a particular data type can change.

echo printing (24)   Printing input data directly after it is read.

end of file (59)   The end-of-file condition indicates that whatever data was in the input file has been read.

execution, program (8)   A program begins to execute when it starts to do the tasks specified in the program.

file (12)   A collection of the data about a specific area of concern; for example, a payroll file. A file usually consists of several records.

FORTRAN (7)   A programming language often used to solve problems in science and engineering.

GPSS (7)   A programming language often used to solve problems in simulation.

hardware, computer (3)   The physical equipment that makes up a computer or a computer system.

integer data (33)   Numeric data consisting entirely of whole numbers; that is, numbers without a decimal point such as 6, 12, –5.

LISP (7)   A programming language originally designed to solve list processing problems. LISP is also often used by people solving problems in artificial intelligence.

maintenance, program (28)   Modification of an already written and running program.

modularization (91)   The process of organizing a program into modules.

module (91)   A subpart of a program that has the following attributes: (a) the first statement is executed before any other statements, (b) the last statement is executed last, and (c) the only exit from the module is through the last statement.

operating system (2)   A program which allocates a computer's resources and schedules tasks.

package program (12)   A previously written program intended for use by several different people.

PL/I (8)   A structured general purpose language. PL/I can be considered a combination of ALGOL, COBOL, and FORTRAN.

program (2)   The instructions that tell a computer what to do: read, write, store, and manipulate data.

real data (34)   Numeric data requiring a decimal point; for example, 12.621, –0.08, and 15.9.

record (12)   Several related data items gathered together in uniform format; for example, the data necessary to pay a particular employee could be placed in a payroll record. A collection of records of the same format is called a file.

semantics (6)   The semantics of a statement provide the meaning of a statement.

SIMSCRIPT (7)   A programming language often used to solve problems in simulation.

SNOBOL (7)   A programming language often used to solve problems dealing with character strings and patterns.

software, computer (3)   The programs that can be used by a particular computer.

static data storage (191)   The amount of storage space allocated to data of a particular data type cannot change.

stream data (55)   Data is in a stream when the physical boundaries of the input or output records are not considered.

stub (99)   A program statement or statements which stands in for a more extensive collection of program statements that have yet to be written. This allows a program to define the overall structure of a program before all of the details are completed.

syntax (6)   The syntax of a language is the language's grammar. Syntax provides the rules specifying how statements can be formed and how statements can be used with each other.

system software (3)   The programs that control the actions of a computer system.

tape, magnetic (3)   An auxiliary storage medium which is used to store data. The magnetic tape used in a computer system are similar to the magnetic tape used in a stereo system.

terminal (3)   An input/output device. Terminals resemble either a typewriter or a television set with an attached keyboard.

top-down analysis (16)   A method of analysis used in problem solving which proceeds by first considering the entire problem and then progressively subdividing the problem until all of the tasks in the problem can be simply and clearly stated.

update a file (324)   Add new data or modify existing data in a file.

variable name (37)   The name that is used in a program to identify storage space for data.

INDEX

The terms in capital letters are reserved identifiers.